MW01257125

Critical Concepts™ Series . . .

Largemouth Bass Fundamentals

Foundations For Sustained Fishing Success

Critical Concepts™ Series . . .

Largemouth Bass Fundamentals

Foundations For Sustained Fishing Success

Expert Advice from North America's
Leading Authority on Freshwater Fishing

THE IN-FISHERMAN STAFF

In·Fisherman

Critical Concepts™ Series . . .
Largemouth Bass Fundamentals—Foundations For Sustained Fishing Success

Publisher *Mike Carney*
Editor In Chief *Doug Stange*
Project Editor *Steve Quinn*
Editorial Compilation *J. Z. Grover*
Editors *Dave Csanda, Steve Hoffman, Jeff Simpson, Matt Straw*
Publisher Emeritus *Stu Legaard*
Copy Editor *J. Z. Grover*
Art Director *Jim Pfaff*
Cover *Jim Pfaff*
Layout & Design *John Jambor*

Acknowledgments

Kevin Brant, fish illustrations, Chapters 1, 8, 10
Russell Browder, *Habitat Management — Brushpiling*, Chapter 8
Jan Finger, photographs, Chapters 1, 2, 5, 6, 7
Ron Finger, illustrations, Chapters 5, 10
Tim Goeman, *Too Much Emphasis on Hatcheries*, Chapter 8
Alan Heft, photograph, Chapter 7
Merlyn Hilmoe, photograph, Chapter 5
Peter Kohlsaat, cartoons, Chapters 9, 10
Bill Lindner, photograph, Chapter 1
Ralph Manns, selected *Bits & Pieces* columns, and features
Minnesota Historical Society, photographs, Chapters 1, 8
Paul Prorok, *Seasonal Reservoir Sections & Patterns*, Chapter 4
Gord Pyzer, *Tracking Bass*, Chapter 7
Tom Seward, illustrations, Chapter 5
Allan Tarvid, photographs, Chapters 1, 2, 5
Matt Vincent, *The Bassmaster Top 25*, Chapter 1
Don Wirth, *Fishing Muddy Water Bass*, Chapter 7

Largemouth Bass Fundamentals—Foundations For Sustained Fishing Success

Printing Edition 10 9 8 7 6 5 4 3 2

Library of Congress Cataloging-in-Publication Data
ISBN: 1-892947-34-X

Dedication

T o all those involved in bass fishing, bass population management, media, youth education, and the fishing and marine industry who have strived to make the sport of bass fishing the sustainable, vibrant activity it is today.

Contents

A Quick History Of Fishing For Black Bass

A ngling surveys indicate that for the past 25 years, black bass have remained the most popular group of gamefish. This, however, has not always been so.

By Dr. James A. Henshall's time (late 1800s), bass had garnered a devoted, if small, following. Henshall was the first writer of note to discuss the merits of these, his favorite fish, in his book, *Book of the Black Bass*, published in 1881. It was he who declared black bass, "*inch for inch* and pound for pound (italics Henshall's), the gamest fish that swims," one of the most often quoted lines in fishing.

Preceding Henshall and beyond him, well into the mid-1900s, trout and salmon, fish admired by English writers, were considered the species of most merit. Henshall objected. "That he (the black bass) will eventually become the leading game fish of America is my oft-expressed opinion and firm belief," he argued. "This result is inevitable; if for no other reasons, from a force of circumstances . . . "

As Izaak Walton was the first popular proponent of angling, and Henshall was the first popular proponent of fishing for black bass, so was Jason Lucas the first real rhetorical champion of bass. Where Henshall, a physician, often wrote with a measure of scientific detachment, Lucas was apt to write passionate essays, given his considerable experience and firmly held beliefs. As the fishing editor of *Sports Afield*, during the 1940s, 1950s, and 1960s, he was the most influential fishing writer of his time. When his book, *Lucas On Bass Fishing*, appeared in 1947, bass were generally accorded the same status as when Henshall fished for them. By the time the third edition of Lucas' book appeared in 1962, however, bass were the most popular fish in North America.

> "inch for inch
> and pound for
> pound, the
> gamest fish
> that swims,"

Of course, it can be argued that the transition from trout to bass was bound to occur, that Lucas only served to speed and perhaps galvanize the process. Where bass were adaptable to most of the thousands of reservoirs and ponds created during that era, trout were not. Trout, too, were more easily overfished in small streams. Natural fish often were replaced with less compelling and even less adaptable hatchery trout. Trout habitat also was more sensitive to increasing environmental problems.

The 1960s—about the time Lucas was ready to retire—was the beginning of the modern age of bass fishing. Buck Perry, with his ideas about how bass relate to structure and about the necessity for speed and depth control with lures, had recently entered the arena. Where Perry most often trolled with Spoonplugs, Lucas was a caster. Lucas, every bit the all-around angler, appreciated the skill necessary to troll successfully, but he was apt to dismiss the option as an "unfortunate" way to have to resort to catching fish.

Lucas also considered fishing with livebait unsportsmanlike, and in the 1962 edition of his book, registered his disapproval of other changes taking place in bass fishing. He wrote, "Pork chunk black eels, plastic worms and jigs really do embody new principles for the freshwater fisherman. But . . . the more advanced angler, who fishes for sport rather than just dead fish, usually dislikes using black eels, plastic worms or jigs, since they must be fished slowly, much like live bait."

The monumental changes of the 1970s and 1980s may have been bound to happen, but certainly were sped by Ray Scott and his Bass Anglers Sportsman Society (B.A.S.S.). Their first tournament was held at Beaver Lake, Arkansas, in June, 1967. As the South was caught up in the aura of B.A.S.S., so too were the best anglers in the North influenced by the gospel according to Buck Perry, preached from the pages of Fishing Facts magazine.

Meanwhile, *In-Fisherman* magazine entered the scene in 1975, offering revisions to Perry's theories of fish movement; along with the opportunity to understand Calendar Periods; lake, river, and reservoir classification; fish moods; and much more. In-Fisherman also was the first in the popular press to tie scientific research directly to sportfishing, using a staff educated in scientific processes to turn difficult research into fishing opportunities for anglers.

This, then, has been the golden age of bass angling, featuring great advances in tackle manufacturing, in fishing education, and in conservation practices. Where once the problem was finding bass and understanding the presentation processes needed to catch them consistently, today the problem often is managing the plethora of tactics and the array of tackle options that have proven to be applicable to the process.

Even Henshall sensed the impending change. "In the days of good old Father Izaak Walton," he wrote, "angling was as stated by him in the title of his famous book, the 'contemplative man's recreation.' While this is no less true in our own day, the art of angling has extended its sphere of usefulness by becoming, not only the recreation of the contemplative man, but of the active, stirring, overworked business and professional man, as well. While in the comparatively slow-coach days of the quaint Walton, it was rather a recreation of choice, it has, in this age of steam become, in a measure, one of necessity."

Doug Stange
Editor In Chief

Introduction

From the Editors —
A Word About This Book

Successful bass fishing can be learned. The basic process is quantifiable and predictable. Its basics are simple but quickly can become complex and confusing. The deeper you dig into bass fishing, the more study and time on the water it will require. The fish themselves and the sport of catching them will keep luring you deeper into its mysteries.

Today, too many anglers seek shortcuts to success — a secret never-fail spot, a new lure, a faster boat, or a more high-tech reel. To an extent, the fishing industry, the media, and professional anglers contribute to the mirage that success in fishing can be bought. Deep thinking, time on the water, mental fortitude, and patience are more valuable in the long run. The foundation for solving any puzzle in bass fishing lies in the first eight chapters of this book. They provide the basis for the F + L + P = S (Fish + Location + Presentation = Success) conceptual formula devised by Ron and Al Lindner in the years prior to the formation of In-Fisherman in 1975.

Veteran In-Fisherman readers will recognize in the initial chapters of this book the heart of the In-Fisherman system of fishing knowledge as it was introduced more than 25 years ago. A generation or two of top anglers have grown up in the sport, infused with the belief that understanding the nature of the bass, its favored haunts and seasonal location and behavior shifts, is the key to successful bass fishing. These elements form the basis of true pattern fishing.

To apply this information about largemouth bass to particular bodies of water across North America and beyond, you need to recognize different characteristics of natural lakes, reservoirs, rivers, and ponds. Fortunately, nearly all those bodies of water fall neatly into a dozen or so categories that with a bit of experience become readily recognizable. Lessons learned or information gathered about one body of water is easily transferred to similar waters.

No angler can progress past the most basic stages of fishing without a clear understanding of the way structure and cover form the world of the largemouth bass, and how they provide clues to bass location and attitude. The edge effect, bass feeding strategies, and preferred prey all enter the equation for successful fishing. In recent decades, research using radio and ultrasonic telemetry has provided new insights into bass behavior that benefits anglers. These results and other scientific research on bass behavior and management are condensed and included in this volume.

As you will see, there are no fast routes to being a successful bass fisherman, except reading, communicating with other anglers, and spending lots of time on the water with an open mind. All anglers are learning whether with their first rod in hand or after winning countless bass tournaments. That's the very definition of fishing and the reason the sport never tires for those who love it. Great success on the water tempts us back time and again, but not any faster than a day of rejection on the part of our quarry. So, we venture forth to work further to solve the equation and tempt reluctant bass to bite.

It is, after all, fishing. But sooner or later, theory and practice come together, the science and the poetry mesh. Thousands of exceptional bass anglers are testament to the power of the process we present in this book. You can be, too.

Chapter 1

The World of the Largemouth Bass

Minnesota Historical Society

All About This Favorite Fish

HISTORICAL PERSPECTIVES

The largemouth bass is the most important gamefish in North America. Care to argue? Probably not, since in all likelihood you're already a bass fan. Every five years, the U.S. Fish and Wildlife Service, with the Bureau of the Census, conducts a national survey of hunting, fishing, and wildlife-associated recreation. They find the black bass clan ahead in the number of anglers who target them and the number of days spent in pursuit of bass. In the latest edition of the survey, published in 1996, trout are the first runner-up group, including at least four popular species, followed by panfish, which comprise a far greater variety of fish species.

Within the black bass group, the largemouth is the unquestioned king in geographic distribution, size, and countrywide popularity. In some areas, of course, the wonderful smallmouth bass is the dominant member of the black bass, attracting the bulk of anglers, while in a few others spotted bass are a prime attraction. Suwannee, shoal, Coosa or redeye, and Guadalupe bass have fans, too, within the limited areas they inhabit.

An early written record of the largemouth bass comes from René Laudoniere of the French Ribault expedition, who discovered and described species caught in a reed trap built by the Indians of northern Florida. In 1764, the English naturalists John and William Bartram described the Seminole Indians "bobbing" with deer hair lures, but spearing was a more common fishing method. The bass was slow to become a sportfish. European settlers, not familiar with the bass, thought of it as a "coarse" fish, a "blackguard and tough." Then, too, the leisure class who fished for sport developed earlier in northern states, which were rich in trout but not in bass. In Kentucky, however, wealthy sportsmen developed an interest in bass by the early nineteenth century.

The bass's modern popularity can be traced to the writings of Dr. James A. Henshall in the late 1800s. A physician from Baltimore, Henshall was the poet, promoter, and father of bass fishing. "Inch for inch and pound for pound the gamest fish that swims," he called it in his benchmark classic, *Book of the Black Bass*. "That [the bass] will eventually become the leading game fish of America is my oft-expressed opinion and firm belief. This result, I think, is inevitable."

His prediction proved accurate, but it took at least 80 years for those words to come to pass. Until then, black bass were ignored or even despised in much of

the eastern United States and little known west of the Mississippi River and north of 40° north latitude. Trout reigned supreme except in the Southeast, where they were found only in cooler waters. In the Sunbelt, bass, catfish, bream, and crappie have remained the favorites of anglers.

Elsewhere, people had to learn about bass, and they found them easy to like—scrappy and catchable. The pugnacious yet capricious nature of black bass makes them sometimes aggressive assassins, sometimes sullen rejectors of all offerings, but always tough battlers when hooked.

Jason Lucas, fishing editor of *Sports Afield* from in the 1940s through the 1960s, was the first modern apologist for the largemouth bass. Bass were becoming more widespread in the post-World War II era, when construction of hundreds of impoundments provided new habitat for the species from the Colorado River to Canada. The boom in farm pond construction also provided new habitat. Throughout his career, Lucas's enthusiastic prose encouraged millions of anglers to try bass fishing, and most of them were hooked as surely as their quarry. By the time the third edition of his classic *Lucas on Bass Fishing* was published in 1962, the black bass had risen to the position Henshall had predicted in many regions of the United States.

From Lucas, the torch was passed to Ray Scott, founder of the Bass Anglers

Sportsman Society (B.A.S.S.), who dreamed of an empire centered around bass fishing. The organization he founded now numbers over 600,000 members in 52 countries and every state of the union, including Alaska, which has no bass. Scott's promotion of tournaments made the black bass the cornerstone of a huge fishing tackle industry, on which today's freshwater anglers have erected an impressive monument, to the tune of annual expenditures of over $30 billion.

The varied techniques for bass fishing have encouraged development and production of an incredible array of rods, reels, lures, and fishing lines. Similar specialization has spread to other species groups, but none to the extent of the product line marketed to the largemouth devotée. Ranger Boats founder Forrest Wood's development of the modern bass boat also laid the groundwork for a huge boating industry, which now caters to anglers who target other species like walleyes, catfish, crappie, and muskies as well.

Largemouth Bass Distribution

Native largemouth bass distribution   Present largemouth bass distribution

DISTRIBUTION

With the final retreat of the Pleistocene glaciers, largemouth bass spread northward from southeastern North America to establish populations near the headwaters of the Mississippi and the Great Lakes drainage, and east into New York and Vermont. The native range of the species included the waters of the lower Great Lakes into southern Ontario and Quebec, the central part of the Mississippi River system south to the Gulf of Mexico, and north along the Atlantic coast to Virginia.

After the largemouth bass gained popularity with American anglers, stocking and immigration extended their range. In the years following the Civil War, a frenzy of stock transfers began. Between 1870 and 1894, largemouths were stocked in almost every state they didn't naturally inhabit, and soon they were also stocked in five Canadian provinces. The building of railroads facilitated stocking. In *Book of the Black Bass*, Dr. Henshall quotes a report from the

Baltimore American (June 1874) that illustrates the zeal of early bass enthusiasts:

> It was twenty years ago, that Alban G. Stabler and J. P. Duke-
> hart, together with Forsythe and Shriver, brought a small lot of Black
> Bass in the tender of a locomotive from Wheeling, West Virginia,
> and put them in the Potomac. From this small beginning, spring
> the noble race of fish which now swarm the river.

The first bass in Nebraska escaped into the Elkhorn River when a railroad car tumbled into the stream and liberated them. Establishment of hatcheries, or "fish cultural stations," as they were then known, provided the fry and fingerlings for such stockings.

THE BLACK BASS CLAN

The largemouth bass, *Micropterus salmoides,* is the largest member of the sunfish family, known to ichthyologists as the Centrarchidae. This name can be roughly translated as "troutlike fish with a small fin." This family contains 34 species, which inhabit the temperate waters of North America. The Sacramento perch is the only member of the family to occur originally west of the Rocky Mountains. Other prominent members of the family are the sunfishes, like the bluegill, pumpkinseed, and redear, the two crappie species, and the four species of rock bass.

The largemouth bass is the biggest and most widespread of the seven species of black bass, a common name used to distinguish these fish from the striped bass and its kind in the genus Morone and from the various saltwater "basses."

SMALLMOUTH BASS

Smallmouth bass, *Micropterus dolomieu,* is the second in distribution, size, and popularity of the *Micropterus* clan. The native range of this sporty fish is bounded on the east by the Appalachian Mountains, on the south by northern Georgia, Alabama, and Mississippi, on the west by the western edge of the Mississippi River basin, and on the north by the Canadian fringes of the Great Lakes basin.

Smallmouth bass were also widely transferred by fish managers, and some old hatchery records list only "black bass," thus clouding certain definitions of the smallmouth's original habitat. Stocking began in the mid-1800s, at a time when many early fish culturalists regarded smallmouths as superior to largemouths. Smallmouth bass now swim in waters as far west as California, north to Washington State and British Columbia, and south to central Texas. Waters that once contained no smallmouths now offer world-class angling.

Smallmouths and largemouths differ in many ways, the most obvious being the size of their mouths. The jaw of the largemouth extends past the eye, while the smallmouth's jaw is much smaller. The dark vertical bars and bronze coloration of the smallmouth contrast with the greenish hue and dark horizontal line of the largemouth.

Both black bass species are opportunistic predators, occasionally attacking any animal small enough to fit in their mouths. With their pointed jaws, smallmouths

Smallmouth Bass Distribution

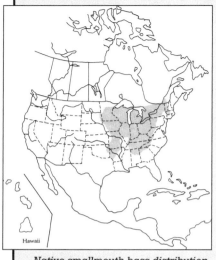

Native smallmouth bass distribution

Present smallmouth bass distribution

are better adapted to picking crayfish from rocky terrain. Their streamlined bodies and longer tails allow for quicker movement in river currents.

The upper reaches of many rivers contain smallmouth bass, while largemouths predominate toward the mouths, where the waters become warmer, slower, and murkier, and where bottom substrates shift from rock and gravel to silt and aquatic plants. In natural lakes, however, both species may be found feeding on shiners, crayfish, and small sunfish. In reservoirs, threadfin and gizzard shad may support both species.

Smallmouth bass approach maximum size at the northern and southern edges of their range. Great Lakes and Ontario waters produce fish over 7 pounds, rivaling the largest commonly taken in Tennessee. The world record—10 pounds, 14 ounces—was caught in 1955 from Dale Hollow Reservoir on the Kentucky-Tennessee border. Dale Hollow has produced other smallies over 10 pounds. Like the largemouth record, this mark seems unlikely to be broken.

SPOTTED BASS

Until 1931, most ichthyologists recognized only largemouth and smallmouth black bass. That year, at a meeting of the American Fisheries Society, Dr. Carl Hubbs noted characteristics of a third species, the spotted bass, which was later named *Micropterus punctulatus*. Hubbs originally called this fish, which he had researched throughout the 1920s, the Kentucky Black Bass. That label has continued in some regions, though Hubbs himself soon regretted its regional connotation.

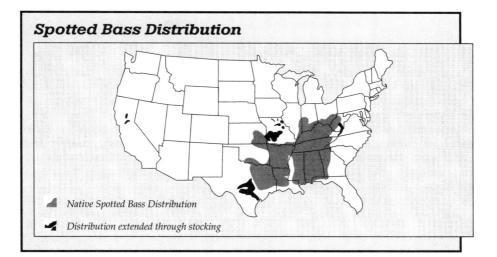

Spotted Bass Distribution

◢ Native Spotted Bass Distribution

◤ Distribution extended through stocking

Ichthyologists speculate that the original range of spotted bass included all of the lower and central Mississippi River drainage from Missouri to northern Louisiana, as well as the Gulf Coast drainage from the Chattahoochee River in northern Georgia to the Guadalupe River in Texas, and most of the Ohio River drainage from Ohio to Tennessee. Transfers have expanded the species's range to California, but the fish hasn't been as widely stocked as largemouth or smallmouth bass.

Spotted bass are less tolerant of cold water than are largemouths and smallmouths, so they seem restricted to waters south of central Ohio and West Virginia. Ecologists describe typical spotted bass habitat as larger streams and rivers with gradients of fewer than 3 feet per mile. Many other characteristics, including mouth size, tail shape, and favored depth, are intermediate between those of largemouths and smallmouths.

Spotted bass have a dark horizontal line like largemouth bass, but it's broken into diamond shapes. Below the lateral line, they have several rows of scales with dark dots in the center, giving the fish a spotted appearance.

Most ichthyologists recognize two subspecies of spotted bass, the Alabama (*Micropterus punctulatus henshalli*) and the northern (*M. p. punctulatus*), sometimes called Kentucky bass. A third putative subspecies, the Wichita spotted bass, is now considered a hybrid between the spotted and the smallmouth bass. The Alabama spotted bass grows faster than the others and reaches a larger size. Studies in the Coosa River have found that spots there average over 17 inches at age 5, larger than an equivalent-aged largemouth bass.

Transplants from Alabama to California have exceeded 9 pounds, including the 10-pound, 4-ounce record caught from Pine Flat Reservoir in 2001. In Alabama, the 8-pound, 15-ounce record fish came from Lewis Smith Lake. In some rivers and reservoirs, northern spotted bass grow slowly and don't live more than 6 or 7 years, producing mediocre fisheries and sometimes competing with young smallmouth or largemouth bass.

Spotted bass tend to spawn deeper than other black bass, though in several regions, introduced spots have hybridized with native smallmouth bass, harming valuable fisheries. For this reason, introductions are infrequent and are made only after considerable research on possible negative effects.

REDEYE BASS

After Dr. Hubbs proclaimed the spotted bass the third member of the black bass clan, confusion remained about other southeastern bass that didn't fit the description of largemouth, smallmouth, or spotted. Confusion stemmed from three factors: similarity in body shape among all black bass, including skull and fins; basic color similarity among species, although variability exists among bass from different populations, waters, even ages and moods; and the many scientific names early ichthyologists had given to black bass species, subspecies, and populations.

Hubbs and Dr. Reeve Bailey, Hubbs's colleague at the University of Michigan, formally designated the redeye bass *Micropterus coosae* in 1940. Native distribution of redeye bass, also called Coosa bass, is the largest of the four less-known species of black bass. Redeyes inhabit streams of the upland drainages from the Black Warrior River in Alabama east to the Savannah River on the Georgia-South Carolina border.

In Alabama, they occur primarily in the upper Coosa, Tallapoosa, and Alabama river systems; in Georgia, in the Oconee and Savannah River drainages; and in Tennessee, in Sheed and Cohutta creeks. Redeyes occur in the South Carolina portion of the Savannah River and north to the headwaters of Lake Jocassee in North Carolina.

Redeyes haven't been widely transplanted because of their small size and rigid habitat requirements, but adults were stocked in several California streams beginning in 1959. Stocking expanded their range slightly in Tennessee and into Kentucky. In small streams, redeyes reach a maximum size of about 13 inches and 1 pound, though the largest on record is Georgia's 3-pound, 3-ounce fish, caught in the Tugalo River in 1990.

Redeye bass thrive in Lake Hartwell on the Savannah River and in lakes Keowee and Jocassee in South Carolina, where fish from 1 to 2 pounds are common. In the more fertile impoundments on dammed streams, native redeyes have declined because of altered habitat, new prey bases, and competition from larger black bass species.

The redeye is named for its blood-red eye, which can be startling, particularly in prespawn males. This beautiful little fish displays a blue tinge on the lower jaw and a distinctive tail marked with white or clear margins. Young fish have an orange spot at the base of the caudal fin; their fins are translucent orange.

The redeye's brilliant coloration (for a bass) and its preference for small, rocky, clear, cool streams have led anglers and fishery workers to refer to it as the brook trout of the South. Like trout, redeyes feed primarily on terrestrial and aquatic insects, also taking small fish and crayfish when they're abundant. Redeyes grow slowly on this diet, reaching 6 inches in length at maturity (about 4 years).

SUWANNEE BASS

In 1949, Hubbs and Bailey added the Suwannee bass, *Micropterus notius*, to the clan, basing their description on specimens collected from Ichetucknee Springs, a tributary of the Santa Fe River

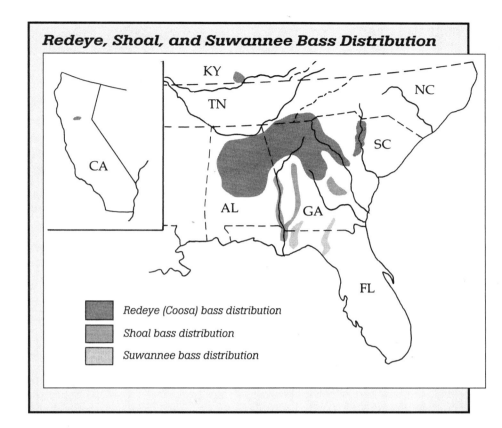

Redeye, Shoal, and Suwannee Bass Distribution

Redeye (Coosa) bass distribution

Shoal bass distribution

Suwannee bass distribution

in Florida. This robust bass is abundant in the lower Santa Fe as well as in the Suwannee River, which flows from the Okefenokee Swamp in southern Georgia to the Gulf of Mexico. It also inhabits the Ochlockonee River from south of Cairo, Georgia, to the headwaters of Lake Talquin in Florida and the Withloacoochee River, a tributary of the Suwannee, which begins near Quitman, Georgia.

Suwannee bass coexist with largemouths throughout their range, but Suwannees favor riffles, rocks, and fast water, leaving the backwaters and snags to the largemouths. Studies of diet show that crayfish dominate samples from Suwannees' stomachs, while largemouths also rely on fish.

Suwannee bass are distinctively colored, with dark blue on the lower portions of their gill covers and throats, and dark green along their backs and sides. Their large mouths, broad, rounded tails, and short, stubby bodies are unique. A 15-inch Suwannee often weighs over 2 pounds.

The International Game Fish Association recognizes a 3-pound, 14-ounce fish caught from the Suwannee River in 1985 as the all-tackle record. The National Fresh Water Fishing Hall of Fame recognizes the 3-pound, 9-ounce fish caught in Georgia's Ochlockonee River in 1984 as its record.

Florida lists the Suwannee bass as a threatened species because of its habitat restrictions and the threats to that habitat from development and chemical-agricultural pollution. Angling for Suwannee is legal, however, and statewide regulations apply.

GUADALUPE BASS

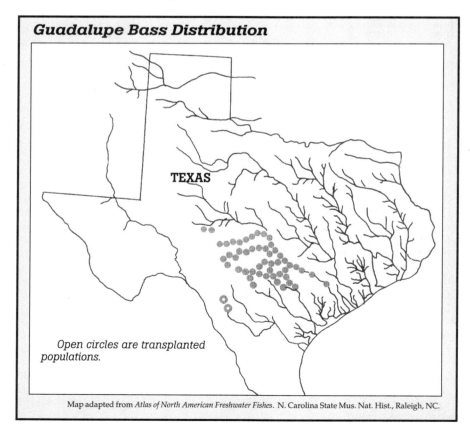

Through the 1940s, Carl Hubbs and Reeve Bailey considered Texas's native Guadalupe bass a subspecies of spotted bass. Then Dr. Clark Hubbs, Carl Hubbs's son, found Guadalupes and spotted bass coexisting in the San Marcos and Guadalupe rivers without inter-breeding, which indicated that they were distinct species. In 1953 the Guadalupe bass was designated *Micropterus treculi*.

This species is native to the San Antonio, Guadalupe, Colorado, and Brazos rivers, all of which drain the Edwards Plateau just north of San Antonio. Rivers in this system are tough environments for fish: flooded by heavy rains, then almost dried up during droughts. In this natural habitat, Guadalupe bass reach only about 12 inches.

In several impoundments, "Guads," as Texans affectionately call their state fish, have thrived, growing as large as the world record—3 pounds, 11 ounces—caught in Lake Travis in 1983. Since then, anglers have submitted larger species for recognition, but genetic testing has proved that they have hybridized with introduced smallmouth bass.

Guadalupe Bass Distribution

TEXAS

Open circles are transplanted populations.

Map adapted from *Atlas of North American Freshwater Fishes.* N. Carolina State Mus. Nat. Hist., Raleigh, NC.

Hybridization is more than a source of frustration for record seekers and confusion for record keepers. It's a threat to the existence of this bass species. All central Texas reservoirs with strong populations of Guads have been stocked with smallmouths, so genetic damage may continue, despite the fact that the Texas Parks and Wildlife Department has discontinued stocking smallmouths there. The agency maintains a pure genetic stock of Guadalupe Bass at Lost Maples State Park near Bandera. Streams with nearly pure stocks include the Llano, upper Colorado, Pedernales, and Guadalupe rivers.

SHOAL BASS

The shoal bass is the seventh member of the black bass clan; it only recently was given a proper scientific name, *Micropterus cataractae*. Before acquiring its Linnaean name, the fish had been called the Chipola bass by Dr. Carl Hubbs. Other ichthyologists considered it a variety of redeye. The taxonomic process moves slowly, but anglers on the rivers in Alabama, Georgia, and Florida, where this fish is found, have long recognized its special qualities and appreciated its size and its smallmouthlike behavior. On Georgia's Flint River, local anglers call it the "Flint River smallmouth."

The all-tackle record of 8 pounds, 3 ounces was caught on a section of the Flint near Thomaston, Georgia. Shoal bass also thrive in the Apalachicola and Chipola rivers in Florida, the Oconee and Ocmulgee rivers in Georgia, and sections of the Chattahoochee River in Alabama, notably Hallawakee Creek, where the 6-pound, 8-ounce state record was caught in 1993.

Shoal bass occupy a niche similar to that of the smallmouth in northern rivers. Both hold behind current breaks like boulders and snags, in middepth holes, and in tailraces. They disappear from impounded waters. Unfortunately, record-keeping organizations have lumped together the shoal bass and redeye bass, a practice that may have prevented record-sized redeye from being recognized, since they are much smaller than shoal bass.

LARGEMOUTH BASS GENETICS

There are two subspecies of largemouth bass, *M. salmoides salmoides* (northern largemouth) and *M. salmoides floridanus* (Florida largemouth). These interbreed freely when inhabiting the same water, producing hybrid or F_1 largemouths. Further spawning among hybrids or between hybrids and parental types produces backcrosses and intergrades, sometimes called Fx generations.

Florida bass from semitropical peninsular Florida can't tolerate water that approaches freezing. A large natural intergrade zone from South Carolina through Mississippi, including northern Florida, contains largemouth bass intermediate between northern and Florida bass; the natural intermediates seem well adapted to that zone. The world-record largemouth bass, 22 pounds, 4 ounces, caught from the Ocmulgee River in Georgia in 1932, came from this intergrade zone. The largest pure northern-strain largemouth, 15 pounds, 8 ounces is apparently the

Distribution of Largemouth Subspecies and Intergrades

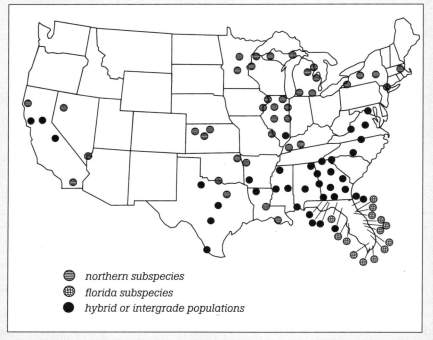

⊜ northern subspecies
⊞ florida subspecies
● hybrid or intergrade populations

Dr. Dave Philipp, a fish geneticist at the Illinois Natural History Survey, checked the genetic makeup of largemouth bass from 90 populations across the United States. He and his colleagues determined bass identity with a process called electrophoresis, which chemically identifies proteins that are characteristic of genetic types. Florida and northern subspecies have slightly different physical characteristics, but these aren't always reliable indicators of a bass' identity. And bass that are hybrids of the subspecies or intergrades (offspring of spawning among hybrids or of hybrids and parent species) can't be identified without protein analysis.

Pure Florida bass were found only in peninsular Florida. Genetically mixed populations occurred throughout the Southeast. And bass samples from most other areas were pure northern subspecies.

A natural "intergrade zone" apparently extends from South Carolina through Mississippi, including north Florida. Bass in this region are adapted to environmental conditions intermediate between north temperate waters and semitropical peninsular Florida. Their genetic patterns show their intermediacy.

Genetic mixtures outside this zone were due to stocking bass with Florida genes outside their native range. Many fishery biologists and anglers were surprised at the extent of genetically mixed largemouth bass populations when Dr. Philipp published his results in the early 1980s. Further stocking of Florida bass has expanded the zone of genetic mixing.

Massachusetts state record fish or the 15.86-pound fish from Canyon Lake, Arizona (which was not tested genetically).

California began stocking Florida bass in 1959, and anglers began to catch immense fish. Texas introductions have also stimulated production of bigger largemouths. Introductions into cooler climates, however, haven't achieved similar successes. Moreover, recent genetic research indicates that forcing introduction of genetic stocks can damage native populations by interbreeding and adding genes that hurt rather than help growth, survival, and spawning success. Northern bass populations may lose their tolerance to cold winter conditions if Florida bass are introduced and if the fish, during unusually mild conditions, survive and crossbreed with native populations. As a result, biologists generally move most cautiously when considering the introduction of new stock. Many conservation geneticists recommend against this practice in all cases.

The BASSMASTER TOP 25 (as of May 2002)

Compiled by Matt Vincent, BASSMASTER staff writer and editor of *B.A.S.S. Times*.

☆ 1.	22 lbs, 4 oz *	Montgomery Lake, Georgia	George Perry	June 2, 1932
☆ 2.	22 lbs, 1/2 ounce (22.01 lbs)	Lake Castaic, California	Bob Crupi	March 12, 1991
☆ 3.	21 lbs, 12 oz (21.75 lbs)	Lake Castaic, California	Mike Arujo	March 5, 1991
☆ 4.	21 lbs, 3½ oz (21.19 lbs)	Lake Casitas, California	Raymond Easley	March 4, 1980
☆ 5.	21 lbs, 1/2 ounce (21.01 lbs)	Lake Castaic, California	Bob Crupi	March 9, 1990
☆ 6.	20 lbs, 15 oz (20.94 lbs)	Lake Miramar, California	David Zinmerlee	June 23, 1973
☆ 7.	20 lbs, 14 oz (20.86 lbs)	Lake Castaic, California	Leo Torres	February 4, 1990
☆ 8.	20 lbs, 12 oz (20.75 lbs)	Lake Dixon, California	Mike Long	April 27, 2001
☆ 9.	20 lbs, 4 oz (20.25 lbs)	Lake Hodges, California	Gene Dupras	May 30, 1985
☆ 10.	20 lbs, 2 oz (20.13 lbs)	Big Fish Lake, Florida	Fritz Friebel	May, 1923
☆ 11.	19 lbs, 8 oz (19.50 lbs)	Lake Miramar, California	Keith Gunsauls	March 7, 1988
☆ 12.	19 lbs, 4 oz (19.25 lbs)	Lake Mira Mesa, California	Chris Brandt	March 22, 1998
☆ 13.	19 lbs, 3 oz (19.19 lbs)	Lake Morena (California)	Ardon Hanline	February 17, 1987
☆ 13.	19 lbs, 3 oz (19.19 lbs)	Lake Wohlford, California	Steve Beasley	February 3, 1986
☆ 15.	19 lbs, 1/2 ounce (19.06 lbs) **	Lake Miramar, California	Sandy DeFresco	March 14, 1988
☆ 16.	19 lbs, 1/2 ounce (19.04 lbs)	Lake Castaic, California	Dan Kadota	January 8, 1989
☆ 17.	19 lbs, 1/2 ounce (19.03 lbs)	Success Lake, California	Larry Kerns	January 27, 2001
☆ 18.	19 lbs, 0 oz (19.0 lbs)	Lake Tarpon, Florida	Riley Witt	June 21, 1961
☆ 19.	18 lbs, 15 oz (18.94 lbs)	Lake Isabella, California	Keith Harper	April, 1984
☆ 20.	18 lbs, 14 oz (18.86 lbs)	Castaic Lake, California	Dan Kadota	February 12, 1988
☆ 21.	18 lbs, 13 oz (18.81 lbs)	Lake Isabella, California	Joe Weaver	February, 1984
☆ 21.	18 lbs, 13 oz (18.81 lbs)	St. Johns River, Florida	Buddy Wright	April 12, 1987
☆ 23.	18 lbs, 12 oz (18.75 lbs)	Lake Otay, California	Bob Eberly	March 9, 1980
☆ 23.	18 lbs, 12 oz (18.75 lbs)	San Vicente Lake, California	James Steurgeon	March 1, 1981
☆ 23.	18 lbs, 12 oz (18.75 lbs)	Lake Castaic, California	Manny Arujo	January 25, 1991

Sources: International Game Fish Association; National Fresh Water Fishing Hall of Fame; Jim Brown of the City of San Diego Lakes; Dennis Lee of the California Department of Fish and Game; the Florida Game and Fresh Water Fish Commission; Western Outdoor News.

*Only undocumented bass on The BASSMASTER Top 25. No photographs of this fish exist, and it was not weighed on certified scales.

**Highly publicized catch was originally submitted at 21 lbs, 10 oz. But during examination, a diving weight was found inside the fish's stomach. Less the weight of the object, the National Fresh Water Fishing Hall of Fame accepts the fish at 19 lbs, 1 ounce. It is not recognized by the International Game Fish Association.

New technologies for assessing genetic differences have increased the knowledge of this complicated aspect of fish management. Protein electrophoresis, a technique introduced about three decades ago, allows quick and sure differentiation of bass subspecies and intergrades. The study of mitochondrial DNA even allows identification of bass siblings. Biologists and fishery administrators must fret over which differences among natural and introduced populations are ecologically significant, a far more difficult task.

REPRODUCTION

Male largemouth bass have been found to mature when as small as 9 inches and at just 1 year old. More often, male spawners range from 12 to 18 inches, considerably smaller than females. Mature females less than 1 pound have been documented, but generally they range from 1¾ pounds to fish as large as the population produces.

When water temperature rises into the low 60°F range in spring (sometimes as early as December in southern Florida or Mexico), male bass instinctively move to protected shallow bays and flats to build nests. In unusual circumstances, spawning may occur in the high 50°F range or into the mid 80s. Within one body of water, temperature may vary from section to section. This protracts the spawn, reducing the possibility of an entire year-class being wiped out by severe cold fronts, floods, or other events.

Largemouths typically begin spawning earliest in the upper reaches of a reservoir, where warm, shallow bays with darker water are more common; they spawn latest in the lower portions near the dam. Mature males select sites with harder bottom, often with objects like sticks, mussel shells, or stones adjacent to or in their round nests. Larger objects reduce the area males must guard from egg and fry predators like bluegills, perch, and shiners. Beds are often built on the same spots year after year, as long as water levels don't fluctuate much.

Males sweep away fine silt and organic debris to form rounded beds. In eutrophic waters, bass may bed on roots of aquatic plants or on flat wood surfaces. Nests are commonly built in 1 to 4 feet of water but may occur as deep as 15 feet in clear waters. The murkier the water, the shallower the bass spawn.

When his nest is complete, the male courts a female who may be cruising or holding in the vicinity of the warm bay, feeding on abundant prey or warming her body as part of the final maturation of her eggs. He nips, bumps, and pushes her as they perform elaborate rituals that include movements and color changes that immediately precede egg laying and fertilization. Spawning may take place at any time of day, though night spawning is common.

The female releases several thousand eggs while the male fertilizes them as they fall into the nest. The female may deposit additional batches of eggs hours or days later, often in the nest of another male. He, in turn, may spawn with another female in that nest. Annual egg production or fencundity depends on the female's size; large females may contain up to 150,000 eggs. Often not all eggs get laid. After spawning, the female typically leaves the nest area, and the male remains to guard the eggs and young fry.

The tiny yellowish eggs (about 1.5 millimeters in diameter) stick to the bottom until they hatch in about two days. After hatching, the tiny larvae look obese, each resting on its yolk sac, absorbing the nutrients it provides. After 5 or 6 days, the largemouth develops that mouth that makes it famous. It becomes free-swimming about 2 days later. Researchers believe that the "black fry" must feed within 5 or 6 days or die of starvation, though some nutrients from the yolk sac remain. Rates of hatching and early development are linked to water temperature; all phases proceed faster in warmer water.

Bass fry, often moving in small schools, feed on the small zooplankton plentiful in these shallow bays where the fish have hatched. In turn, they're eaten by fellow basslings, as well as by many species of fish and invertebrates. The fry's metabolism is fast, so it must feed almost continually, unlike an adult fish. Studies show that fry evacuate their gut about three hours after eating, while an adult bass may make a meal last for an entire day.

Numbers of small bass fall rapidly through the combined effects of predation, starvation, and competition with other young bass and other species of fingerling fish, as well as adult preyfish. Even under the best conditions, only a fraction of 1 percent of fry reach catchable size. The term *recruitment* refers to fish reproduction and survival—the ability of the young to reach the fishable population.

Other factors that limit recruitment are related to changeable spring weather. Optimal conditions for good recruitment include high and stable water levels and slowly rising temperature. But spring is unpredictable, and often cold fronts drive guardian males from their nests, leaving eggs and fry to preda-tors. Storm-driven wind and waves reduce survival of bass fry and fingerlings. Fluctuating water levels may cause nests to be abandoned or fry to be pushed out of protective shoreline cover. Muddy water hinders egg survival and impairs feeding. Lack of submerged vegetation or shallow brush can also deprive small bass of food and cover.

GROWTH AND ABUNDANCE

To overcome these threats to survival, little largemouths grow quickly, switch-ing from a zooplankton diet to larval insects and crustaceans, and then to small fish. Making the transition to a fish diet boosts young basses' growth. Often, how-ever, young bass approach their first winter from 1½ to 4 inches long, depending on the climate and growing season, water productivity, and available food. Larger bass typically survive better; overwinter mortality can be severe in northern regions.

Bass growth rates vary greatly across the species's range. In northern waters, largemouth bass often take 5 or 6 years to reach 12 inches, and even in southern impoundments, fish may take 3 to 4 years to reach this length. But bass in a newly flooded southern reservoir or pond may reach 12 inches in the first year.

George Perry's World-Record Bass

A graphite replica of George Perry's world record. The lure is a Creek Chub Wiggle Fish.

Largemouth bass, like other species, may well live much longer than we pre-viously thought, as shown by recent tag-ging studies and new aging tech-niques. One large-mouth bass from New York was 23 years old when recaptured, while a New Hampshire smallmouth of 26 years was documented in 1999. Analysis of bass otoliths (ear stones) shows the age of older fish more accurately than the traditional scale method, particularly in warmer climates and for bass more than 8 years old. That method has shown some 10-pound bass from Florida to be 10 years old. Yet a captive largemouth in a Texas aquarium grew from 14 to 19 pounds in 2 years.

Wherever they live, bass growth rate declines after maturity, as fish devote more energy to production of eggs and spawning. Male bass typically grow more slowly than females and do not live as long. Aged bass may persist in poor conditions for several years, not spawning and losing weight. These senescent bass have large heads, thin bodies, and ragged fins. Some are blind in one or both eyes. They may bite slow-moving lures eagerly, because natural prey may elude them.

The world-record largemouth bass, the 22-pound, 4-ounce fish pulled from Montgomery Lake, a slough off the Ocmulgee River, by George Perry in 1932,

In the 1990s, the Texas Freshwater Fisheries Center in Athens housed an enormous and fast-growing bass. She weighed 14 lbs. when caught in Brady Branch Reservoir, but a diet of koi carp, sunfish, and shad ballooned her over 19 pounds within two years.

was a natural intergrade between the Florida and northern sub-species. All other largemouth bass over 16 pounds have been fish with some Florida genes, residing in warm climates. Florida bass stocked into California reservoirs have shown the most potential for breaking this old record; Bob Crupi landed a 22-pound largemouth from Lake Castaic in 1991.

Among northern-strain largemouth, the largest is thought to be one from Canyon Lake, Arizona, which weighed 15.86 pounds, followed by the Massa-chusetts state record of 15 pounds, 8 ounces, caught through the ice of Samp-son Pond in 1975. Northern-strain bass over 14 pounds have also been taken in Arkansas. Although genetic problems can follow stock transfers, the increase in gigantic bass in Texas, Oklahoma, Arizona, and Louisiana, as well as Cali-fornia, can be traced to introduction of Florida bass or hybrids.

PREY

Adult largemouth bass most commonly feed on a wide array of fish, notably gizzard and threadfin shad in temperate or southern waters where they occur, and shiners, small sunfish, yellow perch, silversides, and alewives in other waters. They also favor the many species of crayfish that occupy nearly all bass waters of North and Central America. Though not particularly nutritious from a caloric standpoint, crayfish are relatively easy to capture, despite their impos-ing claws, which probably accounts for their prevalence in the diet of bass conti-nentwide.

Less common prey include small ducks, snakes, mice, frogs, and salamanders. Studies show that young bass quickly learn to leave turtles alone, for the rep-tiles scratch and claw their mouths and throats, causing the fish to spit them out. Bass also ignore bullfrog tadpoles because of tox-ins in their skin.

Bass may try to eat prey almost as large as themselves, or they may settle for the larger forms of

tiny zooplankton. The lower limit of prey seems determined by several factors. Prey must be large enough to be visible and worth chasing. Bass rarely waste more energy chasing food than they get from digesting it, but large mouthfuls of tiny prey may be nutritionally advantageous at times.

The upper limit of prey size is determined by the gape of the mouth and throat and the ability to catch and hold strong, struggling prey. Bass readily eat thin preyfish like shiners or shad in longer sizes than thicker sunfish. Adult bass occasionally eat prey up to 60 percent of their own length. Typically, however, they eat prey between 10 and 50 percent of their own length, as shown by stomach samples. The most common range of prey size is 20 to 40 percent. Fish of this size offer the best balance between energy needed to capture them and energy gained from eating them.

Common prey in a body of water are, of course, some of the most important guides to lure and livebait selection. Successful bass anglers match crankbaits, spinnerbaits, and even jigs to colors of preyfish and crayfish, particularly in clear water. Topwater lures appeal to the largemouth's generalist attitude. Any crippled-looking creature on the surface is fair game if it fits into that expansive maw.

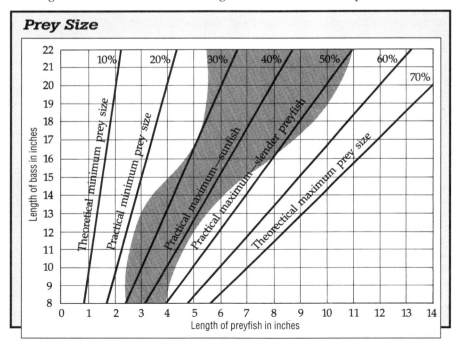

Prey Size

At times, seasonal movements of prey can make bass highly selective in their feeding. Surfacing fish may be intent on baitfish of a particular size and color; they may ignore even similar profiles. When frogs are abundant in the shallows in spring, or when they migrate into lakes in fall, bass and other species single them out.

The lower jaw of the largemouth is large and underslung, a feature that allows the fish to quickly engulf large prey. But it also makes the fish less adept at picking food off bottom, especially prey in rocky crevices. The more tweezerlike jaws of the smallmouth allows it to more readily pick crayfish off bottom.

BASS PHYSIOLOGY

Like all fish, bass are "cold blooded"; their body temperatures remain at or close to the temperature of surrounding water. They may metabolically warm up 1 or 2°F above water temperature while resting, but they cool to ambient temperature when moving because faster-breathing, active fish move more water over their gills, which cools their blood.

Bass use a variety of enzymes to modify their temperature balance in different temperature ranges. As water temperatures change, they chemically readjust for peak efficiency. If water temperatures drop rapidly by more than about 7°F, bass must readjust and may become temporarily inactive.

Like most cold-blooded creatures, bass become most metabolically efficient within a specific temperature range. Within this range, they swim fastest and digest food and grow most rapidly. They tend to be sluggish in cold water and become increasingly more active as optimal temperature is reached. Waters warmer than optimal also slow bass metabolism.

The three primary black bass species—largemouths, smallmouths, and spotted—share nearly the same optimal temperature range: 78 to 86°F. Tests have not been published for the four minor species, but presumably they have similar thermal limits. Under ideal conditions, black basses are found in water temperatures of this range. In typical circumstances, however, bass move away from optimal temperatures to seek prey, locate suitable habitat, and reduce competition with other fish.

In reservoirs and lakes, largemouths usually occupy water near the optimal temperature range. Smallmouths tend to seek out slightly cooler water, partly

Temperature Tolerance

- 110°F — lethal, even for fish acclimated to high temperatures
- 100°F — stressful temperatures can injure or kill fish
- 90°F — summer norm in southern range
- 80°F — optimal growth in lab tests
- 70°F — summer norm in northern range
- 60°F
- 50°F — winter norm throughout southern range
- 40°F — winter norm throughout northern range
- 30°F

to avoid largemouths and partly because the northern waters of their preferred habitat are cooler than those farther south. Spotted bass seem to have more flexible temperature responses, but they are found more often in deeper, cooler waters than either largemouth or smallmouths in streams where all three species coexist. Yet the northern limit of their range (central Ohio) suggests that they don't cope as well with cold temperatures as smallmouths.

Northern-strain largemouths, smallmouths, and spotted bass tolerate water just above freezing, and largemouths of the Far North exist under ice cover for 5 or even 6 months of the year. Largemouths tolerate water up to about 95°F. Prolonged exposure to hotter water can be fatal, but black bass acclimated to warm water can enter water up to 103°F for brief periods to feed, which may occur in reservoirs with thermal discharges.

Bass can sense temperature changes of 0.2°F and can follow temperature gradients toward optimal conditions. There is, however, no evidence to show that black bass in natural waters actively seek thermal optimums as do large striped bass, northern pike, and coldwater species. Instead, they congregate near suitable habitat and abundant prey, adapting to local temperatures.

Bass sense pH, oxygen, and CO_2 concentrations, acclimating themselves to whatever conditions exist so long as minimal requirements are met. They tend to move away from areas with dissolved oxygen below 3 parts per million (ppm) or pH below 6 or above 9.

Largemouth bass are typically freshwater fish, but in coastal rivers, from the Sacramento-San Joaquin Delta in California to the Mississippi Delta in Louisiana to the Hudson River in New York, bass occupy brackish water as well. Adults can tolerate salinity as high as 10 parts per thousand—about one-third the concentration of seawater. Spawning fails, however, in salinities greater than 4 parts per thousand, and in such waters, growth is slow.

Bass are chunky fish with lots of fin area. This shape makes them maneuverable in confined areas but capable of fast attacks and short bursts of speed. Bass can swim about 2 mph for extended periods, and their burst speed has been estimated at 12 mph, about five times faster than you can retrieve a lure.

Largemouth bass are adapted to living in cover, usually weeds or wood. They blend into their habitat. Their backs and sides are dark and their bellies light, and in murky water, their color fades, making them less conspicuous. They can also change color in response to background and mood—for example, during spawning and active feeding.

SENSES OF THE BASS

In addition to the typical five senses, bass have a sixth, lateral line sensitivity that we humans lack. Sensory systems convey environmental information that bass require. Reliance on particular senses varies with the environment. In clear water, bass rely heavily on sight, particularly during the daytime. In murky water, sight is still important at close range, but lateral line perception and hearing gain importance.

Bass use these senses to locate favorable habitat, capture prey, and avoid predators. They relate to and identify nearby objects using all their senses, and at longer ranges they detect objects and animals by sound or smell.

Vision—Vision is the primary sense of black bass, although it's limited to a few inches in murky water and to about 100 feet in crystal-clear water. Whenever possible, bass use sight to identify threats and to find and catch prey. Other senses are used to gather additional information, alert the fish, or fill in when vision is restricted.

The eyes of bass contain rod and cone cells. Rods, sensitive to low levels of blue-green light, provide excellent night vision, allowing bass to hunt and capture prey during the darkest nights. Two sets of cones, believed to have peak sensitivities in the red-orange and green light wavelengths, give bass a wide range of color vision during daylight and twilight. Tests suggest that bass can discriminate between slight differences in greens, reds, and oranges. And they apparently have some ability to detect differences between dark blues, violets, and blacks, and between whites, light grays, and light yellows. So there's biological justification for those massive tackle sacks stuffed with plastics every color of the rainbow.

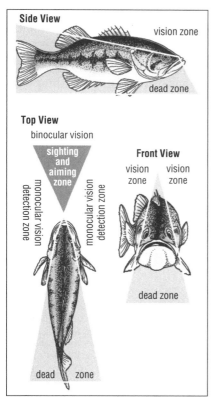

Side View

vision zone

dead zone

Top View

binocular vision

sighting and aiming zone

monocular vision detection zone

monocular vision detection zone

Front View

vision zone

vision zone

dead zone

dead zone

Bass eyes are located on the upper front sides of the head, providing a visual coverage of almost 360°, with a small area of bifocal vision directly in front and upward from the snout. As a result, black bass move and feed forward and upward with relative ease. Feeding downward requires tipping or rolling the body to see and capture prey.

Although black bass can feed and function comfortably in bright, clear water, many prey species have sharper bright-light vision, offering them an escape advantage under well-lit conditions. At night and in twilight and heavy shade, bass see better than most preyfish, giving them a hunting edge. In other words, vision influences their feeding times and tactics.

Vision is, however a product of the interaction between eyes and brain. Although the eyes of bass are physiologically as good or better than human eyes in low-light situations, their smaller brains limit the type of images they see. No child, for example, would mistake a Rapala or spinnerbait for a minnow, yet bass do. The visual images routinely used by bass are simple and undetailed. They apparently identify prey by reference to typical shapes, movement patterns, and flashes of color. As research has shown, however, bass do learn. They're able to see fine details, like hooks or 6-pound-test line, once experience teaches them to focus on these details.

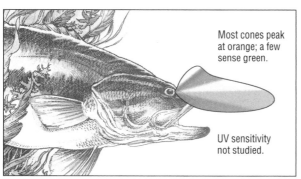

Most cones peak at orange; a few sense green.

UV sensitivity not studied.

Bass have no eyelids, but the eye's rod and cone cells automatically move into and out of dark protective pigment in the retina to adjust for overly bright or faint light. In addition, water rapidly absorbs light, acting like sunglasses to reduce bright sun. Sunlight does not harm basses' eyes at normal depths, but actively hunting bass may move into shade to better detect and stalk prey in bright areas.

Hearing—The inner ears of bass are located inside the skull and are sensitive to sound waves between about 20 and 3,000 Hertz (cycles per second). Humans can hear higher frequencies than bass, but bass can detect most water-generated noises that we can hear.

The inner ears of bass function much like radio signal detectors. Sounds emanate from an object and move toward a bass in a particular direction—say, 90° if the object lies directly to the fish's right. It's difficult for a fish to differentiate a sound in that direction from a sound emanating from 180° directly to its left, until the sound increases or decreases in loudness when object and fish grow closer or farther apart. Bass seem able to gauge the correct angle of sound approaching from noisy prey, lures, or boats.

Hearing and Lateral Line in Fish

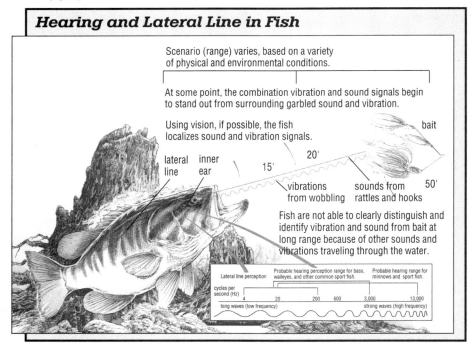

Lateral line—The lateral line, which runs along a bass's sides from head to tail, senses low-frequency vibrations or sounds from about 5 to 200 Hertz. Fish use their lateral line to position themselves relative to nearby cover objects, currents, or other fish in a school. The lateral line apparently also can detect wave echoes from far shores to help bass navigate.

Lateral lines detect the movements of prey and help bass move close enough to see, feel, and attack them in muddy or dark water. By themselves, however, lateral lines aren't accurate enough to help bass catch evasive prey. In tests, bass using only lateral line senses had to repeatedly strike prey in small aquarium tanks.

Sense of Taste

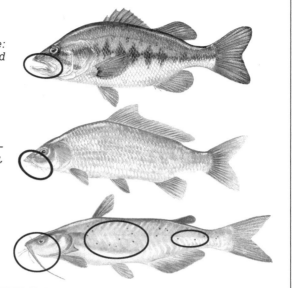

Bass, Walleye, Pike: taste buds centered around mouth and lips.

Carp: Taste buds centered around mouth, lips, and especially barbels.

Catfish: Taste buds centered around mouth, lips, and especially barbels, but also distributed over body.

Sounds travel far underwater, and waves and water currents produce low-frequency noises that compete for a fish's attention. Bass quickly learn to discriminate between random or familiar noises and those associated with danger. They may, for example, ignore outboard motors in a lake with heavy boating use but flee from electric motors associated with fishing.

Smell—Bass have a fairly sensitive sense of smell. Odors in the immediate area that are associated with feeding may stimulate higher activity levels and increase hunting behavior. Bass may follow scent trails toward food if the trail is strong and distinct. But current quickly destroys scent trails and limits the usefulness of scent as a way to track and attack specific prey or lures.

Taste—The taste of objects is the final arbiter, determined by taste receptors located inside a bass's mouth. Bass test potential foods by biting them. Objects that feel and taste edible are usually swallowed. Objects that feel too hard or don't taste like food are rejected. Scientists have identified several amino acids that black bass seem to prefer. Some anglers believe that flavors like anise, garlic, salt, and WD-40 appeal to bass.

Other senses—Bass swim straight across lakes without referencing distinctive structures or cover. They apparently navigate based on the sun's position, aided by a biological clock that compensates for changes in the angle of sunlight throughout the day. Recent research suggests that bass can see polarized light, which would explain their ability to orient with this sun compass on cloudy days (polarized light passes through clouds).

This same sense of solar positioning may also allow bass to anticipate the time of minor solunar periods. They may also sense the position of the moon and sun to identify major solar feeding periods, using an unidentified sensory system.

Secrets to Seasonal Periods of Response

CALENDAR
PERIODS

N o creatures are physically less affected by seasonal changes in the environment than humans. We may feel cheerful on a warm spring day or down after a week of rain; we dress light when it's sultry and cover up when it's cold. But in all seasons, our metabolism remains about constant. We eat three meals a day, go to work, raise the kids, walk the dog, and sleep on a similar schedule year-round. Scientists call us *homeotherms*—creatures with stable body temperatures, regardless of the outside environment.

Other mammals and birds also are homeothermic (often called warm-blooded), although many of those species are more likely to migrate or hibernate, eat less, or grow extra fur during cold seasons. We don't feel such constraints, but most animals also mate, give birth, and raise young only during certain seasons that allow adults to eat heavily and feed their young while forage is most abundant.

Fish like bass are affected far more than birds and mammals by seasonal and even daily changes in weather and water temperature. The feeding activity, digestion, metabolism, and growth rate of bass are all influenced by season and water temperature in accordance with the fishes' genetic makeup. Angling success, therefore, depends in large part upon understanding the changing seasonal activities of bass.

Calendar Periods

Prespawn	Spawn	Post-spawn	Pre-summer	Summer Peak	Summer	Post-summer	Turnover	Cold Water	Winter
1	2	3	4	5	6	7	8	9	10

In-Fisherman founders Al and Ron Lindner developed the concept of Calendar Periods before publishing the first issue of *In-Fisherman* magazine. They used this concept in their early days of guiding and promoting fishing tackle. It worked like magic. Indeed, they termed their traveling fishing show, which often produced fish (including bass, walleyes, and pike) on waters where local anglers weren't catching any, their "magic act."

So it was that Al and Ron, who learned to fish in natural lakes in the northern United States, became particularly interested in how seasonal changes affect fish behavior and determine successful angling techniques. The seasonal changes we note here are most dramatic in the North, where water temperatures range from around 80°F in the heat of summer to just above 32°F for several months of winter. Yet the more subtle and gradual changes that occur in southern waters, even in the tropics, also profoundly affect fish behavior. The In-Fisherman Calendar includes 10 periods in an annual cycle. Dividing the annual continuum into 10 periods is arbitrary; indeed, the periods sometimes overlap. The 10 time frames, however, focus on subtleties in changing water conditions and in fish response. The In-Fisherman Calendar Periods don't follow the 12-month Gregorian calendar, since fish have no regard for such artificial schemes.

The Lindners based the original In-Fisherman Calendar of Fish Activity on the behavior of fish in lakes and reservoirs, but the same seasonal trends occur in rivers, with the exceptions of the Turnover Period and, sometimes, the Frozen Water Period. Other periods, like Summer Peak and Postsummer, occur in rivers, though their timing may differ from the same periods in nearby lakes. The reactions of bass in running waters are different, too; bass in rivers often migrate much farther after spawning and before winter than lake fish.

Practical application—Understanding the In-Fisherman Calendar of Fish Activity is one basis for learning the movement and behavior patterns of bass and developing the skill to find them. The calendar serves as a reference. Understanding that fish progress through distinct periods of activity that vary only in their length from year to year, based on changes in weather, allows anglers to note similarities and differences in fish behavior from one activity period to the next. You can move from one body of water to another, even in different regions, and noting the Calendar Period will still give you a general idea of what bass will be doing.

In discussions among anglers, therefore, the Calendar Period is often a critical factor. It does little good for bass anglers to discuss the application of a lure like a plastic worm, for example, without first noting the Calendar Period in question. Soft plastics are commonly used during the Summer Peak and Summer Periods, but modifications in shape and size and rigging can make this category deadly during the Coldwater Periods in Spring and Fall. They may also be a good choice during the Prespawn, Postspawn, and Presummer Periods in some types of waters, the subject of the next chapter.

Some of this information may at first seem like a return to high-school science class. In a sense, we suppose it is. But as In-Fisherman applies it, this is practical information that has revolutionized fishing for millions of anglers. Many of them were certainly puzzled at first about the relevance of this information to their every-day fishing but have found that understanding Calendar Periods is one basis for consistent fishing success on a variety of lakes, rivers, reservoirs, pits, and ponds.

Calendar Period Regional Timetable

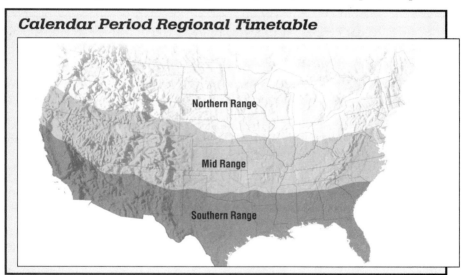

ABOUT LARGEMOUTH BASS AND THE SEASONS

In North America, largemouth bass range from southern Quebec to central Mexico. Bass behave similarly throughout this wide range, but the timing and the length of their prespawn activities, hibernation, and other behaviors vary. Our 10 Calendar Periods of fish response categorize bass behavior by season and allow for subtleties of observation.

Water temperature, for example, is one important impetus for the seasonal shifts, but it doesn't work like a switch. No magic water temperature pulls bass into the shallows for a prespawn feeding spree or triggers them to spawn.

• Bass respond to temperature trends more than to degrees on a thermometer.

• Temperatures in one part of a lake or reservoir can vary substantially from temperatures elsewhere in that body of water. Bass activities in each location vary accordingly.

• Individual bass respond differently to temperature and other environmental factors. Behavior depends on fish size as well as individual differences among fish.

Calendar Period Regional Timetable

1. Prespawn   4. Presummer   7. Postsummer   10. Winter*
2. Spawn   5. Summer Peak   8. Fall Turnover
3. Postspawn   6. Summer   9. Coldwater   *Coldest water of the year.

Gregorian Calendar	Jan	Feb	Mar	Apr	May	June	July	Aug	Sept	Oct	Nov	Dec
Northern Range		10	9	1	2 3 4	5	6		7	8	9	10
Mid Range		10	9	1	2 3 4 5		6			7 8	9	10
Southern Range	10	9	1	2	3 4 5		6			7	8	9 10

Some Calendar Periods are triggered by events other than temperature. The Presummer Period, for example, is tied to the development of weedy cover, which is dependent on weather.

COLDWATER PERIOD (SPRING)

Water Temperature: Cold but rising
General Fish Mood: Inactive to neutral

This period occurs as early as late January in the South and as late as the end of April in the most northern part of the largemouth range, as water warms from the low 40°F range into the 50s.

Bass move from deep wintering sites toward the shallows, where they resume feeding and will later spawn. Bass in reservoirs typically move along creek channels or over deep flats. They sometimes hold in large aggregations where cover and baitfish are present. In deep, cool reservoirs, 10 to 20 feet is the average depth of bass during early spring.

Bass in lakes move shallower more quickly because deep cover is sparse. The spring Coldwater Period is short in northern lakes, where water warms rapidly. Soon after ice-out, bass move into shallow, black-bottomed bays or canals. They're spooky but can be caught on slowly worked presentations like tube jigs or unweighted plastic worms. In some northern states and provinces, bass season is closed at this time, and where it's open, fishing can be inconsistent because of changeable weather.

In the South, where bass shift areas over a longer period of time, fishing can be good, especially for big fish. Observant anglers can find holding areas that bass visit each year for a week or two, often called *staging areas*. Typical locations are timbered holes in submerged creek channels near expansive flats or sloughs. As water warms, bass scatter toward shallower spawning and feeding sites.

PRESPAWN PERIOD

Water Temperature: Cool but rising
General Fish Mood: Positive

As the water warms, bass move shallower. Dark-bottomed bays, particularly those on northwestern shores, warm first, drawing panfish, minnows, and predator species. Insect activity also is greater here than in the main lake. Bass gather around limited available cover, including weed and lily pad stalks, stumps, and fallen trees.

Seasons of Change

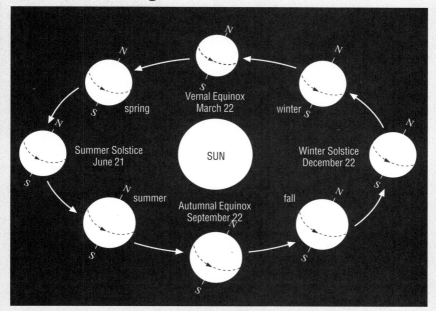

Spring, summer, fall, winter. The pendulum swings between seasons, bringing evident changes on land, but more difficult-to-define changes underwater. Studies show that photoperiod (length of daylight) influences the tempo of the environment, from microorganisms to top-of-the-line predators. The intensity and duration of light in a yearly cycle influences migrations, spawning, and feeding.

Warming coves and shallow creek arms in reservoirs draw prey species. Clear water that's warmer attracts bass, so dead-end creeks and sloughs provide better fishing than creeks with current. Because bass see better and therefore bite better in clear water, upper reservoir reaches muddied by late-winter rains often don't produce well. Clearer shallow coves in the lower third of the reservoir often yield better catches when water temperatures are in the 50°F range.

Bass movement toward the shallows sometimes is tentative. They move into warming shallow bays, but retreat during wind or cold fronts to the first drop-off with substantial cover. Under adverse conditions, they are more likely to remain in coves with thick cover.

Most preyfish species move shallow during the Prespawn Period. Bass must feed heavily to complete the maturation of eggs and sperm and to store energy for the Spawn Period. Water levels in natural lakes, reservoirs, and rivers typically are higher than at any other season. Seek active bass in shoreline cover and in flooded brush, trees, and terrestrial plants.

Late in the Prespawn Period, bass are aggressive and catchable. Cold blustery weather turns fish off early in the Prespawn Period, but as the spawn approaches, they're almost always active, especially in northern waters. Warm, stable weather for several days can produce fantastic fishing. Often the best fishing is toward evening on sunny days.

Periods of stable sunny weather quickly warm shallow water in spring, attracting minnow forage and bass.

To stretch out productive prespawn fishing as long as possible, switch lakes. By moving among several bodies of water, you can find prespawn fishing conditions for more than a month in northern waters, two months in the South. Water temperatures must steadily rise into the low 60°F range and remain there before spawning will begin. Bass in the South typically remain in the Prespawn Period at higher temperatures than bass in northern regions, who spawn at lower temperatures.

SPAWN PERIOD
Water Temperature: Moderately warm and rising
General Fish Mood: Neutral, but aggressively defensive

Several factors trigger the spawn, the most important being length of daylight and water temperature. Water temperature rising into the low 60°F range shifts male bass from prespawn feeding to nest preparation. But bass in a body of water don't all spawn at the same time. Indeed, they've spawned in water temperatures from the high 50s to the low 80s. Water temperature also may vary among sections of a body of water. This scattered spawning protects an entire year class from being destroyed by adverse weather.

In reservoirs, bass usually spawn earliest in the upper reaches, latest in the lower portion, because upstream coves and creek arms usually are shallower and darker colored and thus warm faster. Spawning may continue for four to six weeks in a reservoir. Larger bass tend to spawn earlier than smaller bass; a spawning area filled with small fish may indicate that the spawn is almost completed.

Largemouth bass have spawned successfully in water from 6 inches to more that 15 feet deep, but they typically nest in water 1 to 4 feet deep. The murkier the water, the shallower they spawn. This spawning versatility is yet another aspect of bass adaptability.

Because silt can smother and destroy fertilized eggs, and because predators seek eggs for their protein content, male bass must choose nest sites carefully. They

Male bass guard fry until they reach an inch or so in length.

often choose sites in channels, coves, bays, and along wind-protected shores. In rivers, bass seek quiet backwaters with medium to hard bottoms. Females remain shallow only until they've expelled their eggs. They will strike various baits at this time. Where fishing is legal, many trophy bass are caught during the spawn.

Males remain to defend the nest and fan the eggs to provide oxygen, remove waste products, and

Typical Spawning Months

AREA	MONTHS
Florida	February and March
Mississippi	March through early April
Missouri	April
Pennsylvania	May
Minnesota/Ontario	mid-May to late June

The timing of the largemouth bass Spawn Period illustrates the region-by-region progression of Calendar Periods. Latitude, water temperature, weather trends, length of daylight, competition for habitat, and internal biorhythms are some of the factors influencing the exact timing of the spawn.

Not all bass spawn at the same time, even in the same body of water. While most adult bass in a lake may spawn during a couple weeks of ideal conditions, some spawn earlier, some later. Regionally, the onset of largemouth bass spawning may begin in February in the South and late June in Ontario.

prevent siltation. During the spawn, males often strike lures cast into or over the nest. The aggressiveness of their defense depends on weather conditions, fishing pressure, and the stage of egg development. Males fan and guard their eggs for two to five days until the eggs hatch. Hatchlings, sustained by their yolk sac, remain in the nest for up to a week. As fry become free swimming, they aggregate in a dark ball, which the male guards until the fry swim off and begin eating zooplankton.

Because of erratic spring weather, the success of a spawn varies. Even under the most favorable circumstances, only a fraction of one percent of fry reach catchable size. During the spawn, fishing varies from poor to easy. Males are particularly vulnerable while guarding nests. Females also are vulnerable while in shallow areas where they're sometimes visible and where lure presentation is easy.

In many northern states where the spawn is most synchronized and bass are most vulnerable, regulations entirely prohibit fishing for bass during the spawn or severely restrict harvest to prevent overfishing.

POSTSPAWN PERIOD

Water Temperature: Warming through the 70°F range
General Fish Mood: Inactive to neutral

Postspawn is a short transition period between completion of reproductive activities and the onset of summer patterns. Bass leave shallow bedding areas and move toward areas they'll use all summer, lingering at times in emerging lily pads and submerged weedbeds growing outside spawning areas.

During the Postspawn Period, bass scatter and usually don't move as a group, though numbers of fish may hold in particular areas. They're also not aggressive, due apparently to the physical demands of spawning. Fishing typically is difficult.

Until water warms and weeds reach the surface, bass tend to remain near bottom. Surface lures and spinnerbaits aren't as effective as when bass were massed in the shallows or feeding more aggressively. In a given body of water, however, individual bass may be in the Prespawn, Spawn, Postspawn, or Presummer Period.

PRESUMMER PERIOD

Water Temperature: Warm and rising
General Fish Mood: positive

As the water warms and weeds develop, bass move to depths with the best available cover and prey. In natural lakes, large flats often provide this habitat. At first, bass cluster among weed clumps on flats. Later, they move deeper when weeds sprout along deeper breaklines. Active bass feed on the outside or inside edges of weedlines or over the weeds.

In reservoirs, bass move toward the mouths of small sloughs and shoreline points, especially those near a deeper channel with stumps or timber. They often begin preying on shad that move over main-lake flats. Bass typically are aggressive, feeding to recover from spawning. They are catchable on a variety of presentations.

SUMMER PEAK PERIOD

Water Temperature: warm and rising
General Fish Mood: Positive

Summer Peak is a short period when bass first occupy their typical summer locations. Lily pads have formed but aren't covered with algae. Most aquatic plants have developed, producing well-defined inside and outside weededges. Oxygen levels are high and the water is clear. Lakes are just beginning to stratify.

Food is plentiful, as newly hatched baitfish grow. Adult preyfish and panfish have spawned and are vulnerable to large predators. Bass feed aggressively unless early summer cold fronts are severe. In reservoirs with strong shad populations, some bass begin to shadow schools of shad offshore, particularly at dawn and dusk.

Summer Habitat

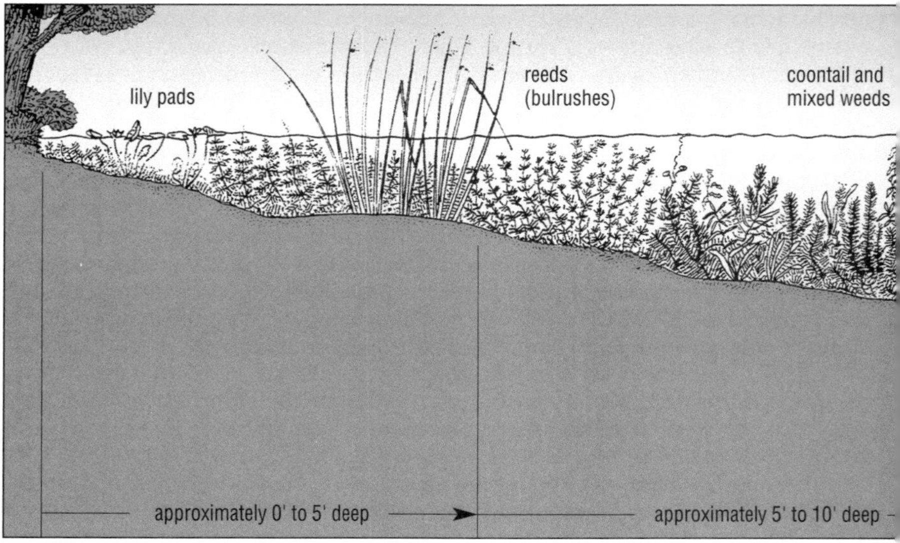

lily pads

reeds (bulrushes)

coontail and mixed weeds

approximately 0' to 5' deep ⟶ approximately 5' to 10' deep

Bass location varies. Some fish are in heavy cover in shallow water, while others prowl deep weedlines, timber, and stumpfields. Catch rates typically are high, but large bass are scattered.

Bass may hold in deeper water if forage fish are available. Moderate water temperatures and high oxygen levels allow bass to inhabit various depths. Deeper lying bass are harder to locate but are reliable biters because they aren't so likely to change their activity level with minor weather changes. Aggregations are common on prime structure. Fishing can be terrific.

SUMMER PERIOD

Water Temperature: Maximum for each body of water
General Fish Mood: Variable

During the Summer Period, water temperatures reach their maximum. Waters that stratify are divided into three zones—a warm surface layer (epilimnion); a layer of rapidly declining temperature (thermocline or metalimnion); and a deep cool layer (hypolimnion), which typically has insufficient oxygen to support bass in fertile lakes and reservoirs.

Minnows, shad, sunfish, and other prey are plentiful in the upper layer. Bass feed heavily, but often briefly, because the abundance of prey reduces competition for food. Fishing may become difficult as bass become finicky and concentrate on specific prey during specific times. In fertile waters, presenting lures or livebait can become difficult because of dense weedgrowth. Very weedy waters also may have low oxygen levels at dawn, which hurts early morning fishing.

Groups of bass may hold in many different habitats. Fishing at dusk or at night may provide the best action when large bass leave heavy cover to prowl flats. Summer is one of the most stable and predictable periods. It's also the longest period in southern climates, up to six months in Florida.

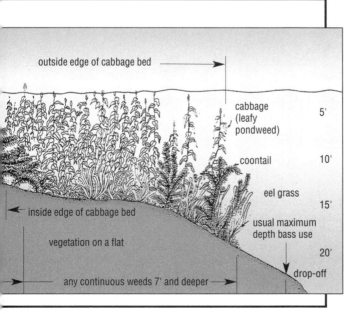

By Summer Peak, bass have settled into areas they use throughout summer. In lakes and many reservoirs, weedbeds become the focus of bass activity. Three general areas include heavy shallow weeds (slop); moderately deep weeds on the flat; and weeds along the deep weededge.

Doug Hannon, the "Bass Professor," has offered many trendsetting observations about largemouth bass in the pages of In-Fisherman *magazine. While many fishermen consider Prespawn the peak period for giant bass, Hannon focuses on the Summer Period for most of his hundreds of bass over 10 pounds. According to Hannon, summer brings stable weather, stable water conditions, and stable fish reaction. Fishermen, therefore, can key on peak daily and monthly periods of lunar influence.*

POSTSUMMER PERIOD

Water Temperature: Warm but cooling
General Fish Mood: Variable

Declining daylight and cooling water gradually alter summer behavioral patterns of largemouth bass. Plants begin to die. Shallow vegetation declines first, then deeper weeds when water becomes murkier due to wind action and plankton blooms. Bass in shallow areas hold near remaining cover, gradually moving to clumps of green weeds that remain in deep water in protected areas such as inside turns.

Bass in reservoirs often move to shallower cover as water temperatures moderate and shad move inshore. Some fish move into small creeks when temperatures decline, but they evacuate these restricted areas when temperatures fall into the low 50°F range. Eventually, dropping water temperatures also reduce the metabolism and feeding requirements of bass.

Postsummer is a transition period. Fishing can be good or poor, depending on how weather conditions affect the variables that give each body of water its unique characteristics.

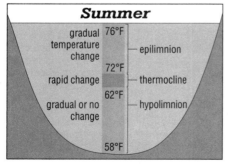

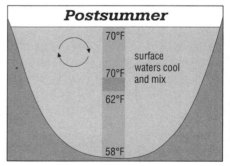

The upper (warmwater) layer may be from 12 to 40 feet thick, while the thermocline may be 2 to 15 feet thick. The lower (cold-water) level usually contains less dissolved oxygen than the upper layer.

The surface of the water radiates heat to the atmosphere at night as water above the thermocline gradually cools. The thermocline remains intact but becomes closer in temperature to the layer above. Oxygen-poor water remains trapped below the thermocline.

TURNOVER PERIOD

Water Temperature: Upper to low 50°F range
General Fish Mood: Inactive

Fall weather cools surface water, making it heavy enough to mix with cooler water in the thermocline. Wind furthers the mixing as the thermocline narrows and finally disintegrates. As water mixes from surface to bottom, it may become muddy, due to rising bottom debris. Hydrogen sulfide and other gases that were trapped on the bottom may produce a musky or sulfurous smell.

Fishing becomes difficult. Conditions leading to turnover may extend

Imminent Turnover

64°F — cooling continues

62°F — thermocline not as marked

60°F — and deeper

58°F

The thermocline shrinks as it approaches the same temperature as the uniform mass of water above.

over several weeks and contribute to poor fishing throughout a region. On a particular lake, however, turnover rarely lasts more than a week before conditions stabilize and the body of water enters the fall Coldwater Period.

COLDWATER PERIOD (FALL)

Water Temperature: Declining to seasonal lows
General Fish Mood: Moderately active to inactive

Following turnover, water usually is in the low 50°F range. Cold temperatures and the breakup of summer fishing patterns end the season for many anglers. But this period can yield the biggest bass of the season. Outstanding catches occur when anglers locate groups of bass.

Bass aggregate around remaining cover. In some waters, they move to steeply sloping structure where they can change depths without moving far horizontally. These areas become winter sanctuaries for large numbers of bass.

Bass that have been buried in shallow weeds all summer move first to cover on flats and finally to cover on or near drop-offs. They're accessible to anglers, often for the first time since spring. In reservoirs, bass aggregate in creek channels and along outside edges of weedy flats. Where shad school offshore, bass in deep reservoirs remain near deep structure.

Green weed patches, usually on drop-offs, key location for bass in natural lakes. Not all weeds die off at the same time. Coontail, for example, thrives in cool water, and lily pads and milfoil hold up late into the season. As fragile species of weeds decline, those that remain attract and concentrate bass.

While water temperatures remain in the 50°F range, bass may feed aggressively, often chasing lures. Slow presentations generally maximize the catch in cold water, however, and slower works best for lunker bass. So fish large baits slowly. And when action slows, try smaller, more subtle baits like grubs, downsized jigs, and small worms.

WINTER OR FROZEN WATER PERIOD

Water Temperature: At its coldest for an extended period
General Fish Mood: Inactive

Winter is a long period characterized by the coldest temperatures of the year. It can't be defined by precise environmental conditions, since bass are found in such a variety of geographical areas. In northern Minnesota, water on lakes and

In northern regions, ice coats lakes, reservoirs and rivers, sometimes to a depth of 3 feet. Ice fisherman frequently catch bass, sometimes in good numbers, indicating that some fish remain active at certain times.

even parts of rivers is under 3 feet of ice. Water temperatures range from about 32°F directly under the ice to 39°F on the bottom. In southern states, water temperatures usually are in the 40°F range, mid-50s in Florida.

Bass in shallow eutrophic waters are affected by declining oxygen levels in winter, because all organisms use oxygen and none is replenished from the air or by photosynthesis. In some lakes, oxygen deprivation in deep water forces bass to move shallower. In shallow lakes in the far north, winterkill may occur.

Usually, though, largemouth bass hold in the deepest water they use all year. They move deep to water that's slightly warmer and more stable than water near the surface. Just how deep depends on many circumstances; 20 to 30 feet is common in natural lakes, 50 feet in deeper reservoirs. Preyfish generally also are concentrated on middepth flats in or near the lake basin. In shallow reservoirs or ponds, bass are in or near the deepest available water. Bass in rivers seek backwaters with adequate oxygen and away from current.

Largemouth bass often gather in huge winter aggregations. In reservoirs, these aggregations often suspend in timber near deep creek channels. Even though bass are inactive, aggregations are so large that a few fish are usually active enough to hit lures.

Cold water reduces bass metabolism. Fish feed infrequently, becoming active only periodically, especially early and late in the Winter Period. Ice fishermen, who usually seek other species, commonly catch largemouth bass through the ice. Lunkers are common just prior to ice-out.

Chapter 3

Categorizing Lake, River, and Reservoir Types

BASS HABITAT FACTORS

When *In-Fisherman* first began publication in 1975, several principles were offered as part of a learning package that guaranteed anglers they could learn to fish successfully, or their money back. Chapter 2 of this book discussed the Calendar Periods that largemouth bass move through as the seasons pass. The ability to identify Calendar Periods remains one overriding factor in understanding how bass are affected by their environment—

where they may be and how they may react to an angler's choice of presentation.

Calendar Periods also serve as a reference point and therefore as a basis for communication. Anglers who understand the system can discuss fish response and place it in context. If two anglers are both referring to the same Calendar Period, say—postspawn behavior or turnover behavior—some comparisons may be valid, even if one is referring to a lake in Minnesota and the other to an Arkansas reservoir.

Classifying lakes, reservoirs, and rivers is another critical concept *In-Fisherman* offers for understanding the structure of different bodies of water. Learning to classify waters helps the angler to note similarities and differences in fish behavior, in context. For example, an angler discussing bass behavior in a canyon reservoir might sound outlandish to an angler accustomed to fishing bass in a middle-aged natural lake. Surprisingly, the thousands of lakes, rivers, and reservoirs across North America generally fall into little more than a dozen divisions that are easy to grasp.

NATURAL LAKES

Obviously, no two lakes are exactly alike. Broadly, though, all lakes can be classified into one of three environmental age groups: oligotrophic (young), mesotrophic (middle-aged), and eutrophic (old). Factors like the lake's predator-prey relationships, the amounts and types of aquatic vegetation, and many other structural considerations help determine a lake's classification and ultimately help you determine where bass should be located within each Calendar Period.

No matter where your favorite lake is located, it's changing. Lakes age naturally, over eons. This aging process is often called *eutrophication* (increase in fertility), and all lakes pass through it. The initial stages of eutrophication may take thousands of years. The final ones may happen quickly, especially with the addition of manmade factors. A lake grows older not only in time, but in condition. In some waters, visible change may take centuries; in others, changes can be seen in a few years.

Throughout this process, the lake environment—structural makeup, food web, vegetation levels, and dominant fish species—changes. Cultural (man-caused) eutrophication, or aging, is in part due to expanding human population and waste disposal. Man may accomplish in a generation what might otherwise take many hundreds of years.

Because of the manmade changes on most North American lakes, we classify natural lakes according to their environmental condition rather than their chronological age. Each category is a point of reference. Anglers quickly learn to recognize similarities in bodies of water and can readily transfer what they've learned on one lake to another with similar characteristics. This is one method for patterning bass and applying those patterns to bodies of water an angler has never fished before but nevertheless recognizes.

As lakes age, their character changes. Environmentally young lakes are deep and clear, while older lakes are shallow and murky. The young lakes are oxygen-rich and support lake trout, whitefish, walleyes, and smallmouth bass. Old lakes are weed-choked and oxygen-poor, and these support carp, bullheads, and perhaps some largemouth bass. Between these extremes fall most lakes, each one more or less hospitable to certain fish species. Largemouth bass thrive in middle-aged (mesotrophic) lakes and in early-stage eutrophic waters but may also occupy small fertile zones in oligotrophic waters. The three basic categories of natural lakes can be regrouped into nine or even more specific categories. First, though, consider the three basic categories.

Middle-Stage Oligotrophic

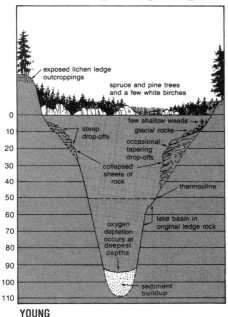

exposed lichen ledge
outcroppings

spruce and pine trees
and a few white birches

few shallow weeds
glacial rocks
steep
drop-offs
occasional
tapering
drop-offs
collapsed
sheets of
rock

thermocline

oxygen
depletion
occurs at
deepest
depths

lake basin in
original ledge rock

sediment
buildup

Depth in Feet

0
10
20
30
40
50
60
70
80
90
100
110

YOUNG

Middle-Stage Mesotrophic

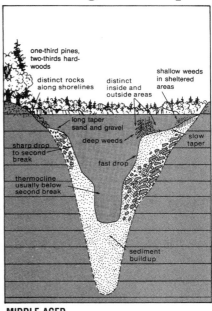

one-third pines,
two-thirds hard-
woods

distinct rocks
along shorelines

distinct
inside and
outside areas

shallow weeds
in sheltered
areas

long taper
sand and gravel

deep weeds

sharp drop
to second
break

fast drop

slow
taper

thermocline
usually below
second break

sediment
buildup

MIDDLE-AGED

Middle-Stage Eutrophic

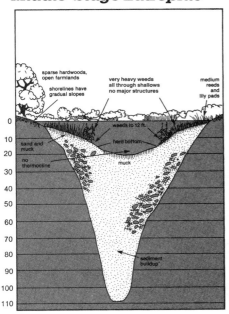

sparse hardwoods,
open farmlands

shorelines have
gradual slopes

very heavy weeds
all through shallows
no major structures

medium
reeds
and
lily pads

weeds to 12 ft.

hard bottom

sand and
muck

no
thermocline

muck

sediment
buildup

Depth in Feet

0
10
20
30
40
50
60
70
80
90
100
110

OLD

The Aging Processes

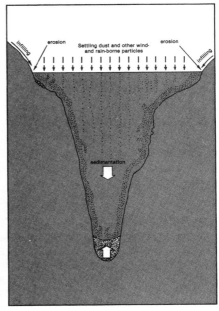

infilling

erosion

Settling dust and other wind-
and rain-borne particles

erosion

infilling

sedimentation

OLIGOTROPHIC LAKES

The youngest, most infertile lakes typically have rock basins and are found almost exclusively in the northern latitudes of North America. They usually have steep, sharp drop-offs, few weeds, and conifer-studded shorelines. The nutrient level of the water is low and oxygen is available in deep water, the zone called the *hypolimnion* (coldwater layer) that lies below the thermocline. Oligotrophic lakes are typically crystal clear.

Oligotrophic lakes usually support low gamefish populations; a few pounds of gamefish per acre is common. You'll find smallmouth bass in these lakes, but largemouth bass are absent from many oligotrophic northern waters, though they may occupy the more shallow, productive bays of large oligotrophic lakes. Bass in these waters tend to grow slowly but may live more than 15 years, so a few lunker-sized fish are possible. Lakes at the more productive end of this category tend to have larger largemouth populations.

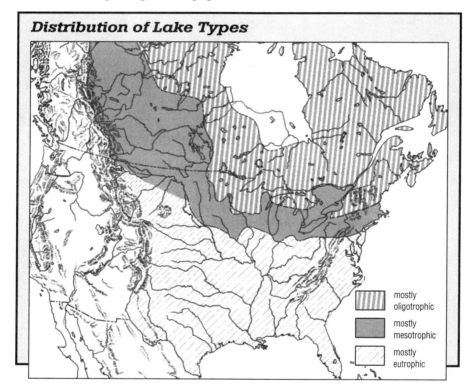

Distribution of Lake Types

mostly
oligotrophic

mostly
mesotrophic

mostly
eutrophic

MESOTROPHIC LAKES

In middle-aged lakes, shorelines are less gorge-like and drop-offs less abrupt. Big boulders give way to smaller rocks, and sand and gravel are more prevalent. Weed-growth abounds on shallower flats. Shoreline terrain is more varied and aquatic plants more diverse. The water receives more nutrients, fostering moderate fertility and strong populations of many species of fish. Lakes of this sort are found from coast to coast at temperate latitudes. Many of the top largemouth lakes of the north-central, northwestern, and northeastern states fall into this category.

EUTROPHIC LAKES

Initial stages of lake aging and the physical changes that result may take place over thousands of years. Later, when aging processes accelerate and the natural process is further accelerated by human activity, the process is called *cultural eutrophication*. The environmentally oldest lakes are warmwater environments, generally shallow and rich in nutrients.

Shallow weedgrowth is thick as long as the water remains somewhat clear. Lake bottoms consist of muck or clay, and shorelines taper gradually to the waterline. Often there are no secondary drop-offs. Marshy areas often abut lake edges. Hardwood trees and flat shorelines are the rule.

NATURAL LAKE TYPES AND SELECT FISH SPECIES

OLIGOTROPHIC			MESOTROPHIC			EUTROPHIC		
EARLY	MIDDLE	LATE	EARLY	MIDDLE	LATE	EARLY	MIDDLE	LATE

CONDITIONS OF ENVIRONMENT

COLD WATER	TRANSITION STAGES	COOL WATER	TRANSITION STAGES	WARM WATER

LAKE TROUT

BULLHEAD

WALLEYE

LARGEMOUTH BASS

CATFISH

Some eutrophic lakes are called *dishpan lakes* because of their overall shallow depth and uniform shape. Typically, these old lakes have dense fish populations, though the bulk of the biomass may be preyfish, small panfish, or nongame species like bullheads and carp. Largemouth bass thrive in these rich, warm environments from Minnesota to Florida. In late-stage eutrophic lakes (sometimes called *hypereutrophic*), however, fish kills due to oxygen depletion become increasingly common. At this point, gamefish species like bass decline, ceding the water to hardy fish like bullheads, bowfin, gar, and carp.

RIVERS

Rivers come in many sizes and provide habitat for many fish species. Different stretches of the same river can have contrasting personalities and different fish species assemblages. For example, a young, clear, coldwater river plunges downhill, flowing over and cutting through solid rock. Here, trout thrive but certainly not largemouth bass. As a river matures, it becomes increasingly fertile, flows more slowly, and begins to meander. A coolwater, moderate-flow environment favors walleyes and smallmouth bass. Finally, a river winds through a floodplain as it approaches the coast or its confluence with a larger river. This slow-flowing, warmwater environment supports excellent largemouth bass populations that inhabit backwaters, oxbows, and slower sections of the main river, as well as many other species of game and nongame fish.

Slow-flowing, shallow rivers with broad floodplains offer complex backwater areas with abundant cover in the form of stumps, fallen trees, and aquatic plants. Side channels provide connections to other prime spots, and largemouth bass use them for travel during all seasons and for feeding during the warmer months.

River Type Continuum

1. Headwater Stream

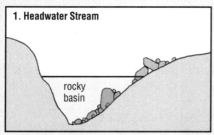

rocky basin

Bottom rocky; water cool and clear; depth shallow; width narrow; gradient steep; current fast; no aquatic vegetation. No largemouth bass habitat; smallmouths in lower reaches.

2. Major Tributary

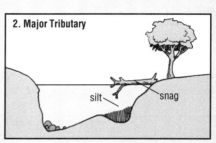

silt   snag

Bottom variable; deeper pools common; water warmer and more turbid, especially after rain; gradient and flow rate reduced; typical riffle–pool–run sequence. Fair largemouth habitat.

3. Medium-sized River

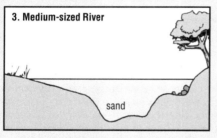

sand

Bottom variable; riffle–pool–run sequence occurs, but not as well defined; vegetation may be present on shallow banks; tributaries common. Good smallmouth habitat; fair for largemouths.

4. Navigable River

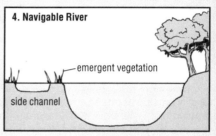

emergent vegetation

side channel

Current moderate; channel complex, possibly dredged; aquatic vegetation locally abundant; bottom soft; water murky and warm. Largemouth bass abundant in backwaters.

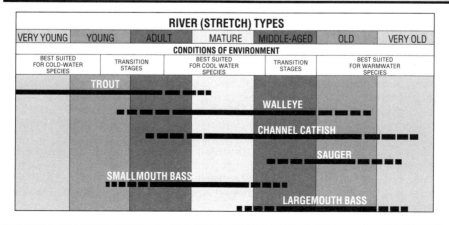

5. Tidal River

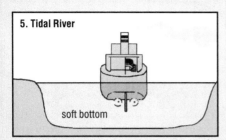

soft bottom

Water subject to tidal influence; salinity varies with location, tide, and rainfall. Largemouths inhabit backwater ponds, feeder creeks, and river structure, but move seasonally in response to flow and salinity.

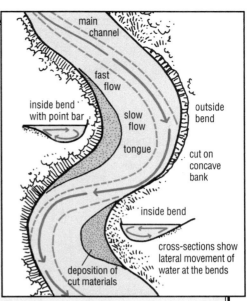

main channel

fast flow

inside bend with point bar

slow flow

tongue

outside bend

cut on concave bank

inside bend

cross-sections show lateral movement of water at the bends

deposition of cut materials

The force of water is constantly remodeling the riverscape. Over time, rivers change their course. It is this change that constructs adjacent flood plains. If a river stretch does not have an extensive adjoining flood plain, it means that its bed is stable or the river is geologically very young. Water is a universal solvent; given time, it can chew away granite, dissolve iron, and move mountains!

In streams, the action of water along with the meandering effect cuts materials on the outside bend where current flow is swift and deposits other materials on the inside bend where current speed and force is reduced. Notice how the current has created a tongue-like structure. The deepest part of any river stretch is always on the outside bend.

Because they live in current, river bass are notoriously tough and powerful.

Typical Impound Features

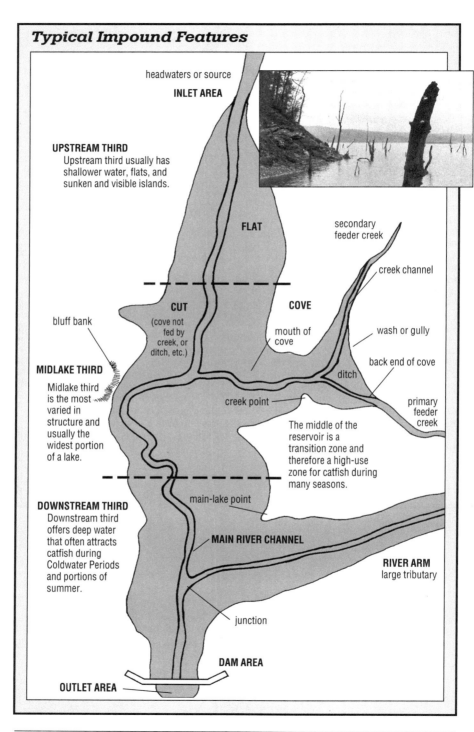

headwaters or source
INLET AREA

UPSTREAM THIRD
Upstream third usually has shallower water, flats, and sunken and visible islands.

FLAT

secondary feeder creek

creek channel

CUT
(cove not fed by creek, or ditch, etc.)

COVE

bluff bank

mouth of cove

wash or gully

back end of cove

MIDLAKE THIRD
Midlake third is the most varied in structure and usually the widest portion of a lake.

ditch

creek point

primary feeder creek

The middle of the reservoir is a transition zone and therefore a high-use zone for catfish during many seasons.

DOWNSTREAM THIRD
Downstream third offers deep water that often attracts catfish during Coldwater Periods and portions of summer.

main-lake point

MAIN RIVER CHANNEL

RIVER ARM
large tributary

junction

DAM AREA

OUTLET AREA

---

44   Critical Concepts . . . Foundations For Success

RESERVOIRS

A reservoir is a body of water impounded behind a dam. Water floods the landscape—marshes, plains, hills, mountains, plateaus, and canyons—depending on the geographic area. In general, reservoirs in the North, West, and Northwest provide cooler water environments than those in the South, Southwest, and Southeast, but nearly all impoundments offer habitat for the adaptable largemouth bass.

Taking a cross section of North America, we see that some regions are low, swampy, and flat. These are old flood plain regions. Other regions are hilly or have mountains with highland ridges that form foothills. Reservoirs built within different land forms inherit their basic configuration; that is, they have a similar cross section and shape. Canyon reservoirs, for example, are long and snakelike with towering, sharp, almost vertical walls. Waters impounded in flood plains are wide and offer expanses of shallow flats.

Reading Reservoir Features

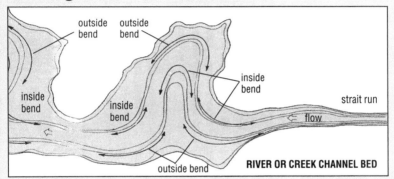

This illustration shows the difference between an inside and outside bend. The outside bend of a river or creek is "washed" the hardest by the water flow. Tongue areas are especially attractive. Remember, obstructions such as a fallen tree can slow the flow and provide cover.

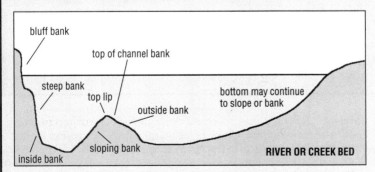

River and creek channels with the proper depth are the "main highways" in a reservoir. Bends, the degree of bank slope, the make-up of the bank top, the amount of timber or bush at the top of the banks, and obstructions in the channel itself affect the exact location of fish.

The shape of an impoundment is the key factor in determining its classification. By studying a topographical map, you can usually determine what classification an impoundment falls into. Other facets of a reservoir's personality include (1) annual fluctuation of water level; (2) water clarity; (3) fertility; and (4) temperature.

IMPOUNDMENT CLASSIFICATION

We classify reservoirs into six categories: canyon, plateau, highland, hill-land, flatland, and lowland (or wetland). These classes are based on regional and geological aspects of North America's various land forms. Both natural and manmade characteristics determine what class an impoundment fits into. There are, of course, exceptions: smaller reservoirs are hard to classify exactly, and some reservoirs have portions characteristic of different classes, just as lakes and rivers do.

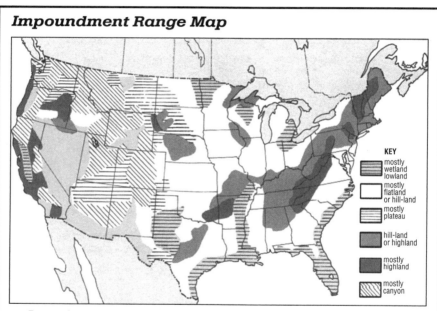

Impoundment Range Map

KEY
- mostly wetland lowland
- mostly flatland or hill-land
- mostly plateau
- hill-land or highland
- mostly highland
- mostly canyon

Reservoirs constructed in similar landforms, even when they're in different parts of the country, are enough alike to fit into six basic groups: canyon, plateau, highland, hill-land, flatland, and lowland (or wetland).

In general, the reason for building a reservoir determines its form and function. Its purpose—flood control, electrical generation, water supply, pumped storage, or recreation—determines its size, geographical shape and geological location, flow rates, and other important characteristics. Physical features limit type and abundance of fish that inhabit it.

While shape is the basis for reservoir classification, fertility also affects its suitability for largemouth bass. Flooded lowland and flatland rivers usually have fertile flood plains that add to a reservoir's productivity. Nutrients foster growth of tiny floating plants called *phytoplankton* that feed small swimming crustaceans called *zooplankton*. Young fish and adults of some species that are important prey for largemouths (like shad and sunfish) prey on zooplankton. The prey base determines predator abundance and size.

LOWLAND IMPOUNDMENTS

Lowland impoundments are the shallowest category of reservoir, sometimes with a maximum depth of fewer than 15 feet, usually found in the old creek channel. A small dam blocks a small river, causing a wetland to fill and spread greatly due to the low, flat terrain. In Wisconsin, lowland impoundments called *flowages* provide multispecies fisheries, as do lowland impoundments on bayous in Louisiana. Particularly in southern latitudes, largemouth bass are the dominant sportfish, often reaching large size.

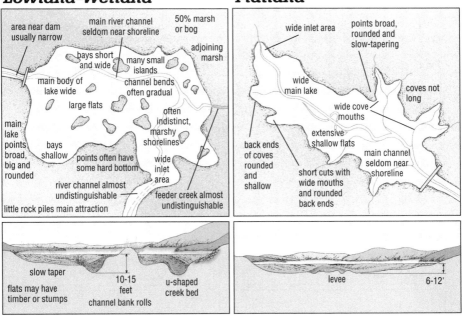

Lowland impoundments feature vast flats with cover provided by the flooded timber and thick vegetation that sometimes grows in rich soils. Some such waters have many small, low islands and may contain old pond dams in the basin, offering a bit of structure. Current is minimal and fishing patterns are typically similar to those in natural lakes.

FLATLAND IMPOUNDMENTS

Many of the nation's most famous largemouth bass fisheries fall into the flatland classification. Waters like Greenwood Lake on the New York-New Jersey border, Lake Seminole on the Florida-Georgia line, Kentucky Lake, Santee-Cooper in South Carolina, and Ross Barnett in Mississippi offer a broad, shallow basin extending from a main river channel that meanders through farmland and low hills. Several broad arms define former tributary creeks that may run only during the rainy season.

Because of the shallow, fertile basin, aquatic plants typically thrive, sometimes covering 50 percent or even more of the surface area of the reservoir. Weed fishing patterns predominate in these waters, though flooded timber and stumps also offer cover for bass, particularly in flatland impoundments that are murky and thus have little plant growth. River channel ledges in the 12- to 20-foot range also hold bass, where the fish await passing schools of threadfin and gizzard shad.

Baitfish and bass are very abundant, and other species including white bass, hybrid stripers, crappies, and catfish are common, too. These older reservoirs were the birthplace of many bassin' techniques and continue to offer excellent fishing.

HILL-LAND IMPOUNDMENTS

Hill-land impoundments provide the classic reservoir shape, with many small fingers branching from a main basin that surrounds a major river channel. These impoundments are deeper than flatland impoundments but not as wide, because hills on either side of the river constrict them. Creek arms are narrower and deeper, with extensive submerged timber, though this form of cover has been declining over the many decades since most of these reservoirs were built.

Hill-Land

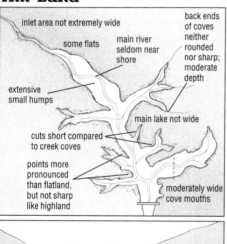

inlet area not extremely wide
some flats
main river seldom near shore
extensive small humps
cuts short compared to creek coves
points more pronounced than flatland, but not sharp like highland
back ends of coves neither rounded nor sharp; moderate depth
main lake not wide
moderately wide cove mouths

one side may be steep
30-60 feet
slower taper
small dish-shaped bed

Highland

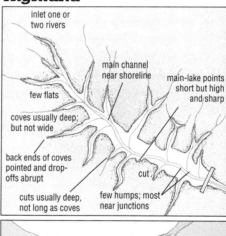

inlet one or two rivers
main channel near shoreline
main-lake points short but high and sharp
few flats
coves usually deep; but not wide
back ends of coves pointed and drop-offs abrupt
cut
cuts usually deep, not long as coves
few humps; most near junctions

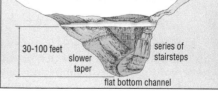

30-100 feet
slower taper
series of stairsteps
flat bottom channel

Abundant shad and mild climate foster excellent populations of largemouth bass, and in several areas they are joined by smallmouths and spotted bass. Water color ranges from fairly clear with a greenish tinge to stained. The color may vary seasonally, with spring rains making the water murky and summer plant growth fostering clear water in creek arms. The upper end of the reservoir tends to be murkier where the main river enters, with silt gradually falling out as water approaches the deep basin near the dam. Bass often undertake seasonal shifts in location, particularly during the Prespawn, Postspawn, and Turnover, and Cold Water Periods.

HIGHLAND IMPOUNDMENTS

The dams on highland impoundments usually are constructed in steep, narrow ravines. This category of reservoir is therefore narrow but very deep, where high bluff walls border long, narrow creek channels. The basin itself is also narrow and extends from higher elevations down to the dam. The deep basin offers few or no islands, but tributary creek arms may include islands and underwater humps. Most bass fishing occurs in the upper end of creek arms; smallmouths and spotted bass may coexist there and may range into the main body of the reservoir.

Clear water with little cover is also a challenge for anglers. Largemouths may live in available shallow cover or hold in water deeper than most anglers are accustomed to fish. Preyfish are not abundant, which limits largemouth numbers. Lack of competition among bass in some highland reservoirs makes them trophy fisheries, however. Stripers, walleyes, and other coolwater species share the baitfish supply. Night-fishing is popular on these waters, because bass roam shallower and seem to feed more actively after dark.

CANYON IMPOUNDMENTS

Huge concrete dams across steep, narrow canyons form canyon impoundments, the dominant type in the Southwest and West. These waters are the most capacious and deepest reservoirs, often over 200 feet. They're also ultraclear, a result of the sand and rock that form the basin. These substrates yield little plant life, so cover is in the form of sparse stick-ups, boulders, and sheer canyon walls with occasional rock slides. Canyon impoundments are narrow and very long, with long tributary arms.

These oligotrophic impoundments typically feature a deep, oxygenated hypolimnion that supports stocked rainbow trout. Warmwater species like largemouth usually inhabit shallow bays and tributary arms, but large fish or schools

Canyon

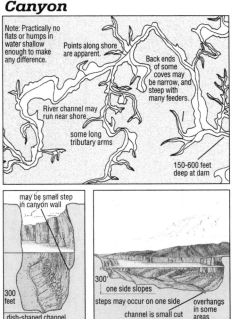

Plateau

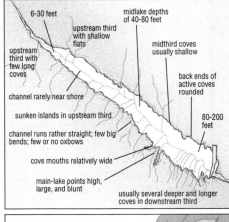

of small bass may roam the open water, feeding on shad and the occasional trout.

Canyon bass fishing patterns are a study in contrasts. Many anglers catch bass by working plastic worms along deep breaks and shelves, sometimes taking bass in water over 50 feet deep. At the same time, canyon impoundments are known for great topwater fishing, with opportunistic fish rushing to the surface from deep shade to nail poppers and other baits. And while small soft plastics are commonly successful, lunker hunters employ giant plugs and soft plastic baits that imitate rainbow trout.

Due to low fertility and competition from striped bass for prey, largemouth bass don't reach high density in many canyon impoundments. In some smaller western waters, however, stocking of Florida bass has yielded huge bass, threatening the world record in California.

Comparative Impoundment Characteristics

Impoundment Classification	Depth	Main River Channel Characteristics	Feeders	Cuts and Coves
Flatland	20-40′ at dam 6-12′ upstream.	Seldom near shoreline, meanders, greatly altered, straightened with levees, dikes. Trees and brush along banks. Oxbows where channel has been straightened.	Creeks or ditches usually less than 20′ wide. 1-6′ deep, V-shaped bed.	Coves are short, shallow with a small feeder creek running through, and have wide mouths. Short cuts with wide mouths and rounded backs. May contain weeds, brush & timber.
Hill-Land	45-175′ or more depending on region.	Near center of reservoir. Natural state, usually quite straight. River bed is usually rounded.	Most have a distinct channel with sloping banks, brush and/or treelined.	Coves are deep downstream, and may have large timber stands. Upstream much like flatland coves. Short cuts.
Highland	60-200′ or more depending on size.	Often runs near shoreline. Natural state has many junctions of creeks and river channels that are mostly too deep for bass use. Flat channel with steep walls.	Some are "drywet" (carry water only after heavy rains), rock bottoms.	Coves are deep but not wide, and can be very long. Brush and timber common, sharp rocky points, some steep walls, some flatter, shallower. Deep cuts, not as long as coves.
Plateau	50-200′ depending on location.	Runs through center of reservoir, quite straight, usually not deep with flat beds. Banks are generally clean, some brush may be found. Downstream ⅓ is generally too deep for bass use.	Little gullies or washouts from flash floods. Main feeders have high walls. Feeders most prevalent on downstream third. Short and wide at mouth.	Coves have flat basins, short, usually wide in relation to length. Some brush may be present. Shorelines are steep in deep coves, flat in shallow coves. Short cuts with high sloping walls in downstream ⅓. Not as prevalent upstream.
Canyon	500-600, downstream; a few feet to 40 or 50 ft. at the inlet.	May run near shore. Less distinct downstream. Very distinct, dish-shaped gorge upstream. Usually is too deep to be used by bass.	Very long creeks and small rivers. Can be 40-60 mi. long, and are shaped like main channel.	Almost all coves are creek or river-fed. Some "dry-wet" with wide mouths can be very long. Some with 2 or 3 creeks.
Wetland Lowland	Depends region.	The diversity of lowland impoundments makes them difficult to categorize.		

PLATEAU IMPOUNDMENTS

In the high plains and low plateau regions from the Missouri River west to the eastern base of the Rockies, plateau impoundments prevail. These long, windswept reservoirs have a maximum depth in the 50- to 90-foot range. Though they may have long tributary arms, most coves are short and wide, not providing much protection from wind and waves. Due to wind, wave action, and loose substrate, vegetation is sparse. Largemouth bass are absent from some plateau impoundments and maintain low-level populations in shallower, more protected sections of other waters. In recent years, smallmouth bass populations have prospered in plateau impoundments on the Missouri River, joining walleyes as key sportfish. White bass and channel catfish also are common in Plateau reservoirs.

Points	Shoreline	Bottom Content	Brush, Timber, or Vegetation	Common Man-made Features
Broad, rounded, slow tapering. Some with brush; usually lack timber.	Mainly long, slow tapers. Steeper bluff bank s on rare occasions.	Black soil, mud flats, some hard clay.	Standing timber in main lake is common—mainly cypress and willow. Brush in backs of coves. "Moss" is main vegetation.	Dam, roadbeds, causeways, ponds, levees, building foundations, rip-rap, cemeteries.
Rounded, usually with standing or cut timber. Some rare cases have boulders.	Slopes quickly to 7-12' of water, then gradually to main river channel.	Sand, clay, loam, some mud flats, extensive small humps.	Brush and timber in coves, "moss" on shallow flats in main lakes. Has most weed growth of any reservoir type in the South.	Dam, rip-rap, high lines and pipe lines, fence rows, rock piles, road beds, cemeteries, drainage ditches, railroad beds, building foundations, marinas.
Short, but very sharp and steep. Some slick; some with trees or brush. Mostly rocky.	Varies from heavily-timbered, moderate slope to cliffs. "Stairstep" ledges in some cases.	Sand, clay, rock, shale, limestone.	Timber is mainly hardwoods or pines and cedar. Brush varies regionally. Moss or weeds not common.	Same as hillland except causeways, bridges, and riprap are not as common.
Vary depending on region from very sharp to rounded.	Steep bluffs downstream; gradual slope upstream.	Varies from rocky to sandy, to silt depending on region. Usually clean. Upstream ⅓ has shallow flats.	Quite limited. Some in backs of coves. Some vegetation in upstream third.	Dam, roadbeds, marinas, spillways, others as mentioned above not common because of low populations.
Very distinct along sheer walls of reservoir and downstream portions of cove. Most composed of jagged rock. Can rise 1200 feet above water and drop 300 feet below water.	Sheer cliffs with mainly, some broken rock, slightly sloping solid rock faces or "mesas."	Mainly rock, some sand and gravel in backs of coves.	Some sage brush or other scrub vegetation found occasionally. Cottonwood trees and some highland cedar at extreme backs of coves.	Very few, some marinas, dams.

SMALL WATERS

Small waters of various kinds provide a large portion of total bass habitat and fishing opportunities in the United States. Bass are commonly stocked in farm ponds ranging from 1 to 100 acres, where they do a double service: they're both a sportfish and a predator that controls populations of bluegills or other sunfish to prevent stunting.

Largemouth bass spawn well in ponds, so usually only an introductory stocking is necessary. Cover options in ponds are generally limited, making bass easy to locate. Where fishing pressure is light, pond bass are often aggressive and amazingly easy to catch. Proper pond management requires that harvest be limited so bass can fulfill their predatory role. Ponds are fascinating but require a lot of work to maintain good fishing, because natural forces and overharvest can easily throw them out of balance.

Anglers looking for top fishing ponds should find out the species present, balance, stocking schedules, and management plans. They also should consider pond structure, function, size, and shape. The size and type of watershed (the area around a pond that brings runoff to it) determine the water level, water clarity, productivity, and characteristics like pH and stratification.

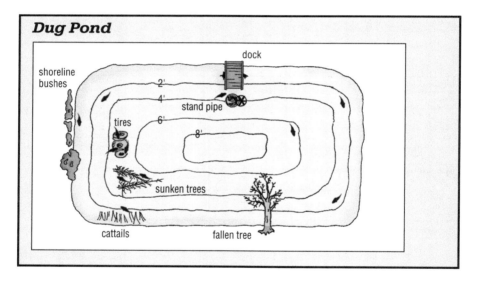

Dug Pond

dock
shoreline bushes
2'
4'
stand pipe
tires
6'
8'
sunken trees
cattails
fallen tree

DUG PONDS

Farm ponds with shallow, featureless basins are dug with earth-moving equipment. Water running off adjacent land keeps the pond full, but supplemental pumping from wells may be necessary during dry periods. Although most dug ponds are smaller than 5 acres, management such as fertilizing can make them productive for bass, sunfish, and catfish.

Active fish cruise along shallow banks or hold near available cover—docks, fallen trees, and weedbeds. Bluegills often gather in shade from shoreline trees and bushes. When better cover is scarce, corners and depth breaks hold fish. In winter, fish occupy the deep basin. During summer, the deep areas lack oxygen and fish avoid them.

BUILT PONDS

Building a dam across a low area will create pond if the watershed and soil type are adequate. The dam backs up runoff, forming a pond from 2 to 50 acres. It is deepest near the dam, with gradually shallower water toward the upper end.

Cuts, points, humps, and flats with weeds or timber attract bass, sunfish, and catfish. In summer bluegills may cruise open water to feed on zooplankton or hold near willows or other overhanging trees to nab falling insects. Emergent vegetation and submerged weedlines also are good fishing areas.

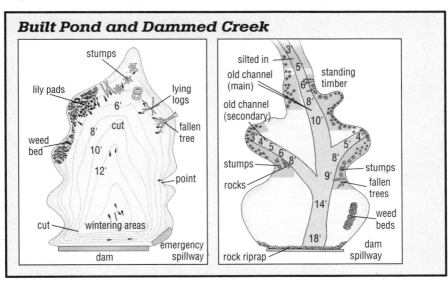

Built Pond and Dammed Creek

DAMMED CREEKS

Creeks are dammed to power mills, irrigate, and for fishing. Most of these ponds cover from 10 to over 100 acres. Standing timber and stumps near deep water attract fish. When creeks prevent ponds from stratifying, fish may move deep in summer. Structure and cover are diverse, and often many species are present, as wild fish enter from the creek.

Low fishing pressure can mean superb fishing, particularly for bass and catfish. Competition with wild fish, however, may inhibit bluegill growth. Dammed creeks usually aren't fertilized, because water quickly passes through them. Fish production on a per-acre is lower than in smaller ponds, but giant bass may be present.

PITS

Pits created by mining operations often fill with rainwater, springwater or groundwater from the water table. Where water chemistry is suitable, bass and many other species thrive. Pits are typically deep and clear, with manmade structure such as shelves, roadbeds, mine shafts, and spoil piles. Clear water fosters weedgrowth if soft sediments and shallow flats are present. Stumps and flooded timber also hold fish.

Pits range from a couple of acres to over 1,000, and the fish composition varies from only bullheads to dozens of species. Check with property owners or fishery agencies to learn about stockings and management strategies.

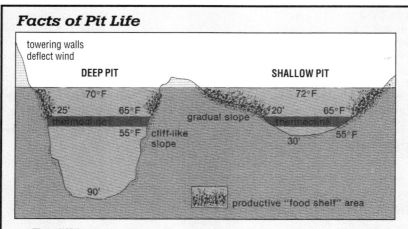

Facts of Pit Life

towering walls deflect wind

DEEP PIT   **SHALLOW PIT**

70°F   72°F

25'   65°F   20'   65°F
thermocline   gradual slope   thermocline

55°F   cliff-like   55°F
slope   30'

90'

productive "food shelf" area

The clifflike walls of most deep pits provide little productive shelf. They're infertile compared to most shallow pits.

Towering wall surrounding many deep pits deflect wind. You can comfortably fish them even on windy days; but without wind, the depths don't reoxygenate to support much aquatic life below the thermocline. These pits may look like deep Canadian trout lakes. But despite their wilderness appearance, they're often infertile with limited ability to produce fish.

Explore pits during the day, but expect best results during low-light periods and at night. Biomass is usually low due to infertile conditions, but trophy fish are possible. Some Florida phosphate pits are fertile and produce extraordinary bass fishing where the harvest is controlled. And the world-record 4-pound, 2-ounce bluegill was caught in Ketona Lake, a flooded limestone mine in Alabama. Presently, it's a poor fishery, which shows the importance of releasing large fish—and of fishing pits when they're producing big fish, before masses of anglers discover them.

There are some undiscovered small waters. Highway construction often requires excavation of thousands of cubic feet of earth, leaving broad and shallow holes that make good bass habitat where winterkill isn't a problem. These ponds are always easily accessed, but are often overlooked. In southern climates, small waters like canals and golf course hazards often hold big bass.

THE ADAPTABLE BASS

Largemouth bass have adapted to and have thrived in a great variety of waters; they do best when these environments offer moderately clear, moderately warm water with plenty of oxygen. But they turn up in freshwater, brackish estuaries, mucky prairie lakes, and stone-walled mining pits. They thrive among alligators in tropical lakes and in water that's frozen over five months a year.

This adaptability is one of the most attractive attributes of the largemouth. Wherever you are, a bass isn't far away. Thanks to stocking, they occur in every state but Alaska, absent only in the Rocky Mountains and some arid regions of the Great Plains.

Locating and catching bass within these various waters depends upon understanding details of the kinds of structure and cover each offers, and how bass relate to them—the subjects of the next two chapters.

Chapter 4

Reading Bass Structure

THE KEY TO ESTABLISHING FISHING PATTERNS

Understanding how bass behavior changes through the Calendar Periods and classifying bass waters are good starts in learning to locate bass and establish fishing patterns, but no angler can progress past the most basic stages without understanding another set of factors: structure, cover, and edge effects.

Structure is the shape of bottom in a body of water, its changing depth, points, flats, islands, drop-offs. *Cover* refers to any object on structure. Piers, wood, rocks, weeds, old cars in the water—all these things are sometimes loosely referred to as structure, but these are cover. These two concepts must be considered together. A bank might have great cover—say, fallen trees or stumps—but unless it's near deep water (and therefore near some breakline, hole, or channel), the chances of finding large fish after the spawn are poor. On the other hand, merely fishing sharp drop-offs probably will be unproductive unless those drop-offs offer food, cover—something that gives fish a reason to be there at that particular Calendar Period. Chapter 6 will examine more details of what makes attractive cover for bass; here we'll focus on basic bass structures, with only general mention of the many sorts of vegetation that are a bass angler's frequent points of reference.

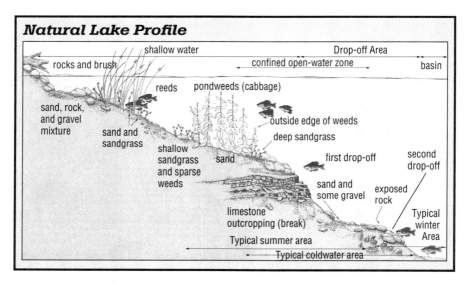

Natural Lake Profile

The concept of edges is critical to understanding both structure and cover. Observers long ago noticed that an area where two habitats meet—meadow and forest, for example—attracts many kinds of wildlife. Even edges have edges; while some kinds of wildlife make use of the entire forest-meadow edge, some species confine their activities only to certain areas, perhaps a finger of forest projecting into the meadow, and these areas are especially rich.

This edge effect is important because fish, including bass, relate to edges. The edge may be obvious, like the outside portion of a weedbed, or subtle, like the edge of a school of baitfish, or the depth of light penetration. Deep lakes may have a lot of depth variation and structure, but in a shallow, almost structureless lake, seemingly insignificant breaklines, such as changes from one weed type to another, transitions from hard to soft bottom, or drop-offs of just 1 or 2 feet, can be the key to bassing success.

THE DEVELOPMENT OF STRUCTURE FISHING

The term *structure* was coined by Elwood "Buck" Perry, one of the most astute anglers of all time. In the 1940s he invented the Spoonplug, a deep-diving metal lure that when trolled rapidly could function as a device for mapping the shape and composition of lake bottom. When sonar become available, he took advantage of that as well. His fishing concepts were based on edge theory; his term for

an edge was *breakline*, and an edge on an edge was called a *break*. He theorized that schools of gamefish lived in deep water, making periodic feeding movements into shallows when they became active. As they moved up, they held along breaklines, the areas of rapid change of depth, and they concentrated at the breaks.

We've since discovered many exceptions to Perry's structure theory, but it nonetheless remains a cornerstone of modern fishing strategy. Certainly his theories were thought-provoking. He put the proper emphasis on eliminating unproductive water; he was responsible for turning attention from the surface to features of the underwater world that concentrate bass and to determining the right depth to find fish.

Buck Perry was a maverick; some of his theories seemed scientific, some merely dogmatic; still, his startling claims were often backed up by astonishing catches. The North Carolina angler traveled the country demonstrating his techniques and selling his lures. The bass-rich South generally rejected his teachings—perhaps anglers found his lures ugly, or they disliked trolling. He brought his barnstorming act north, however, to waters where bass are more scarce, and in the late 1950s, Chicago writer Tom McNally brought Perry's theories to the national fishing press. McNally excited great attention in the Midwest with photos of Buck Perry holding stringers with limits of 4- to 6-pound bass from supposedly fished-out lakes near Chicago.

Bill Binkleman, an avid bass angler and manager of a large Milwaukee hardware store in the early 1960s, bought cases of Perry's Spoonplugs for his customers; he started holding fishing meetings in his store and published a newsletter, *Fishing News.*

Binkleman soon abandoned Spoon-plugs when he found he hated trolling, but he continued to promote structure fishing, with refined livebait presentation. He expanded and reinterpreted Perry's rigid system. And although he became famous for his walleye fishing, he admitted he'd learned all his walleye techniques from catching bass. Binkleman left a large legacy as a fishing educator. His newsletter evolved into *Fishing Facts*, the first magazine to deal seriously with structure fishing and to publish contour maps and underwater views. He also initiated one of the first television fishing shows.

Two young Chicago anglers, Ron and Al Lindner, became friends with Binkleman and frequent contributors to his magazine. In 1975 they made the leap from fishing guides to tackle manufacturers and publishers of fishing information. *In-Fisherman* soon became a comprehensive and collaborative source of fishing information, incorporating scientific studies and management principles, along with how-to fishing tips.

Structure fishing today, or *modern structure theory*, as the Lindners termed it, focuses not just on cover, shape of bottom, and changes in depth, but on understanding everything going on underwater. It looks at what fish need in particular environments at particular times of year.

When considering the kinds of structure available in different waters, then, remember that modern structure fishing looks at the big picture.

BASS STRUCTURE IN NATURAL LAKES

Until perhaps 70 years ago, most largemouth bass lived in weedy natural lakes in the eastern United States or in calm sections of rivers. As bass (and

other species) were transplanted into waters they weren't native to, few innovations in tackle or technique emerged, so bass lagged behind other gamefish in popularity—until the construction of the vast American reservoir system. For manmade impoundments, from 2-acre ponds to sprawling reservoirs of over 100,00 acres, the choice for stocking was the adaptable largemouth bass.

In the cover-laden shallows of new impoundments, bass populations prospered. In bass fishing circles, talk turned to fishing timber—trees, stumps, and logs. It detailed tactics for fishing riprap, bridges, dams, channel edges, bluffs, and creek arms. Classic bass behavior in natural environments became less important than their behavior in reservoirs. Yet this behavior was simply an adaptation of old bass habits. Proof is visible today as reservoirs mature—flooded wood cover erodes and is replaced by weedgrowth. Largemouths shift back to their old behavior patterns in weedy reservoirs that are similar to natural lakes.

The new structure fishing—edges, drop-offs, and points—changed the face of modern angling. Most anglers applied the concepts strictly to changes in bottom. A few innovative anglers fishing natural lakes, however, began applying the concepts to changes within weedbeds. This thinking unlocked the mysteries of bass behavior in natural lakes, resulting in today's better understanding of bass in all environments.

No matter where you fish—lake, river, reservoir, pit, or pond—understanding bass behavior in the structure and cover of natural lakes provides the foundation for catching them consistently.

CRUISERS OF THE SHALLOW FLATS OR CREATURES OF THE DEEP?

Good bass structure in a lake lies at a favorable depth, typically from 2 to 25 feet. Areas with rather featureless depth profiles can be productive, too, if the bottom content is conducive to growing weeds. Areas with little or no depth or shape may grow the best vegetation and host the most bass along distinct physical edges. In most natural lakes, largemouth bass are creatures of shallow flats—food-rich zones less than 20 feet deep. The largemouth prefers warm water and its compact body shape is ideally suited for maneuvering in cover.

Bass can also function in deep, open water if large numbers of more efficient open water predators like pike, walleyes, or muskies aren't present. But when largemouths face heavy competition from other species—the typical condition in midwestern natural lakes—they are generally restricted to shallow weed zones. (Smallmouths, by comparison, are more suited to deep water, so they are commonly found on deep, weedless structure. When both species inhabit the same waters, smallmouths are usually deeper.)

In many impoundments, however, largemouths do use deep, open water. The lack of large competing predators, abundance of suspended forage like shad, relatively high bass biomass, and lack of vegetation all contribute, and bass colonize available habitat. These factors also explain why you can catch bass in 35 feet of water in some New England natural lakes where largemouths were introduced by stocking. These lakes host few if any pike and only a handful of small pickerel to compete with either bass species. Largemouths often inhabit deep water, unless smallmouths are numerous enough to compete for prime deep spots.

In large, deep natural lakes with sparse weedgrowth, localized largemouth bass populations are often restricted to shallower bays or sections of the lake best suited to their basic nature. Deep, open waters will be occupied by other species. Medium-sized lakes usually have more weeds on the flats, and bass may be more common in main-lake areas, though pike or walleyes sometimes dominate deep weededges. Small natural lakes usually have few large pike or walleyes, so bass may be present throughout their extensive weed areas.

If you're unfamiliar with a lake, fish it, evaluate the balance of predators, and determine its "personality." Fish populations increase and decrease, and other physical and biological conditions change. General principles are just starting points—the rest is up to you, which is what makes bass fishing so challenging and so much fun.

STRUCTURE THROUGH THE SEASONS

In most natural lakes, largemouth bass are predominantly weed oriented. Both deep weeds and shallow weeds are potential areas for largemouth use; the structures that host bass vary through the seasons. The key to locating bass is evaluating available weedgrowth and predicting how bass will relate to it. It might be argued that the location of food is more important, but of course the baitfish that bass feed on also relate to weeds.

When spring arrives, winter ice cover or extended cold water have decimated all but the most resilient and deepest plants. As the lake warms and the environment shifts into high gear, however, shallow vegetation quickly sprouts. Deeper weedbeds also thicken in spring sunlight.

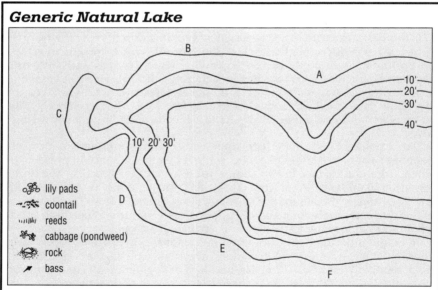

Generic Natural Lake

*Many anglers automatically assume that Areas **A** and **E** are the best spots because they are obvious structure. Not necessarily. Weedgrowth plays an important role. In each example, bland-looking Area **B** is a potential spot even without distinct points or turns. The wide, shallow flat at **B** develops some of the best weedgrowth and bass habitat in the lake. Subtle changes in the weeds could hold many bass.*

Changes by themselves don't attract fish. Changes in habitat do. First find prime habitat. Then look for edges and variations that concentrate active fish.

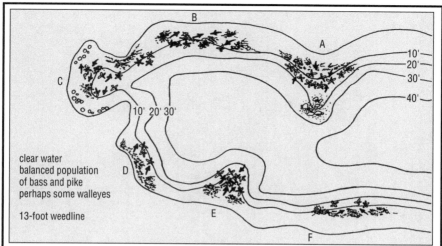

This is a typical condition in many midwestern lakes. Weedgrowth is abundant down to 12 to 15 feet, although significant numbers of shallow open areas with few weeds exist, too. Largemouth bass are free to spread throughout the weed zones, although they must share the deep weededge with pike. Pike can drive them shallower than the deep edge at times, but some portion of the bass population will use the deep weededge during summer and fall.

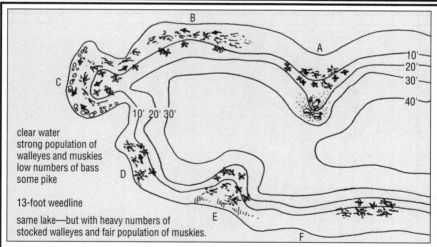

Most largemouth bass will be restricted to the shallow zones, particularly the bays. The bass population is lower than in the previous example.

Summer is often heralded by lush weedgrowth from the shallows to the drop-off. Bass inhabit a variety of shallow zones, taking advantage of the abundant habitat and the prey that seek shelter and food among the plant stalks.

Fall reverses that progression. As days become shorter and water cools, weeds begin to die in the shallows that are most exposed to temperature fluctuations at night. The shallowest habitat becomes progressively less suitable for bass.

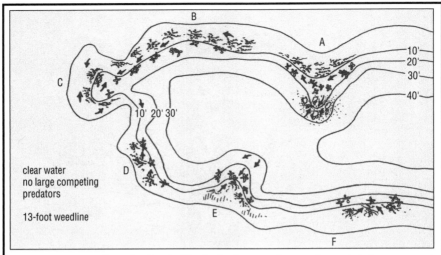

Same lake—in New England. The lack of competing predators lets bass expand throughout the lake and into the deep zones. The presence of small trout or alewives as open-water food sources may promote big bass use of deep structure. Bass are the dominant critters in the lake and can go wherever food and suitable habitat exist. Similar behavior occurs in Florida natural lakes, although the waters aren't as deep. Many pits and ponds fall into the same category.

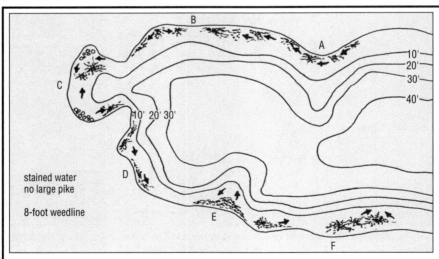

This lake has shallower weedgrowth than the previous examples due to its stained water. Weeds are thick, clumpy, and extensive, however, with few open areas on the flats. Bass are spread throughout the lake, including along the deep weededge. Note that weeds don't grow all the way to the drop-off, creating ragged weededges rather than distinct outside weedlines.

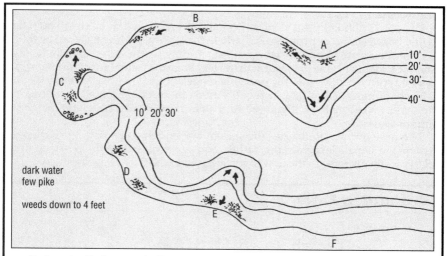

Dark water limits growth. Bass relate to the few weeds they can find. Yet with few other predators present, bass can use the clean points where weeds don't extend all the way to the drop-off. In dark, fertile water, bass can grow quite large but probably won't be abundant. If the lake is infertile, bass numbers and size may be small.

Natural lake environments can be more complex than they appear. Subtle interactions between fish species and available habitat affect bass behavior. In most cases, however, weeds are the key.

By late fall, largemouths retreat to the last stands of healthy green weeds bordering the deep basin of the lake—the last bastion of cover adjacent to the lake's relatively stable deep water zone. A calm, warm period, or Indian Summer, may temporarily reverse the progression, however.

SHALLOW, MEDIUM, AND DEEP BASS

Throughout the year, bass continually shift location, following expanding or diminishing habitat. Small groups of bass may simultaneously inhabit various areas. Seldom do all bass do the same thing at the same time. At most times of the year, some bass in natural lakes are shallow, some are middepth, and some are deep—that is, deep within the typical bass range. The ratio changes from one Calendar Period to another. In Prespawn and Spawn, most are shallow; in winter, most are deep. But during most of the open water season, bass are spread from the shallowest, thickest tangles to the deepest, greenest clumps and in between.

Bass can usually be caught in each depth range during the same fishing trip. Shallow bass often feed aggressively but are usually the first to turn off in response to cold fronts. Deeper bass may be harder to find but are consistent biters once you find them. Most bass probably hold in middepth habitat, but it may take a while to find the best spots, and the fish may be scattered. A good angler develops favorite fishing patterns to use for each of the major depth zones.

Because shallow bass are usually most active in low-light periods, a good general strategy is to work shallow patterns early and move to middepth flats after sunrise. Bass along a deep weedline or in dock shadows turn on later in the day and remain active longer. As the sun goes down, they reverse the cycle and finish the day in the shallows at dusk. So should you.

SEASONAL EFFECTS

Chapter 2 defined the Calendar Periods and provided more detail on where to find bass as the year progresses. Early in the season, finding bass can be tough. A surface water temperature gauge aids in finding warm water. Even when two bays look identical, one may warm up faster. Polarized sunglasses are useful, too, as bass typically move into the invisible range at this time. If you don't see sunfish and minnow activity, bass probably aren't there, either. Small fish move into the shallows before bass; if you see sunfish but don't catch bass, you may be an hour or two early.

The time immediately after the spawn presents its own fishing challenges. Postspawn female largemouths, rather than swimming directly to a deep drop-off, typically disperse to the first cover adjacent to the flats. Developing weeds in

---

Evaluating Flats

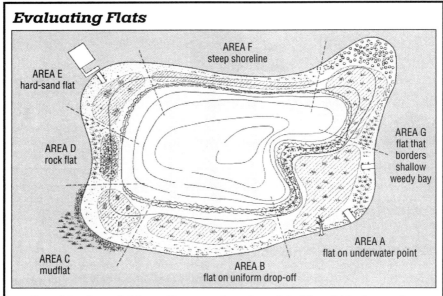

Area A is a large flat formed by an underwater point. It has thick clumps of coontail in the 5- to 8-foot range and a dense band of cabbage along the outer edge. The shoreline has a dense reed bank for spawning and summer use. The area provides a wealth of habitat and should host a large percentage of the lake's bass.

Area B has a thin band of cabbage along the drop-off and a fair coontail bed on the flat. Few distinct points or corners concentrate bass. The deep weedbed is narrow. The area is only fair.

Area C has a bottom content conductive to growing only a few sparse, stringy weeds. A waste of time.

Area D is a rocky flat with a few shallow reeds. It provides little largemouth habitat in mixed-species lakes, though it could attract smallmouths.

Area E is a sand flat with few weeds and even fewer bass.

Area F is a steep shoreline with thin bands of cabbage and coontails. Habitat is limited, with no visible irregularities to concentrate bass.

Area G offers a variety of bass habitat. The lily pad bay should attract a large percentage of the bass population in spring and support a group in summer. The coontail flat should host most of the bass in summer, since the cabbage rim is thin. A good spot.

---

the 4-to 8-foot range often hold clusters of fish, which must be fished slowly and carefully, since females aren't very aggressive at this time. Once newly hatched fingerlings disperse, males join the females on the flats. Bass continually shift location, relating to the best available habitat as the weeds bloom and thicken, progressing from the shoreline toward deeper breaks. It's common to catch several bass in one spot and then find none there the next trip. The fish are in transition, spreading throughout their expanding habitat.

The key is to think about what makes a productive flat. Flats are any region of relatively minor depth change, located anywhere in the *littoral* (shoreline) zone of a lake. Flats are the food-producing zones of lakes and reservoirs, extending from shore to the deep weedline. A productive flat provides an extended area of favorable bass habitat at a depth conducive to growing plants. Sunlight must penetrate for the weeds to grow. But if the bottom is too hard, weeds won't develop.

Not all weedy areas are flats, of course. Steeply sloping banks may harbor clumps of vegetation that offer food and shelter, but not much of either. Such areas have limited areas to hold fish but are worth fishing because they can be quickly checked. Major flats offer a larger food and shelter zone; bass have more choices. Flats can be found on points, in weedy bays, on big sunken islands, along slowly tapering, straight shorelines, and they can be any shape.

Substantial weedgrowth makes a flat productive. Flats with sparse vegetation aren't very attractive to largemouth bass. But some have such thick weedgrowth that it's hard for bass to feed there. The best flats combine thick weeds with many edges.

BASS STRUCTURE IN RIVERS

Many anglers don't think of largemouth bass as river fish. Rivers mean current, more associated with trout, walleyes, catfish, and smallmouths. It's true that largemouths usually avoid fast current, but besides taking advantage of the cover and food in river backwaters, largemouths sometimes feed near current breaks. And they may migrate upstream and downstream through main river channels.

After all, it was through the continent's vast river network that bass traveled to populate most of eastern North America, making their way to southern Canada between 15,000 and 20,000 years ago. Many of our big rivers are prime bass fisheries: the Potomac, the St. Lawrence, the St. Johns, the Sacramento, and especially the Mississippi, which offers good bass fishing from Minnesota to Louisiana.

Man's alterations have created new bass habitat. Locks and dams have been built to aid barge traffic and to control flooding; rivers have been bridged, channelized, dredged. All these have created various problems but have also provided opportunistic, adaptable largemouth with new habitat options.

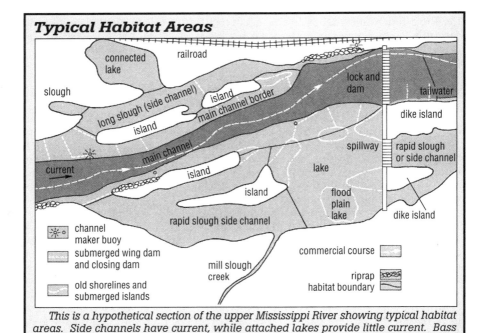

Typical Habitat Areas

connected lake
railroad
slough
long slough (side channel)
island
main channel border
lock and dam
tailwater
dike island
island
main channel
spillway
rapid slough or side channel
current
island
lake
island
flood plain lake
dike island
rapid slough side channel

channel maker buoy
submerged wing dam and closing dam
mill slough creek
old shorelines and submerged islands

commercial course
riprap
habitat boundary

This is a hypothetical section of the upper Mississippi River showing typical habitat areas. Side channels have current, while attached lakes provide little current. Bass spend most of their lives away from the main channel.

RIVER HABITAT AND SEASONAL MOVEMENTS

From fall through the Spawn Period, largemouths favor still, lakelike areas. From late spring through early fall, bass often hold near chutes and cuts with slight current or in wide, slow stretches of the main river. Of course, since many species of river baitfish occupy current areas all year, you can expect bass, as opportunistic feeders, to sometimes be found there, too.

To understand all the regional variations of this pattern and find river bass regularly, you need to think about what bass need. Research has identified five primary factors that determine bass location in rivers: dissolved oxygen, current, water temperature, cover, and prey.

In northern rivers that freeze over, the most critical habitat for river bass is a suitable winter holding area. Backwater wintering areas sheltered from current and with adequate depth (at least 5 feet) tend to be slightly warmer than the main river. But as dead weeds decay under the ice, they consume oxygen. Dissolved oxygen can then drop to critical levels. If oxygen falls below about 3 parts per million, which may occur in late winter, bass shift closer to the current, where water holds more oxygen. But they continue to avoid direct current.

Overwintering areas are scarce in some river systems, and this may limit the number of bass a river section can hold. Research on a 15-mile stretch of the Mississippi River between Iowa and Illinois revealed only three suitable wintering areas for largemouth bass. The river could possibly support more bass if wintering areas were more common. Excavations to create additional winter refuges have been tested with promising results.

Farther south, where rivers don't freeze, winter habitat requirements aren't so stringent. Yet similar shifts in location occur, except in southern Florida, where

Backwater Basics

*Consistent fishing for largemouths in rivers rests with eliminating unsuitable river areas. Largemouths need cover away from heavy current. The obvious largemouth holding spots in this river area include **Areas A, C, and D. Inside Bend Area B** may also attract fish because cover is present, and inside bends usually offer reduced current. Areas like **E** that are adjacent to good backwater areas should hold a few fish. As a rule, however, concentrate on areas away from main current.*

water temperatures rarely fall below 55 °F.

During winter, largemouths occupy deep sloughs off the main channel, where current is minimal. Areas with stumps, standing timber, or rocky holes may attract large aggregations of bass if the number of prime spots is limited. Fishing is sporadic, and bass aren't aggressive, but many fish in clearly defined locations can mean excellent fishing.

In temperate regions, bass leave their overwintering areas at the thaw or just prior to it. Spring locations for river bass are more diverse than wintering areas. Bass initially move toward shallow, woody cover. High water often inundates timbered bottomlands, and bass quickly occupy those areas. They use timbered or brushy pockets early in spring, switching to weeds as they develop.

In northern rivers, bass don't bite well in spring as long as water remains ice-cold and murky. They stay shallow and tight to cover. Lures must be presented slowly and close to the fish to entice bites. On sunny afternoons, however, activity increases. In murky water, bass may bite on lures flipped next to the boat, but to avoid spooking them, you need to be as quiet as possible.

Spawning areas also are critical for river largemouth. They may travel miles to areas offering appropriate bottom type, cover, and lack of current. Tracking

River Habitat

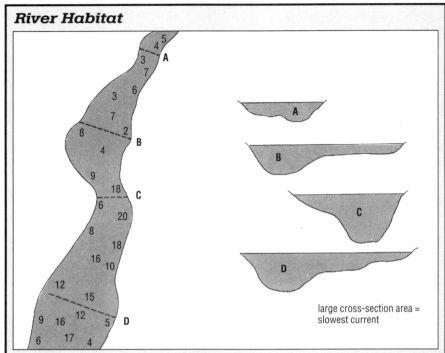

large cross-section area = slowest current

Areas exposed to main current flow are usually not productive for largemouth bass. Main-river areas where current flows may, however, hold largemouths if cover is present. As a rule, the wider the river cross section, the slower the current, and the more chance of large-mouths.

__River cross-sections A__ and __C__ are not largemouth water. __River cross-sections B__ and __D__ most likely offer reduced current flow. But __cross-section D__ is relatively deep and probably isn't largemouth water, either. If the flat in __Area B__ has cover, it may hold largemouths.

studies indicate that river bass know their way around large stretches of river, and they may return to bedding sites they used in previous years. Bass spawn in 1½- to 3-foot depths where hardpan sand or clay may be covered by a few inches of silt. Sandy areas may also be used, and in heavily weeded backwaters, lily pad rhizomes or large stumps suffice. We know little about the spawning behavior of river bass because murky water makes observation difficult, but we assume their behavior in rivers doesn't differ from that in lakes.

Through the Postspawn Period, fishing near isolated stickups will catch bass. Thick wood cover attracts big females, but almost any cover from 1 to 5 feet deserves attention.

After spawning, bass move to summer feeding areas, often backwaters or sloughs with thick cover and reduced current. They'll be cover oriented, often holding in water only 1 to 2 feet deep. During summer, largemouths tend to be homebodies. A bass caught from under a particular stump and carried to a tournament weigh-in may soon return to the same stump; this navigation process isn't well understood, however.

In some rivers during summer, bass move to side channels and cuts that connect backwaters to the main river. Shad, minnows, and other baitfish move through cuts; largemouths hold along weededges, in wood cover, or by wing dams to attack passing prey. In rivers where water flow is moderate in summer, largemouths may hold in the main channel around objects that break current like pilings, navigation towers, and wing dams. Natural objects like fallen trees, boulders, and holes near tributary mouths hold bass, too.

As weeds dwindle in fall, wood cover again becomes the primary bass cover because low dissolved oxygen in dying weedbeds seems to push them out. Moving in stages, bass filter toward their overwintering areas, arriving before ice-up in northern latitudes. In some river systems, they may move 10 miles or more.

Even small, slow-moving creeks no more than a cast across can hold big bass, particularly in the Southeast. Structure and cover may be small and subtle here, but they're still the key to finding bass. Deep holes, frequently located at sharp outside bends, are prime habitat, especially when enhanced with wood cover. These holes give bass space and attract a variety of prey. Creek bass typically hold downstream from cover, even though the current is slight. During rainy periods, when current increases, bass move to more protected areas like stumps, boulders, snags, rock piles, bridge abutments, cypress trees—anything that can blunt current. Bass lie tight to these objects, ready to seize food.

TIDAL SYSTEMS

Tidal rivers and their associated marshes, particularly along the Atlantic and Gulf coasts, offer good bass fishing. The systems are vast and receive less fishing pressure than nearby lakes or reservoirs. Bass in tidal areas typically don't live as long or grow as large as bass in still waters, but they grow strong and fight hard.

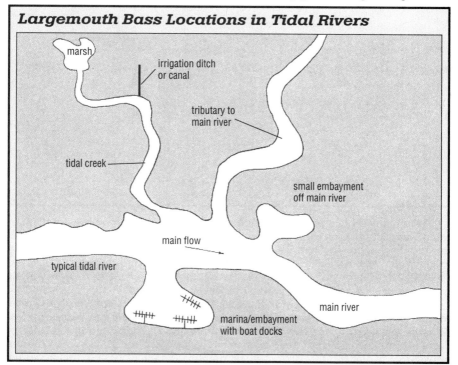

Largemouth Bass Locations in Tidal Rivers

marsh

irrigation ditch or canal

tributary to main river

tidal creek

small embayment off main river

main flow

typical tidal river

marina/embayment with boat docks

main river

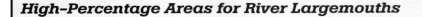

High-Percentage Areas for River Largemouths

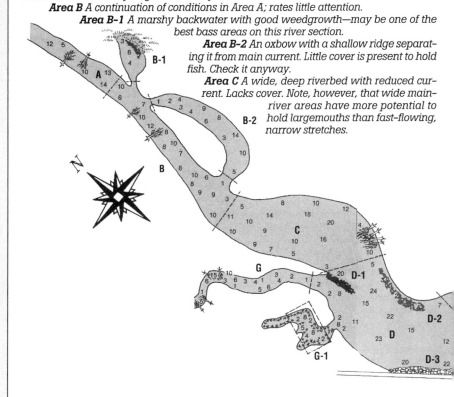

This drawing illustrates a moderate-sized river stretch and some typical location options for largemouth bass.

Area A A main river area with adequate depth and fallen trees to block current. This area should hold many largemouths only where flow is minimal.

Area B A continuation of conditions in Area A; rates little attention.

Area B-1 A marshy backwater with good weedgrowth—may be one of the best bass areas on this river section.

Area B-2 An oxbow with a shallow ridge separating it from main current. Little cover is present to hold fish. Check it anyway.

Area C A wide, deep riverbed with reduced current. Lacks cover. Note, however, that wide main-river areas have more potential to hold largemouths than fast-flowing, narrow stretches.

Almost any estuary from New England to Maryland may contain a good largemouth bass population in areas where salinity is less than 5 to 8 parts per thousand. In spring, when freshwater run-off pushes salt water downstream, bass follow and occupy marshes or sloughs that become too saline in summer. As river discharge declines, the "salt wedge" moves upstream, hugging the bottom, because salt water is denser than fresh.

A typical tidal marsh is a pondlike area ringed with emergent weeds and connected by a creek to a river whose lower reaches are affected by oceanic tide cycles. Most bass fishermen aren't accustomed to thinking about tides, but understanding tides is central to catching bass in estuaries. Twice a day at high tide, ocean water moves inland and fills tidal marshes; their salinity depends on river discharge and

Area D *A wide river area with reduced current and cover. Probably the best main-river largemouth area. Fish the weedbed at the creek point **(D-1)**, the weeds and wood on the inside bends **(D-2)**, plus the riprap and wood on the outside bend **(D-3)**. Expect cover in the inside bend to produce the most bass.*

Area E *Not good largemouth water, although the weedgrowth and bridge abutments may hold a few fish. Note the shallow flat in front of **Shallow Bay F**. If cover is available on the flat, it may be productive.*

Area F *A shallow bay fronting a river section. Not enough depth to serve as year-round bass habitat, but traveling bass that hold here may stay for most of the open-water season. Also good spring and summer habitat.*

Area G *A relatively shallow, barren creek. All backwater areas have potential, but some are better than others. The wood gathered at the outside bend probably means this creek floods in spring. Probably not a good spawning creek. The deep tangles provide a home for some bass, possibly big ones.*

Area G-1 *A creek with depth and cover. Everything you're looking for in a back-water area.*

*Backwater areas and cover are the keys to river bassin'. Concentrate on **Areas G-1, E, B-1**, and **D**. Slip into **Creek G** for a shot at a few large bass.*

Detail of Area G-1

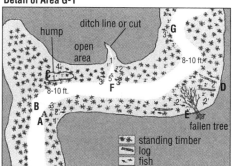

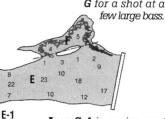

*Area G-1 is a prime spot. Because the creek is full of timber, focus on areas of change in otherwise continuous timber. Where a channel meets a flat is one transition, but expect inside bends **(A)** and outside bends **(B)** to gather more fish.*

*Humps on a flat **(C)** are another transition that attract bass. Horizontal timber **(D)**, as opposed to the abundant vertical timber, is another contrast. So are fallen trees along a continuous bank **(E)**, and small channel cuts that merge with the main creek channel **(F)**. Areas where a channel swings close to a bank may also hold more fish **(G)**.*

the marsh's proximity to the river mouth. The flow of incoming water can be strong enough to reverse the flow of some rivers. Current determines baitfish position and allows optimal feeding by bass, stripers, redfish, and the many other predators that occupy these productive habitats.

Visualize the river trying to push water seaward, the ocean trying to push water inland. The contest goes back and forth as tides rise and fall, and the fish react to changing conditions, even though many species of tidewater fish are *euryhaline*—tolerant of a wide range of salinities.

When the tides recede, a heavy flow of water moves toward the ocean, and marshes rapidly lose volume and become too shallow for bass. Bass seem to have an instinctive concern about being caught in shallow water. They evacuate to

Position of River Bass in Weeds

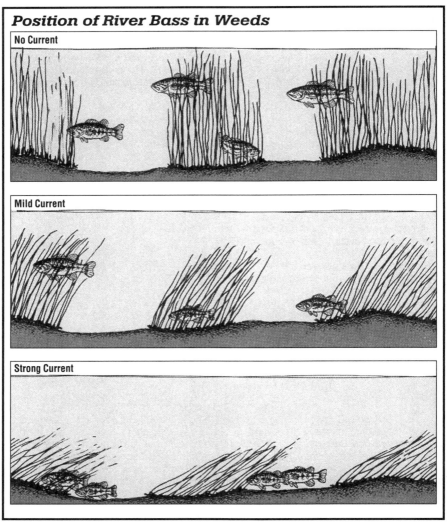

No Current

Mild Current

Strong Current

avoid being trapped in isolated pools, holding in deeper cuts and deeper shoreline cover and feeding less actively.

When tides raise water levels in marshes, bass scatter to thick shoreline marsh cover. They may congregate around the marsh inlet, facing toward the incoming water that brings baitfish. Tidal flows position bass downstream of cover, where they wait to dart out for prey. You may find them holding in little holes or dips in marshes or tidal creeks. When the water levels drop, bass leave the emptying marshes and move to the river or to twisting feeder creeks. You should leave, too, unless you like the prospect of six hours in a muddy hole. Bass may stay close to the inlet mouth, or they may move several miles.

Tides, of course, rise and fall in response to the combined gravitational effects of the sun and moon. Tide tables predict these fluctuations, but the impact is delayed inland, in the marshes where the bass live. The strength of tides is affected

Tidal Positioning

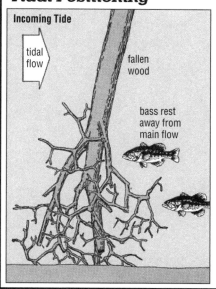

Incoming Tide

tidal flow

fallen wood

bass rest away from main flow

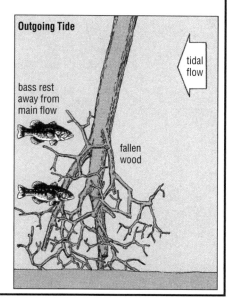

Outgoing Tide

bass rest away from main flow

fallen wood

tidal flow

by moon phase and position, and predicting water levels and their effect on bass is tricky. Typically, the best fishing times are between high and dead low tides, when the water has just begun to move.

Many rivers provide a pleasant alternative to the more familiar fishing offered by ponds, lakes, or reservoirs. Creeks can be waded or fished from shore. On larger waters, canoes and johnboats allow a relaxing float far from the noise of usual water recreation. On big rivers, you may share the waters with tugs, barges, and foreign freighters. But always there are bass, if you know where, when, and how to find them.

RESERVOIR PERSONALITY

Reservoirs are the most diverse type of largemouth bass habitat. They include structural features and habitats of both lake and river environments, as well as complex features of their own. Largemouth bass thrive in manmade waters ranging from shallow, weedy flowages to deep, clear canyon reservoirs. Many reservoirs contain riverine portions and slow water habitats similar to oxbow lakes, river backwaters, and shallow, natural marshes. Some also contain large flats with underwater vegetation, plus a variety of inundated shoreline cover. Every concept, technique, and tactic bass anglers

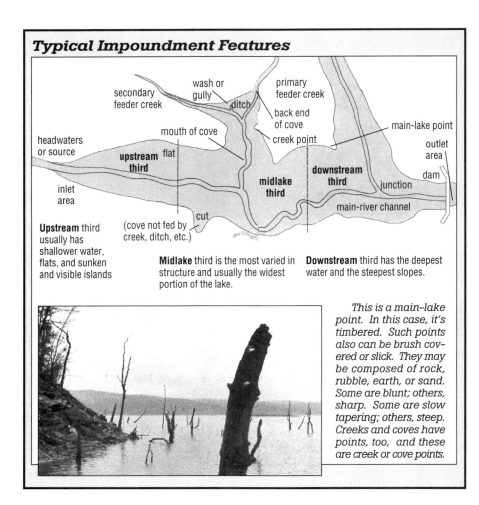

Typical Impoundment Features

secondary feeder creek

wash or gully

ditch

primary feeder creek

back end of cove

mouth of cove

creek point

main-lake point

headwaters or source

upstream third

flat

outlet area

downstream third

dam

inlet area

midlake third

junction

main-river channel

cut

(cove not fed by creek, ditch, etc.)

Upstream third usually has shallower water, flats, and sunken and visible islands

Midlake third is the most varied in structure and usually the widest portion of the lake.

Downstream third has the deepest water and the steepest slopes.

This is a main-lake point. In this case, it's timbered. Such points also can be brush covered or slick. They may be composed of rock, rubble, earth, or sand. Some are blunt; others, sharp. Some are slow tapering; others, steep. Creeks and coves have points, too, and these are creek or cove points.

use in rivers and natural lakes also applies to reservoir fishing.

Many reservoirs offer a wider range of fishing choices than rivers or natural lakes. Impounded waters inundate old riverbeds with scoured edges and rough terrain. They provide more bottom structure, shoreline cover, shallow water, deep water, and open water bass habitat than most natural lakes. Many are so vast and offer so much potential habitat that they overwhelm visiting anglers.

Chapter 3 classified the six basic reservoir types. Knowing which category best describes a reservoir helps you anticipate basic underwater structures, shoreline forms, and depths. The personality of any specific reservoir depends on many physical and biological factors, and these, in turn, influence bass behavior. These include size, shape, depth, current, water level, thermoclines and other clines, water clarity and color, underwater structure, vegetation and other cover, age, climate, weather, fish population mix, purposes and uses, human impacts, and on and on. Discussion of all these interrelated factors is beyond the scope of this chapter. But reviewing a few key structural features of reservoirs can help you locate bass in these complex systems.

SIZE, SHAPE, AND DEPTH

Many smaller impoundments have enough current to prevent stratification. Water quality is similar at all depths, though current-related factors dominate bass fishing patterns. Largemouth habitat is limited, and river-adapted bass species, particularly smallmouths, usually predominate.

At the other extreme are huge lakes formed by large dams that block major river systems. These are wide and often deep, particularly toward the dam. The ratio of the volume of incoming water to the volume of stored water is small, and currents are local, weak, or nonexistent except near inflowing rivers. In the absence of current, water stratifies when the sun heats its surface.

Large impoundments lose riverine traits except at their upstream origin, near feeder rivers, and during floods. They're often nutrient rich near inflows and nutrient poor in the deepest areas near the dam. Drainage areas are large and frequently rich in both silt and nutrients. As a result, reservoirs are murky more often and for longer periods than natural lakes. In addition, heavy rains can create sudden, massive currents that swiftly and drastically change water chemistry and level.

Major impoundments provide a variety of largemouth bass habitat with different depths in different sections. The largest reservoirs have extensive *pelagic* (open water) areas and great expanses of deep, cool areas that are marginal bass habitat. Wide, shallow reservoirs warm quickly in spring, stratify early in summer, and cool rapidly in fall. Narrow, deep reservoirs warm and cool more slowly. Given similar climates, bass in deep reservoirs enter the Spawn Period later and have extended Postsummer Periods. In the South, deep hill-land and highland reservoirs may never cool enough to enter a true Coldwater Period.

Between these extremes of very large and small reservoirs lie a wide range— large and small, shallow and deep. Compared to large reservoirs of the same classification, small waters heat and cool faster and generally offer less diversity of habitat. Small waters also undergo complete water changes more quickly during rainy seasons and have less stable temperature and chemical profiles. Compared to deeper waters of the same size, shallow reservoirs gain and lose heat more rapidly, gather silt and age faster, remain murkier, and are more likely to have *anoxic* (lacking oxygen)areas near the bottom. Weather changes, therefore, have more immediate impact on fishing in shallow reservoirs. In general, small waters provide less consistent bassing.

CURRENTS AND DAMS

The ratio of the volume of incoming and outgoing water to the volume stored, the shape of the impoundment, and directional flow toward outlets determine where currents exist in reservoirs. Wide areas in the path of inflowing water dissipate currents, while narrows concentrate and strengthen them.

Currents flowing along rough bottoms produce eddies, and currents forced to turn by structure produce vertical currents. Such mixing limits the formation of thermoclines and tends to evenly distribute nutrients and silt.

Incoming water seeks its own density. Warm and therefore "light" water flows into and mixes with warm surface water. Cold, dense, incoming water sinks under warm water and mixes with cold water below the thermocline. Salty or mineral-laden water, heavier than pure water of the same temperature, sinks deeper. Pure rainwater floats on cold or salty water, and cold rain mixes with warm surface water as its sinks.

If currents don't mix layers of water, nutrients entering a reservoir can pass through quickly, while relatively stagnant bottom water remains for months.

Seasonal Reservoir Sections & Patterns

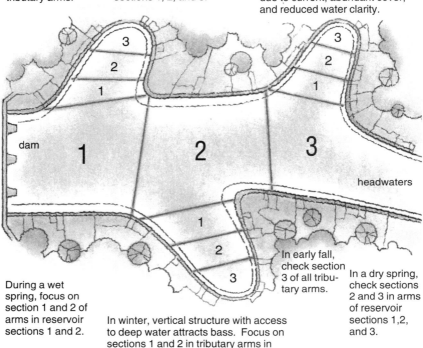

In late fall, bass shift to sections 1 and 2 of tributary arms.

During early and midsummer, check main-lake structure in sections 1, 2, and 3.

In late summer, the upper end of section 3 may offer the best action due to current, abundant cover, and reduced water clarity.

dam

headwaters

During a wet spring, focus on section 1 and 2 of arms in reservoir sections 1 and 2.

In winter, vertical structure with access to deep water attracts bass. Focus on sections 1 and 2 in tributary arms in reservoir sections 1 and 2.

In early fall, check section 3 of all tributary arms.

In a dry spring, check sections 2 and 3 in arms of reservoir sections 1,2, and 3.

To eliminate unproductive water, Rick Clunn uses a system of seasonal location patterns. He divides a reservoir into smaller sections and concentrates on those appropriate for that season. The lower end of a reservoir begins at the dam and extends upstream about one third of the way up the main body of the reservoir, the upstream third includes headwater tributaries. Section #2 is intermediate.

The lower section generally has the deepest and clearest water while the upper end is shallower and more stained. Recent rains affect the upper section first and more strongly. Clunn similarly divides tributary creek arms into three sections that generally follow the depth and clarity characteristics of the main body of the reservoir.

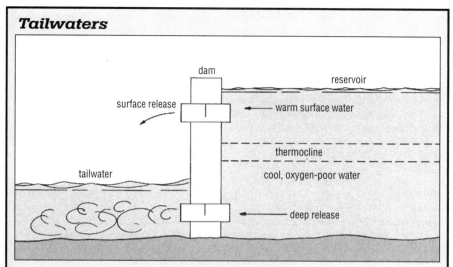

Tailwaters

Reservoirs built with surface outlets release warm water, and bass and other warmwater species often thrive in tailwaters below dams with shallow drains. Deep outlets pass cold or cool water that often holds little oxygen and may be toxic to fish until it mixes with air. Once aerated, deep-outlet water often is better suited to cold- or coolwater species like trout, walleye, or stripers than it is to bass. When bass are present in cold tailwaters, they may avoid aerated outflows and hold downstream where water has time to warm and absorb more oxygen. Some reservoirs release cold, oxygenated water that may support coldwater, coolwater, and warmwater species, respectively, as distance downstream from the dam increases and water becomes progressively warmer.

In big reservoirs, incoming flows spread and dissipate, and outflows create currents only near outlets. Large, deep-draining reservoirs may develop variable temperature profiles and may not have a distinct turnover in fall. These reservoirs provide stable environments and good fall bass fishing when other reservoirs are destabilized by the fall turnover.

The purpose of a dam and its engineering plan dictate how water is released. Outlets near the surface drain surface water and produce warmer surface currents, while deeper outlets drain deeper, colder water, producing deep, colder currents. Deep outlets, by removing the coldest water, raise the average temperature of deep water and lower the thermocline. Shallow drains remove the warmest surface water, reduce its maximum temperature, and may weaken or prevent stratification.

Currents are important to a reservoir's personality and to finding bass, because both preyfish and bass react to them. To save energy, bass avoid strong currents by holding behind cover, though they'll face into weak flows. In still water, bass typically stalk and flush prey along cover edges, or they attack schooling prey in open water. In currents, food items drift or swim past properly positioned bass, so ambush may become a more effective feeding tactic than active hunting.

In strong currents, smallmouths or other riverine bass typically dominate, but regardless of species, currents determine where fish hold. In weak currents, bass may suspend and feed in open water over deep channels or move along shorelines and flats with wood cover or vegetation. When flows force them to swim harder, they shift toward bottom or behind cover objects.

In hydroelectric power reservoirs, bass often match feeding periods to generating schedules. Prey species like shad school tightly and are more vulnerable in currents, so bass feed aggressively while generators are operating. Prey like sunfish and crayfish, however, seek shelter from currents, so where they are the dominant prey, bass may become more active when currents are reduced.

Current direction is affected by reservoir structure. Productive fishing patterns often develop where sharp turns force currents to swerve, because baitfish and bass often concentrate there. Deep layers of cool, dense water also mix upward at these turns. Surface water becomes muddier or clearer, depending on the clarity of the deep layer. Upwellings concentrate nutrients, prey, and bass. Bass may also be more active where deep currents approach the surface. The most obvious upwellings occur in straight reservoirs with strong currents and only a few sharp bends. Snakelike reservoirs with many bends dissipate currents, so effects may be noticeable only at the first sharp turn below inflows.

WATER LEVELS AFFECT BASS

Natural lakes have stable water levels; outflow balances inflow, and except in times of serious drought, depth changes only a few feet between rainy and dry seasons. Many reservoirs, in contrast, alternately store and release water. Inflow and outflow are seldom balanced, and the surface level is often rising or falling.

At hydroelectric dams, generators operate when demands for electric power are high, and peak generation often occurs in hot months, when air conditioners are used heavily. Another seasonal peak occurs in midwinter, when days are short and lights are on longer. Electric demands are highest in the late afternoon and evening, so hydropower reservoirs have daily generation schedules.

Dams built to store municipal water supplies usually fluctuate less but generally decline in summer and fall. In contrast, dams built for flood control or to store irrigation water may fall drastically within a few months. Irrigation needs jump when spring rains stop. Dry seasons increase reservoir demands, while inflows decline. Wet years refill reservoirs, but extended drought forces drawdowns that can damage fisheries.

Water-level reduction exposes banks to erosion that may wash away woody shoreline cover, sand, or organic material conducive to plant growth. Soft soils drift into river channels and shores remain rocky, weedless, and infertile. Such reservoirs usually have a plankton food base, and bass rely heavily on pelagic preyfish. Clear reservoirs with wildly fluctuating water levels are often unproductive bass fisheries.

It's vital to know the seasonal and annual water-level histories of reservoirs you fish. Low water for several years often increases fishing pressure and may reduce spawning success, so bass populations decline. High spring water levels usually produce large hatches of bass, increase cover, and protect bass from harvest. High water often improves fishing several years later, when bass have reached catchable size.

Constantly fluctuating levels often reduce spawning habitat and shoreline cover. This reduces bass populations and may prevent bass from establishing stable home ranges. They're forced to move frequently and often adopt offshore feeding habits. They roam in large groups if their numbers haven't been reduced by fishing, and they often suspend off cover and structure, particularly if other large predators aren't abundant.

Bass that do establish home ranges in fluctuating waterways tend to inhabit steep structures that extend from below the maximum drawdown depth to near the full-pool level. These spots provide what bass need, despite major water-level changes. Steep points and bluffs are prime locations.

Bass in reservoirs with annual drawdowns adapt suspended, open water habits or change habitats seasonally. Shallow flats and banks with gently sloping bottoms are dry too frequently to hold bass, vegetation, and prey. Flats that are frequently exposed are visited by migrant bass only when they reflood.

The recent water-level pattern is almost as important as past history. Traditional lore suggests that anglers fish shallow when water is rising and deeper when water is falling. This isn't always the best advice. Reservoir bass move shallower when it's advantageous. When water inundates shorelines covered with terrestrial vegetation, the new shallows often provide abundant food and cover to attract preyfish. But in reservoirs with barren shorelines above the waterline, increases in level provide little additional food or cover, and bass are likely to stay at their accustomed depths.

Dropping water levels force bass off shallow flats and away from shoreline cover but rarely affect bass on steep bluffs. Sudden drops may expose crayfish as they evacuate their holes, stimulating shallow feeding activity.

Periodic drawdowns that don't lower the surface enough to expose the outer edge of weedlines can form banks of offshore weeds with distinct inside edges. Vegetation near shorelines grows back slowly when water levels are raised, while the outer rings of grass remain healthy. Offshore weed rings are prime bass habitat—high-percentage fishing spots.

Drawdowns lasting only a few days may kill some shallow-water plant species, but not those resistant to drying, like water lilies and hydrilla, or those like milfoil, which rapidly reseed or regenerate from broken plant parts. Milfoil may dominate reservoirs subjected to occasional brief drawdowns.

Long-term drawdowns kill most exposed plants. Here, too, replacement weeds are likely to be species that reestablish quickly by seeds or by regeneration of fragments. By allowing deeper light penetration, drawdowns between 5 and 20 feet increase the likelihood that hydrilla and other deep-rooting species will colonize deeper water.

Fall drawdowns may help bass fisheries by exposing prey sheltered in shoreline cover. Drawdowns also dry and oxygenate bottom and allow terrestrial grasses to grow. Additional cover and nutrients are available when exposed areas become flooded again.

Drawdowns during the spawn can hamper bass production, and early summer drawdowns can force bass fry from protective cover and expose them to additional predation. In general, strong bass fisheries result when water levels are stable or are drawn down in fall, raised to or above normal pool prior to the spawn, and then held at that level until summer.

A few reservoirs have been built for recreational purposes or to support real-estate speculation. They are often held at constant levels that produce excellent fishing—if prey and cover are abundant and harvest isn't excessive.

As impoundments age, however, shallow cover rots, and shorelines eventually become barren. Some fixed-level reservoirs would provide better fishing if water levels were allowed to fluctuate enough to flood terrestrial vegetation during and immediately after spring spawns.

All these variables make reservoir fishing complicated. The quality of fishing is also affected by many management decisions. Public policies are part of

How Water Level Fluctuations Affect Different Reservoir Types

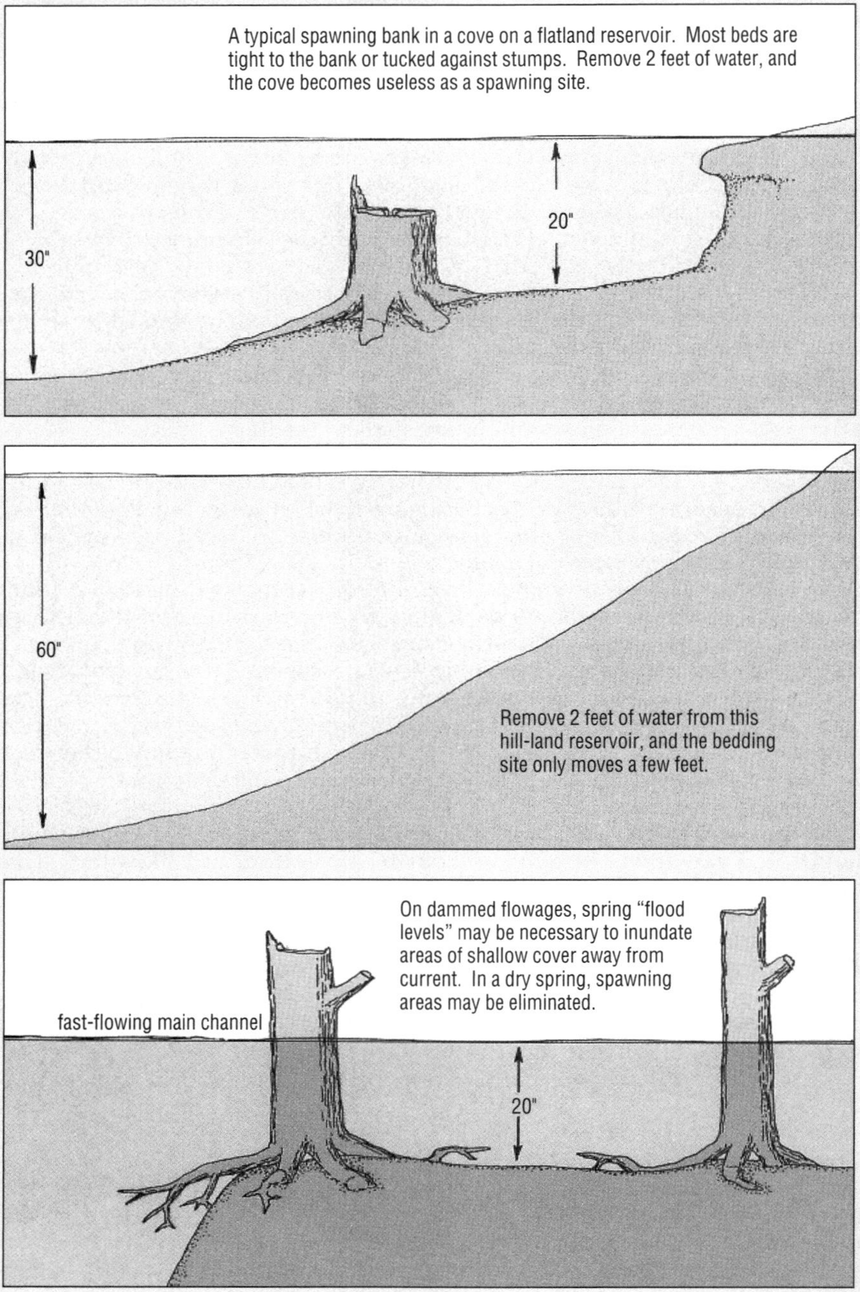

A typical spawning bank in a cove on a flatland reservoir. Most beds are tight to the bank or tucked against stumps. Remove 2 feet of water, and the cove becomes useless as a spawning site.

30"

20"

60"

Remove 2 feet of water from this hill-land reservoir, and the bedding site only moves a few feet.

On dammed flowages, spring "flood levels" may be necessary to inundate areas of shallow cover away from current. In a dry spring, spawning areas may be eliminated.

fast-flowing main channel

20"

each reservoir's personality—not just release schedules, but boating access, sewage treatment regulations, property owners' interests, stocking decisions, limits. But then you wouldn't have bought this book and read this far if you weren't a dedicated bass angler eager to learn the details that improve fishing success.

Make a list of personality factors like the ones in this chapter, and other factors you notice—it will pay off. You may not be able to change release policies, but you can learn release schedules and fish appropriately. Fill in the details. Call power company authorities to learn the depths of outlets and to obtain past and present release schedules and water level and thermocline histories for the last 10 or 20 years. Ask professors of limnology and aquatic biology at a nearby university what they know about your reservoirs. Talk to state fishery biologists, dock owners, guides, and other anglers. Attend tournaments and read magazine articles.

Once you have a complete picture of a reservoir's personality, good and bad days may suddenly be explained. You're on your way to understanding why you caught bass where you did and how you missed a productive pattern. And you'll recognize similar conditions when they reoccur. This kind of knowledge is useful wherever you fish, but it's even more important on reservoirs, which offer the greatest complexity and potential.

PONDS

Now that you've looked at reservoir fishing on the grand scale, think for a moment about the smallest of reservoirs—ponds. These are relatively easy to fish, yet many have the capacity to produce record-class fish. Most fishermen live within a few miles of several ponds. But not all of them yield good bass fishing. Successful angling is primarily finding the right ponds.

The key to a productive pond is good management. You need to know if a pond is well managed or neglected, and what the pond is managed for. Once you've located a productive pond, remember that all the usual principles of structure still apply: a pond has shallows, flats, and "deep" holes—just on a much smaller scale.

Underwater structure and cover shape the world of the largemouth bass. Understanding its forms and functions is a key to successful bass fishing.

Habitat and Feeding

THE CLUES FOR PRESENTATION

Cover is the name of the game in most bass fishing, so the preceding chapters have often referred to cover. You already know the general way that structure and cover together are key to locating bass and the different ways bass relate to cover through the seasons. In this chapter, we'll look more closely at a few kinds of cover and how to fish them.

Cover refers to weeds, timber, boulders, logs, docks, stumps—anything that breaks uniformity. Prime bass cover provides shade. Shade doesn't cool fish, except in very shallow and clear water, but it camouflages and hides them. It provides a visual advantage when they attack prey in bright sunlight. Cover that consistently produces bass often is located on distinct underwater structures or at spots where bisecting structures encourage moving bass to hold. Of all kinds of cover, weeds are by far the most common and important.

WEED WISDOM—THE IMPORTANCE OF UNDERWATER PLANTS

Vegetation concentrates nutrients in shallow water and provides food and cover for preyfish. Bass are attracted to both the prey and the weedy cover. Where underwater vegetation is available, largemouth bass use it consistently. Other cover—trees, brush, or rocks—attracts few largemouth bass when underwater weeds are nearby, unless the bass population is near capacity, or larger and more effective predators occupy the vegetation. Even during coldwater periods, largemouth bass often stay near weeds at moderate depths rather than move to deeper water.

Abundant underwater plants clear water by trapping silt, blunting wave action, and reducing plankton by monopolizing the available nutrients. By limiting plankton and creating a food chain based more on rooted plants, vegetation modifies interactions among fish species. Weedy reservoirs usually hold more bass and sunfishes and fewer open-water species than do waters with food chains based primarily on plankton.

Reservoirs that are usually murky seldom hold much vegetation because plants require sunlight. Some species of vegetation, however, tolerate more shade than others. The exotic weed hydrilla, since it needs little light to root and grow, thrives in dingier water than most native plants. It also roots at greater depths and seems to tolerate wider fluctuations in water level. Hydrilla often creates excellent bass fisheries until it grows out of control and fills more than about 30 percent of a reservoir. Then it clogs shallow areas, compromises dam functions, and reduces bass growth rates. At some point, control measures may be implemented by the reservoir authority.

Native plants generally provide better habitat. Many plant species only grow in specific bottom soils like sand, silt, clay, or mud. Which species will grow in a body of water depends on the presence of these soils at depths reached by ample light.

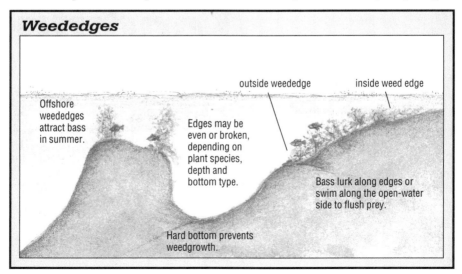

Weededges

outside weededge   inside weed edge

Offshore weededges attract bass in summer.

Edges may be even or broken, depending on plant species, depth and bottom type.

Bass lurk along edges or swim along the open-water side to flush prey.

Hard bottom prevents weedgrowth.

If you find bass in a clump of coontail at 17 feet, for example, you'll probably find other productive patches of coontail at similar depths, in creek beds and channels where enough silt settles to form the soft bottom that coontail requires.

Few plants root in hard rock, so highland and canyon reservoirs seldom hold many underwater weeds. If weeds exist, they'll be in isolated flats and upstream areas where inflows drop sand and silt.

Aquatic plants trap sediment near the bottom, produce oxygen during daytime by photosynthesis, consume oxygen at night, trap surface heat, and decrease currents. This creates local pH-, oxy-, thermo-, and chemoclines under large weedbeds, particularly during early morning hours. Low oxygen and acidic pH conditions often exist near the bottom under weedbeds, so bass in weeds often suspend near the canopy.

Water around weedbeds typically contains more oxygen as the day goes on and steadily loses oxygen at night. If the nighttime oxygen drop is severe, bass hold near the tops of weedbeds while dissolved oxygen is ample but move outside the edges of vegetation late at night. They remain outside until photosynthesis reoxygenates the weed canopy an hour or two after sunrise.

VEGETATION CATEGORIES

Poor Pads

Productive Pads

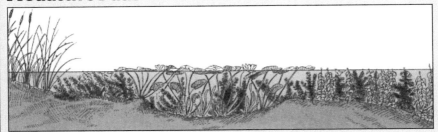

Sparse, isolated lily pads with little surrounding cover are less likely to hold bass than areas with dense cover. Adjacent coontail or cabbage and a mixture of weeds within the pads attracts bass. The area must, however, have enough passages beneath the pads to permit bass movement, though you seldom find areas that are too thick.

Points, turns, pockets, depressions, and variations in pads concentrate active bass. Inactive bass may be only a few feet away, buried beneath the canopy and difficult to trigger.

The term *weeds* commonly refers to a wide variety of aquatic vegetation, each with its own profile, texture, height, stiffness, density, and other characteristics. Plant biologists use the term only for noxious or invading species, however. We can't say one type of weed attracts bass more than another, but there are some common favorites: lily pads on shallow, soft bottom; stands of reeds, maidencane, or other emergent plants on shallow, sandy bottom; coontail or cabomba on middepth or deep flats; cabbage (pondweed) bordering deep drop-offs.

Each lake and reservoir has different combinations, and the attractiveness of each vegetation type varies over the course of the year. Bass react to the changing environment by moving to the most attractive zones. Successful anglers evaluate local conditions and know what attracts bass.

Several things determine which weed species grow in certain areas. Most important are water depth and bottom type. Different varieties of weeds compete with each other for sunlight and growing room; the best flats often contain a variety of weed species.

Lily pads grow in the shallows on soft or semisoft bottom. If there's a layer of sand several inches beneath the overlying muck, bass will construct nests there. Fertile lakes, however, may have several feet of soft muck in lily pad bays, making them unsuitable spawning sites. Developing pads attract substantial numbers of bass during early-to mid-Prespawn Period and host a resident population during the summer. Bass desert pads in early fall when shallow weeds begin to die. Active bass concentrate in pockets, alleys, and outer edges; inactive bass bury underneath.

Reeds or bulrushes are hard-stemmed emergent plants growing in shallow water. They often provide good spawning conditions and also attract bass throughout summer. Thick reeds may hold a resident population of bass; sparse or clumpy reeds attract active bass from a nearby home weed flat. Thick clumps provide the best cover. The shallow back edge of a reedbed often attracts the most bass. Pockets, alleys, and edges bordering heavy cover also concentrate fish.

Maidencane refers to several species of tall, branched, emergent shoreline plants that grow in firmer soil than bulrushes. Pockets and holes in cane are potential summer bass attractors if the water is 2 feet deep or more.

Middepth flats usually offer a variety of weedgrowth. *Sandgrass*, an alga that grows 6 inches to 2 feet off the bottom on sandy soil, offers little cover to bass. Numerous shallow plants grow in stands too thick for bass to use effectively.

Coontail is one middepth plant that's an excellent bass attractor. It grows to the surface and forms umbrella-shaped overhead cover. Dense coontail is difficult to fish, but fortunately a coontail bed usually has pockets, holes, and edges, or grows in clumps with open water surrounding it. Coontail may or may not extend to the deep weededge. It also persists into late fall.

Various species of *cabbage (pondweed)* often form a deep or outside weededge. These tall, leafy plants are prime bass habitat. They're also easier to fish than coontail. Sparse cabbage offers casting lanes between individual stalks. Even thick cabbage is fishable, since a wrist snap cleanly breaks the leaves or stalk, freeing the lure. Try that with exposed hooks in coontail, however, and you'll foul the lure most of the time.

Some weed types are easier to fish than others, making them favorite angling spots. You may like to fish certain weed types and find others exasperating. Your favorite lures may frequently hang up, or you may have to use heavier tackle than you prefer. The bass, however, use the best available habitat, which doesn't always conform to an angler's notions of convenience. To be consistently successful, you

Coontail Clump

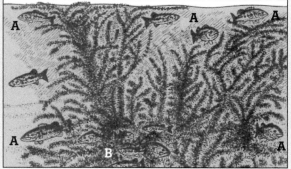

side view

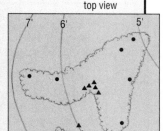

Active bass **(A)** favor points and edges and tend to ride high. Inactive bass **(B)** tend to move to corners or penetrate the weeds and hold tighter to bottom.

▲ Inactive postfrontal bass
• Active stable weather bass

can't just fish lily pads or the deep outside edges of cabbage. Be versatile in your thinking and techniques, and approach each lake in a systematic fashion. Be prepared to sample all weed zones until you identify the most productive patterns. Patterns change not only seasonally but over the course of a day.

WEEDLINES

Edges are critical to predators—edges in structure and in cover. A cover break is any abrupt change in cover. Sharp changes in depth or bottom content will cause obvious cover breaks. Changes from one weed type to another can be more subtle, yet here, too, something ends and something else begins. Any of these cover breaks may concentrate bass.

Weededges are the main type of cover break in natural lakes because bass feed efficiently along weededges, and submerged terrestrial cover is generally lacking. Dense, continuous weeds make it hard for bass to launch successful strikes on prey. Though bass can feed in and around weeds, they're more efficient when they can catch their prey in open water along a weededge. Any weedbed creates an edge, but a secondary edge adds to a spot's potential. Look for breaks in the weedline, pockets, inside turns, and points where the vegetation grows out along an underwater extension.

Deep weedlines—Water clarity determines how deeply sunlight can penetrate and thus where rooted vegetation can grow. The deep weedline of good bass lakes often lies between 10 and 15 feet deep; in lakes with dark water, it may be as shallow as 6 feet, and in clear lakes, as deep as 20 feet. Unusual weather or algae blooms may cause the depth of the deep weedline to vary a foot or two from year to year, or the weeds may be sparser or thicker than the previous year.

Though the deep weedline generally lies at a specific depth, it isn't an exact line unless it's formed by a distinct drop-off. A 12-foot-deep weedline might actually range from 10 to 14 feet, depending on bottom type and slope. Slowly tapering bottoms often have wandering weedlines with ragged, clumpy edges. You can't simply position your boat at a certain depth and assume you'll stay on the edge. Watch your depthfinder for the presence of weeds, look into the water with polarized sunglasses, and feel for weeds with your lures. Following ragged weededges requires careful attention, but it's worth the effort.

Lake Weededge—High Percentage Spots

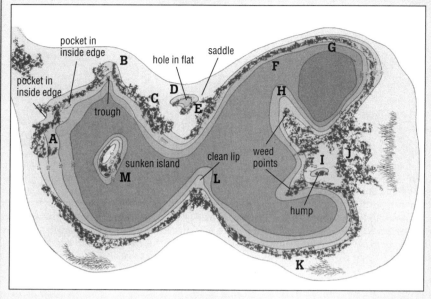

A—Widely spaced, uneven contour lines foster a jagged weededge; look for points, pockets, lots of bass-holding cover.

B—Troughs or "funnels" are prime feeding areas and migration routes for bass.

C—Check inside edges on large flats. An inside edge can hold more bass than an outside edge.

D—A 10-foot-deep hole on a flat—this is a bass magnet.

E—Hole near the drop-off creates a saddle, always attractive to fish.

F—Close, straight contour lines usually mean weed walls. Fish quickly by cranking parallel to the wall. Inside edges aren't as likely to hold fish.

G—A tight inside bend, a likely area for a curved weed wall. Search for active bass.

H—Weedy points near a deep hole must be checked for weed clumps just off the main weedlines.

I—Hump on a flat, an excellent shallow bass attractor.

J—A large flat usually offers a variety of structural elements that attract and hold bass.

K—A small flat, not likely to hold many bass, in contrast to J.

L—A clean lip where weeds end abruptly and the point slopes gradually toward the drop-off.

M—A big offshore hump (sunken island) offering these fine weed-edge possibilities: sloping point; small clean lip; sharp drop for weed wall; wider contours for a jagged weededge; possibility of thick clumps on sloping, main-lake side; and a bald spot on top.

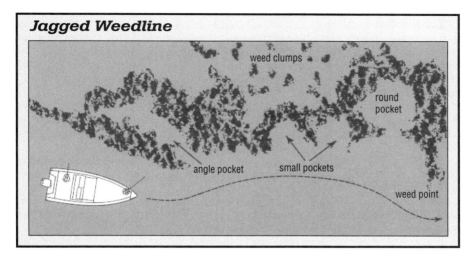

Jagged Weedline

weed clumps

round pocket

angle pocket

small pockets

weed point

Throughout summer, the deep weedline is a great spot to contact feeding bass. Minnows and crayfish concentrate there, and feeding bass patrol above and along the weededge, looking for food. It's also easy to fish because it's so accessible. Position the boat in deeper water and fish to the weedline without the problems of moving a boat in thick weeds. Bass along the deep weedline also tend to be more stable—less easily put off their feed by a passing cold front.

The deep weededge also is a prime bass location in the fall. As the water cools, shallow plants begin to die, first in the extreme shallows, then on the flats. Largemouths leave these areas, moving to healthy stands of vegetation. Fish concentrate in larger and larger groups as habitat diminishes.

By the time the water temperature dips into the low 50°F range, most largemouth bass have gathered in deeper weeds. Even here the weeds will have diminished. The healthiest stands of green weeds typically occur along sharp inside turns along the drop-off. Bass of all sizes stack into these areas from the shallows, flats, and deep edges, gathering into some of the largest concentrations of the year. This is trophy time.

Bass may remain in or near these areas through late fall and into winter. They bite well on jig-n-pig combos, plastic worms or craws, and live bait—until the water drops into the 40°F range. Bass are concentrated then, but not active. You can catch bass till ice-up with slow, precise presentations. They can still be caught at early ice and throughout winter, but for most fishermen, it's a long winter of trip planning, hook sharpening, and tackle organizing.

Shallow weedlines—Vegetation often stops growing on the shallow side of a weedbed, forming an inside edge or corridor of open water between the bank and the thick vegetation. This may be due to wave action in the shallows, water-level fluctuations that eliminate grass during fall and winter, or changes in bottom content. In many lakes, the near-shore zone contains mixed sand and gravel that isn't hospitable to most aquatic plants.

The shallow weedline is rarely as distinct as the deep weedline, often just a patch here and there, yet it sometimes forms a distinct edge in portions of the lake. Don't neglect these inside edges. They don't get as much fishing pressure as deep edges but can be loaded with bass. Shallow weedlines are most productive in early spring or early summer, especially during the morning or evening.

Top weedlines—Weedy flats often have a top weedline, a space between the surface of the water and the tops of most submerged plants. When there's enough room to run a spinnerbait, a spoon, or a shallow-running crankbait over the weeds, the top edge can be great. This edge often is ragged, with clumps and small pockets to flutter lures into. Make accurate casts and steer your bait to key spots with your rod tip, or else make long casts to cover large areas efficiently.

Openings in the weeds—Little pockets within weedbeds sometimes occur where a deeper hole or hard bottom breaks up an otherwise uniform terrain. They're hard to spot, but the surrounding weededges can be fish magnets, and few anglers fish them.

Edges within a weedbed—Get familiar with the categories of vegetation where you fish. A vast, cabbage-covered flat may contain colonies of coontail. These clumps of denser plants often concentrate bass. The same situation occurs when patches of wild rice, bulrushes, or dollar bonnets grow within a vast bed of water lilies. Blindly fishing the whole bed may provide slow action, but focusing on the edge-within-an-edge can yield incredible catches.

Points and inside turns—Weededges can be straight and unbroken, or they can have points, breaks, and inside turns that commonly concentrate bass and other species. Catchable bass along weededges tend to be along points or in inside turns.

Aggressive bass often concentrate around or over the tops of points. They move as far toward edge-oriented food as possible without leaving weedy cover. Inside turns, meanwhile, concentrate bass that are less active though still willing to feed. A bass tucked back in an inside turn is as deep in weeds as it can get and still be near a weededge to grab a meal.

PRESENTATIONS FOR VEGETATION

Active bass patrol edges along the top and sides of weedbeds. Tips of weed points are excellent because they're the junction of several types of edges. Active bass are susceptible to fast-moving horizontal presentations like spinnerbaits,

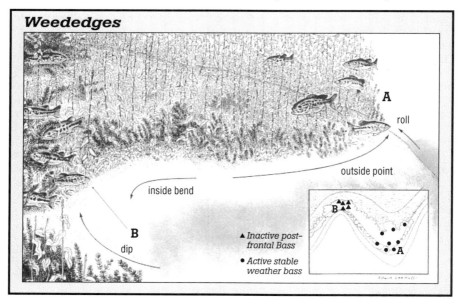

Weededges

A

roll

outside point

inside bend

B

dip

▲ *Inactive post-frontal Bass*

● *Active stable weather bass*

Matching Tactics to Conditions

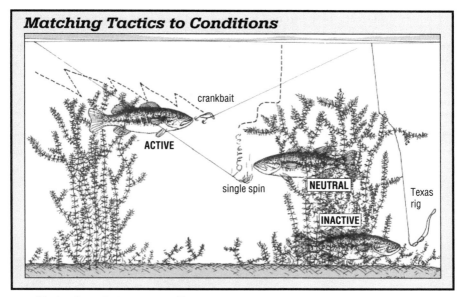

crankbaits, buzzbaits, or weedless spoons.

Inactive bass tend to bury in weed patches or to suspend in open water, holding several feet from their feeding area. During inactive periods, inside corners often provide better fishing than points. Slow, vertical presentations usually are best, like worms or jigs, or near-stationary methods, like topwaters twitched above or alongside shallow cover.

Match your presentation to the type and thickness of the weeds, as well as to bass mood. Crankbaits work well next to edges or over the tops of weeds but hang up continually when weeds extend to the surface. Spinnerbaits or buzzbaits are a better choice over weed tops; weedless worms and jigs can be teased through dense stalks.

Open-hook jigworms work well along deep cabbage edges, where the hook momentarily hangs in weeds before you snap it clear, sometimes triggering nearby bass. In heavy coontail, use a Texas-rigged worm or jig-n-pig. Versatility is essential for consistent success.

SLOP BAYS

The slop bay is a distinctive type of summer flat, relatively shallow with dense weedgrowth. It is often the product of nutrient overload, such as badly maintained septic systems, fertilized lawns, or incoming creeks that flow through fertilized farmlands. Rooted vegetation often reaches its maximum growth in early summer. Coontail, milfoil, cabbage, duckweed, and lily pads—especially lily pads—are typical weeds found in slop bays. In fact, lily pads are often referred to as slop, although the term includes more than pads.

Wild rice patches, common in the northern United States and Canada, function much like slop bays; they often hold largemouths all summer. Rice is even more difficult to fish than slop, and lure choice is limited to a handful of weedless spoons, rats, or jigs and worms for flipping. Wild rice and slop are worth the effort, though. The thickest, heaviest tangles of shallow cover can host the biggest largemouths during summer. Few anglers accept the challenge of tackling them, beyond making token casts to the outer edges of rice or pads.

Slop bays develop when rooted weeds are fully grown, at about the Summer Peak Period. Many nutrients become available for filamentous algae, which lie on the surface like angel hair Christmas tree decoration. They clot together with the rooted vegetation, and form a floating canopy of clingy gunk. This canopy provides overhead cover and shade for bass, from yearlings to trophies. Water temperatures are about as warm under the slop as in sunlit areas, but bass tolerate the warmest temperatures that occur in northern lakes; in southern lakes, temperatures over 95°F can push bass out of slop.

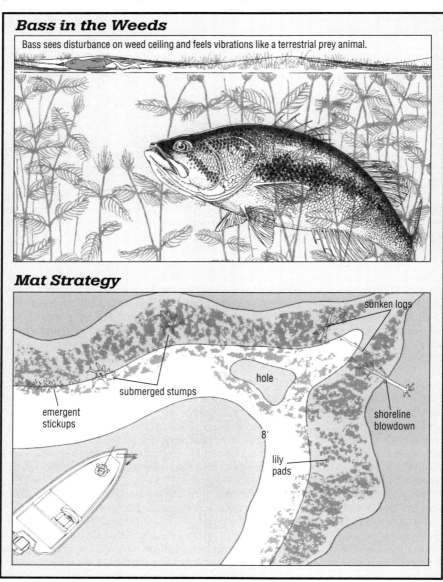

Bass in the Weeds

Bass sees disturbance on weed ceiling and feels vibrations like a terrestrial prey animal.

Mat Strategy

sunken logs

submerged stumps

hole

emergent stickups

shoreline blowdown

8'

lily pads

Bass may remain in slop bays if conditions are adequate and prey abundant; in fact, bass in slop and rice are often homebodies. They remain in their hole or snag, though from time to time they may leave to roam the adjacent flats to hunt food. They frequent slightly deeper holes, fallen trees, exposed roots of stumps, and similar spots in dense vegetation. Incoming springs can also attract slop bass.

Slop bass become almost exclusively ambush predators. They don't see potential prey for long, and in such thick cover, they can't easily run down prey. Slop bass are attuned to surface activity, using a combination of vision, hearing, and lateral line perception to pick up moving objects that might be food. When a possible meal approaches, *KERSPLOOSH!* To catch them, work a lure over the slop and then bring it into small openings where bass can bust it. Spinnerbaits and buzzbaits, two usually good shallow cover baits, may not work well if the turning blades get mired in algae. The best baits are weedless spoons, weightless plastic worms, and weedless plastic frogs.

Fishing slop presents three difficulties. First, it's hard to identify key holding areas when you can't see through the slop. Initially, you must fish the whole area; once you've found favorite holding areas, concentrate on them. Use your eyes. Spot bass by hearing or seeing their feeding swirls. A bass patrolling the shallow water of a slop bay will bump weeds or make a wake that tips you to its location.

Some slop bass specialists prowl bays in early spring to locate stumps, holes, and other spots that will hold bass when slop develops. Later they can fish the bay efficiently, moving from one high-percentage spot to another without making a lot of noise and wasting time hunting for spots no longer visible under the canopy.

Second, it's not easy to move a boat in slop—stumps, drowned timber, weeds, lily pads, rice, and algae. Outboard motors make too much noise, and water pumps can clog and overheat. Even the best weed-chewing electrics bog down when wrapped in filamentous algae and wild rice. In some situations, the best way to move a boat is with a long push pole with a duckbill end, which gets a good bite in the bottom without sticking there. Reconcile yourself to fishing slowly and methodically.

Finally, it's difficult to land a slop bass. You need stout line and heavy, long rods to get a bass on top immediately. Once you've got a bass skidding toward you, you can control even a big fish, but if you give him a chance to get his head down and run for cover, it's all over.

At the first fall cooling period, vegetation in slop bays begins to decay. As temperatures grow unstable in the shallows, bass leave and head for deeper flats to join bass that have been there all summer.

OTHER COVER

WOOD

Where vegetation is limited, wood is usually the most attractive type of cover to largemouth bass. Prime wood in shallow areas provides shade and lies on or near bottom so bass can hold near or under it. Standing timber also attracts bass that suspend to attack pelagic preyfish over deep water. In reservoirs, brushpiles, standing timber, and stumps present more fishing possibilities.

Wood inevitably rots or floats away. Most wood and brush cover that's periodically exposed to air disappears within a few decades. Tree trunks standing below the surface last longer, but once standing trees lose their branches, they're less attractive to bass. After about 30 years, only the hardest wood cover remains, and most reservoirs need habitat improvement to sustain fine-quality fishing for largemouth bass.

Fallen Trees

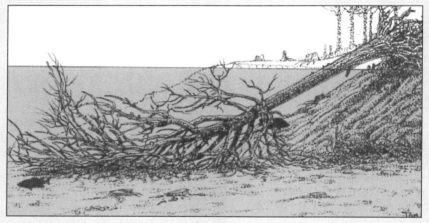

Fallen trees are familiar cover primarily caused by wave-produced erosion from wind and boat traffic. Beavers also fell trees, as do lightning, wind, and state agencies. Fallen trees are best during spring or when trees have fallen with no competing cover.

Consider how recently the tree has fallen, for age affects lure presentation. Clues to look for are the amount of sod remaining in the roots and the number of fine branches visible near the crown.

New trees resemble a broom pushed down by the handle—many small branches near the crown, but not in it. It's tough to get a lure down the trunk past the crown, so peg your sinkers and don't let the lure bury in tightly spaced branches. A new tree offers directional wood; drop the lure down the trunk and bring worms or crankbaits through the sunken crown from 90 degrees to the side. Risks of snags increase, but this is a productive technique that drops a lure through the section of a tree that is most likely to hold bass.

Standing Timber

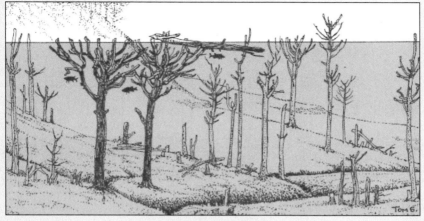

You're faced with searching through hundreds of trees. Only a few combinations exist where nature's work coincides with man's work to create ideal structure plus cover. Few 50-to 70-foot trees have crowns to the exact pool level of a lake, and fewer still grow along a creek channel.

These emergent half-crown trees lie along a midlake creek channel, making them distinct from other trees, suggesting that they'll attract big bass and crappies during spring. Work them from each angle, especially between the crowns and along any horizontal extension, such as lodged driftwood. Don't drop lures farther than the crowns, because bass usually don't relate to bare trunks. These are good spots on spring nights, especially when moonlight helps you approach them.

Approach quietly and be rigged for heavy-duty work. Slide lures through the branches and use a controlled drop at the edges of the crown.

ROCKS

Rocky areas with holes and cracks where crawfish, darters, and other preyfish can hide provide good feeding grounds. Largemouth as well as smallmouth bass hold around rocks large enough to create caves and shadowed areas for protection. Boulders and rock slabs are particularly attractive when they're located in or adjacent to weedbeds.

Riprap placed along dam faces and bridges also represent important bass cover in reservoirs. Its crevices provide feeding opportunities, and the placement of riprap often provides a path from deep water to the shallows that bass use on a daily or seasonal basis.

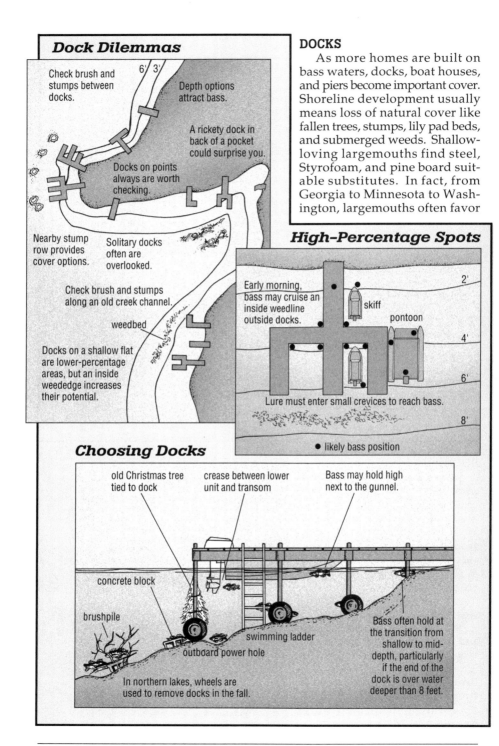

Dock Dilemmas

Check brush and stumps between docks.

6' 3'

Depth options attract bass.

A rickety dock in back of a pocket could surprise you.

Docks on points always are worth checking.

Nearby stump row provides cover options.

Solitary docks often are overlooked.

Check brush and stumps along an old creek channel.

weedbed

Docks on a shallow flat are lower-percentage areas, but an inside weededge increases their potential.

DOCKS

As more homes are built on bass waters, docks, boat houses, and piers become important cover. Shoreline development usually means loss of natural cover like fallen trees, stumps, lily pad beds, and submerged weeds. Shallow-loving largemouths find steel, Styrofoam, and pine board suitable substitutes. In fact, from Georgia to Minnesota to Washington, largemouths often favor

High-Percentage Spots

2'

Early morning, bass may cruise an inside weedline outside docks.

skiff

pontoon

4'

6'

Lure must enter small crevices to reach bass.

8'

● likely bass position

Choosing Docks

old Christmas tree tied to dock

crease between lower unit and transom

Bass may hold high next to the gunnel.

concrete block

brushpile

swimming ladder

outboard power hole

Bass often hold at the transition from shallow to mid-depth, particularly if the end of the dock is over water deeper than 8 feet.

In northern lakes, wheels are used to remove docks in the fall.

docks of all shapes and sizes over natural cover. Often the most unappealing dock produces a bonanza.

Largemouth bass may hold near or under docks in all season except when ice forms, but summer's the best time to fish them. Bass occupy docks after leaving spawning bays, with postspawn females preceding nest-guarding males. Early summer dock fishing often produces the largest average size of the year. The number of bass using docks may build as summer progresses, and small bluegills, shiners, and other preyfish gather on the flats and gravitate to docks.

Hot sunny days seem to drive bass under docks. Timing is crucial—fish too early in the morning, and most of the fish haven't moved to shade; delay too long, and some other anglers beats you to the best ones. You can make good dock catches in the dark, as well as at dawn, dusk, and in pouring rain. At night, lighted docks produce best.

Not all docks are equally attractive; subtle differences may repeatedly attract fish to one dock more than to others. You can't always tell why, but a few guidelines will help you spot prime docks.

Docks with wood pilings usually are better than docks with metal pilings. Reservoir docks often are built to float, lack any pilings to concentrate bass, and may float over deep water. They provide only overhead cover and shade. Docks low to the water offer better overhead cover than high ones. Tight decking usually is better than open cracks. A "T" or "L" extension on a dock makes it considerably better than a simple straight dock. Big docks are better than small ones; docks with boat bays or covered boat lifts are bigger and often more attractive to bass than docks without lifts, although bass may hold in the shade under any boat tethered to a dock.

We once thought docks with deep water nearby were better than docks stranded in the shallows, but we've seen too many good docks that aren't near deeper water. Docks along inside or deep weedlines usually are productive. What counts is the quality of cover the dock offers and the ability of the area to support fish.

Docks often run from shore to depths of 4 or 5 feet, depths bass frequently use. You will find deeper holes formed when the dock owner guns his motor to run his boat onto a boat lift. Sometimes docks are associated with weededges, because property owners clear paths for their boats or rake out a swimming area. The best docks are adjacent to weedflats that hold many bass. Some bass may remain around docks, but many move in from adjacent weeds at prime times, usually midday.

Docks offer the best fishing when sun creates distinct shady areas under them. On overcast days, or at dawn and dusk, bass often hold or feed on adjacent weedflats. When the sun rises, though, patterns that worked on the flats may fade. Then it's time to move to the deep weedline—or find a line of good docks.

Several approaches work for dock bass. Aggressive bass will be out on dock edges ready to chase. Retrieve spinnerbaits or crankbaits right along the dock edge, especially along the shady side. Flipping is great for fishing docks because you can drop jigs with pinpoint accuracy along pilings and in corners where bass hold. Some dock fishing specialists use a spinning rod to skip plastics underneath. The cast is flat and powerful with a slight upswing at the moment of release. Lightly weighted plastic worms, grubs, or tube jigs will skip several times before stopping a dozen or more feet under the dock, where less aggressive bass hold. Some experts execute the skip cast with baitcasting tackle, using a short rod to propel jigs far back, where big wary bass may lurk.

Bass Feeding Tactics from Cover

This 8-to 9-pounder seems to be holding an ambush pose, facing out from under a pontoon boat toward prey. She (bass over about 6 pounds usually are females) had an unobstructed view and attack route into open water. She was hidden in shade (illuminated in the photo by the flash); the sunfish visible in the open sunlit area wouldn't see her unless she moved.

The lunker's fins were flexing and her spiny dorsal fin was folded, suggesting a neutral or semi-active disposition. Perhaps she was waiting for feeding conditions to improve or was pausing during a feeding movement. She hadn't cocked her body into a single bend or S shape, which bass often use to attain maximum striking acceleration and longer range.

The sunfish seem like easy targets, but the bass didn't attack. Some anglers believe bass catch prey easily, but this isn't true. Sunfish are frequently photographed near bass, but divers rarely photograph or even observe attacks. (Many underwater shots that show bass attacking prey are setup situations in aquariums.) Divers may make bass nervous and less likely to attack, but uninhibited bass also don't strike often. Hungry bass may hunt for extended periods but only eat occasionally. In fact, studies of stomach contents show bass often go several days with empty stomachs.

Like the sunfish in this photo, preyfish stay just out of range. To be attacked, they would have to blunder closer or turn so they could no longer see the bass make its move. Underwater photographs seldom show prey near active bass. Preyfish seem to sense when bass become active, and they move away or hide in cover. Yet preyfish often hover 2 to 3 feet from neutral bass and within inches of inactive bass.

DAWN AND DUSK, THE LOW-LIGHT PERIODS?

One important function of cover is to provide shade. When can we expect bass to seek it? Anglers intuitively assume that fish experience changes in daylight as humans do. We presume light underwater is dimmer at dawn and dusk than at midday, and label dawn and dusk the low-light periods.

Before sunrise and after sunset, the amount of available light is low, but once direct sunlight hits the water, almost as much underwater light is available in the early morning and evening as at noon. Because water molecules, suspended particles, and plankton in the water scatter light in all directions, there's almost as much light in the depths shortly after sunrise as later in the day.

FISH-WATCHING:
BASS REVEAL THEIR HUNTING TACTICS TO SHARP-EYED ANGLERS
BY RALPH MANNS

Ralph Manns, Austin, Texas, is a fishery scientist and angling authority who has contributed features and columns to In-Fisherman *for decades. Here he advocates personal observation—fish-watching—to provide answers to angling questions. When we say bass relate to cover, what exactly are they doing? And how does this help us determine an effective presentation?*

She was swimming slowly along the bank, about 3 feet deep. Through the clear water of Lake Wohlford, we could see she was big, maybe 8 pounds. If we'd landed her then, in 1950, she'd have been a real trophy, as this was long before the California Fish and Game Department introduced the Florida subspecies there. We cast crankbaits in her direction for several minutes, hoping she'd bite. Our casting soon alarmed her, and she disappeared into the depths.

It would be many years before I took time to consider what I'd seen and to learn from this sighting. We thought her open water appearance was an exception; at that time, fishing magazines and scientific literature suggested that largemouths typically lurk in cover, ambushing prey and lures. As any angler can observe, however, the reality is quite different.

More than 45 years later, my home overlooks a community pond containing largemouth bass. Day after day, I watch as bass move through the shallows and patrol the shoreline in loosely organized schools of three to six fish. Pausing periodically, they turn to face and search cover edges and the nearby shore for prey.

Occasionally a bass holds for a minute or two under a floating log, in the shade of a vegetation clump, or in open water, but the most active fish typically cruise, searching cover rather than hiding in it. They do not seek shade or lie in ambush while hunting. They ignore any preyfish alert to their approach but attack any unwary preyfish within range.

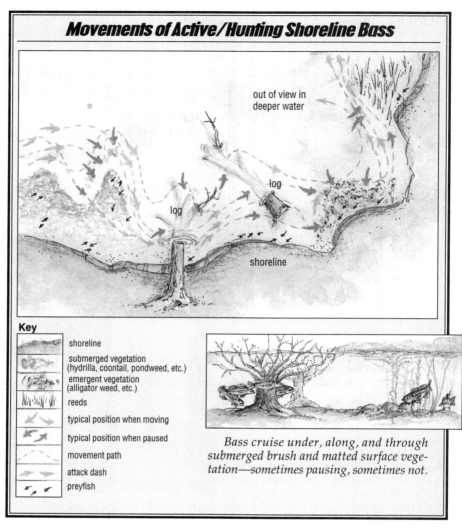

Movements of Active/Hunting Shoreline Bass

out of view in deeper water

log

log

shoreline

Key

	shoreline
	submerged vegetation (hydrilla, coontail, pondweed, etc.)
	emergent vegetation (alligator weed, etc.)
	reeds
	typical position when moving
	typical position when paused
	movement path
	attack dash
	preyfish

Bass cruise under, along, and through submerged brush and matted surface vegetation—sometimes pausing, sometimes not.

In the pond, active bass tend to cruise the shoreline about 3 feet deep, deeper in clear water and shallower in stained water. From their pausing positions, they dart into water as shallow as 4 inches to take minnows or small sunfish. After an attack, a bass school usually moves farther along the shoreline.

I often glance at my Fish-En-Time watch to note the times of solunar periods. I've seen moving bass at all hours of the 12-hour solunar cycle, but I see active bass most often during the solunar major hour and near the minor hours. At morning and evening twilight, it's hard to see bass, but you can detect surface-feeding activity as baitfish jump to escape. This twilight feeding activity occurs whether or not a major or minor coincides.

I became a dedicated bass watcher while studying fish and fishery management at Southwest Texas State University. Almost every day, I'd sit on a high bank overlooking one of the many ponds at the Aquatic Science Facility. Sometimes no bass were visible, but if I studied the bottom and the vegetation through polarized glasses, I'd spot an inactive bass or two lying motionless in holes in the cover. Sometimes, as if on cue, several bass would rise out of hiding to be joined by others. These bass then cruised the shoreline or edges of vegetation in small loose schools, just like the bass in my backyard pond.

Some of the university ponds were clear and easily monitored, others murky. I couldn't see movement or schooling in the stained water, but I did spot bass hovering a few inches under the surface within a foot of cover and facing it. When visibility was low, they apparently moved closer to cover to detect prey at the cover edges. Bass would appear out of the murk, hold for a minute or two, then disappear, only to reappear a few yards down the shoreline. I concluded that bass in murky water hunted much like those in clearer water, but were less likely to move in groups.

Every basser should be able to see this patrolling movement of active bass, even though it's harder to see cruising bass from a bass boat than from a high bank. The idea that bass hunt from ambush inside cover has obscured the reality—most active, catchable bass are cruising along cover edges or moving under lines of cover in a series of starts and stops. They may move in one direction for many yards, or back and forth, but they tend to move rather than lie in ambush. Once this behavior is seen and understood, it's possible to make better decisions on where to cast or how soon to return to a productive spot, or what kind of presentation to use.

At the university, a round pond held catfish, carp, sunfish, and largemouths. I watched as students chummed bread on the water. Bass weren't interested in the crumbs, but catfish and sunfish massed in the area. Bass that had been previously nearly invisible in holes in the vegetation rose and circled the feeding fish. They ignored nearby sunfish that appeared wary and alert, but dashed up to 10 feet to take preyfish that had become distracted by the bread and had focused too long on eating.

When I've tossed live minnows near moving bass, the bass usually strike them immediately. Bass hidden in cover and apparently inactive usually ignore minnows tossed nearby. Yet a series of tossed minnows seems to arouse inactive bass; after several minnows swim within easy striking range, bass start feeding. This situation may be duplicated by repeatedly casting a lure near cover where an inactive fish is hiding. The appearance of many prey nearby gives bass a cue to leave cover and hunt.

While scuba diving in Travis Reservoir, I watched the same predator-prey relationships I've seen from shore. Sunfish that can see bass (bass know this—they can see a preyfish's eye) are ignored, but an injured preyfish or one turned so it might not see an approaching bass is considered vulnerable. Vulnerable prey within striking range are struck immediately by active fish. Vulnerable prey farther away are slowly stalked until they're within range.

While diving, we saw totally inactive bass inside cover, apparently digesting food and totally ignoring nearby prey. Preyfish would hover within inches of these bass. Semiactive bass suspended near cover and attacked only nearby vulnerable prey; they ignored healthy sunfish holding just 3 feet away, but with an eye toward the bass.

Bass became active periodically. We'd see them yawn a few times and form small, loose schools. The schools then moved to patrol the edges of cover and shoreline. These underwater observations confirm behavior anglers can detect if they take the time.

Applying This Knowledge

Merlyn Hilmoe

Imagine a small cove with three or four laydown logs in 2 to 3 feet of water. If you believe bass principally hunt from ambush, you might at most hope for one or two bass to be holding under each log, and after you catch a bass or two, you might look elsewhere. This could be a valid tactic when bass are neutral or inactive and not moving.

If you understand that bass feed by moving, however, you might return again and again to each log, hoping to find new, active arrivals passing through the cove. You might even decide one log is the arrival point and silently wait there, making intermittent casts to catch new arrivals. Similar situations develop in deeper water on points and humps.

Suppose you're casting a rattle-bait and get a hit at a large flat or point. You've seen that feeding bass often travel in small schools and so expect other bass to be there. After a few fruitless casts to the spot where the bass was hooked, decide which way the bass were moving and cast well ahead of their proba-ble course. If this doesn't garner another strike, try another possible route—perhaps a reverse course.

Bass hunt actively, usually moving in small schools along the shoreline and edges of cover. They enter cover to rest, hide from larger predators, and digest food. Semi-active or neutral bass often suspend near cover, where they hunt opportunistically rather than actively. They sometimes strike vulnerable targets that are lulled into approaching too close or that get careless and look away too long. This may account for great catches made by carefully flipping or pitching lures into cover.

Active bass are more eager to bite and easier to tempt with lures, but they're also more wary and easily alarmed while exposed and moving. Casts to cover are effective primarily because active fish pause nearby to look for emerging, vulnerable, careless prey. Anglers who flip or pitch may believe they're catching bass lurking in ambush. Field observations suggest, however, that often they're contacting bass that are cruising open areas near or under brush or vegetation and looking for prey.

You can watch this in clear, shallow areas. Preyfish try to avoid cruising bass and stay about 3 feet away from hovering bass, but they'll closely approach inactive bass. Totally inactive bass—those sleeping or digesting prey—can be seen with prey just inches from their mouths.

Preyfish know when bass are feeding, and they try to avoid them. Bass learn early in life that healthy, alert prey can successfully dodge them. They learn to conserve energy and wait for vulnerable targets. To consistently draw strikes, a lure must appear to be fleeing in panic, trapped against a solid background, injured, or distracted and unaware of the bass. When a lure looks and moves like a healthy preyfish, it must be very close to a bass to be considered a vulnerable target.

For too long, writers and biologists have emphasized the ambushing nature of bass. Take time to look and study for yourself.

Environmental Effects

WHAT WEATHER DOES TO BASS

Local climate determines how much solar energy a body of water receives each year. This energy, and the availability of nutrients, will determine the production of microscopic plants (phytoplankton), algae, and aquatic weeds; these determine the abundance of zooplankton and of preyfish. The abundance of these lower organisms in the food web will ultimately determine the abundance and the growth rate of bass populations.

Each body of water has its own typical heating rate in spring, thermocline pattern in summer, cooling rate in fall, and cycles of plankton and prey throughout the year. Annual events, such as a Prespawn bite or a midsummer slump, often occur at about the same time each year. By observing and recording the unique cycles of favorite fishing waters, an angler can plan trips when good fishing is most likely. There can be wide yearly fluctuations of water level or abundance of preyfish, but studying long-term trends is more informative than just remembering what happened last year.

Water temperature and water clarity affect the location of preyfish and bass. Local weather patterns determine when water levels rise and fall, when inflows are clear or muddy, when winds blow, and the severity and impact of cold fronts. A good angler is a good observer of the weather. In addition, many anglers try to time their fishing trips according to solunar tables, which take account of gravitational forces.

This chapter examines four factors—wind, water clarity, water temperature, and solunar period—using both scientific data and observations made during long hours in a bass boat.

WIND

Wind is both friend and foe to the bass fisherman. Wind can concentrate bass, turn them on, and cover your presentation trail, making it more difficult for fish to detect you. On the other hand, it can disperse fish, turn them off, complicate boat control, and sometimes make fishing dangerous. The effects of wind are complex and often not well understood.

BASIC OBSERVATIONS ON WIND

Most anglers know some things about wind, and most of those are probably correct. *Concentrate on structural elements on the windward side of the lake*, for example, is a solid rule. But does that mean any structural element? Shallow-lying structure? The windward or leeward side of shallow structure? Any time of the year?

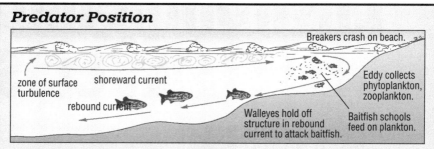

Predator Position

Breakers crash on beach.

zone of surface turbulence

shoreward current

rebound current

Eddy collects phytoplankton, zooplankton.

Walleyes hold off structure in rebound current to attack baitfish.

Baitfish schools feed on plankton.

Many factors affect the direction and strength of wind-caused current, so anglers must understand the physical principles, then assess conditions as they occur in a lake. Areas where current turns abruptly form eddies, where water follows a circular course. Islands, humps, and shorelines are obvious current breaks that often cause upwind eddies.

Strong directional currents collect debris and organisms incapable of strong swimming. Baitfish, including shad, yellow perch, bluegills, and shiners, may quickly congregate to feed on abundant plankton. Larger predators also appear and may hold offshore, facing into the rebound current, or may invade the turbulent shallows to chase prey.

Most anglers also know that winds create currents—in fact, they often over-estimate the strength of wind-induced currents. These currents, however, are complex. In general, prevailing winds, especially when blowing over giant lakes and reservoirs, create weak currents that flow at about a 45-degree angle to the right of wind direction. There are currents that flow along the shore and reverse currents flowing back under the surface. (We'll come back to these angles and currents in a moment.)

In average-sized lakes and reservoirs, wind-generated currents tend to follow main-lake shorelines and circle large bays in the direction of prevailing winds. Structures that constrict this flow often attract baitfish and bass. A narrow pass, or a hump rising to within a few feet of the surface, may compress and accelerate wind-driven currents enough to simulate feeding behavior like that of riverine bass. In small bodies of water and sheltered coves, wind-generated currents are less important or not detectable.

Winds lasting only a few hours create no noticeable currents and affect fishing only by creating ripples and waves that change subsurface light. Wind currents that last several days may concentrate floating plankton near downwind shores. These concentrations sometimes attract baitfish that may stimulate bass activity. Wind-created flows running directly into a shoreline may break up and become chaotic, creating unstable swimming conditions for preyfish and making them temporarily vulnerable to attack. Even larger predators, however, often avoid powerful wave action. Consistent winds also push the warm surface layer of water downwind, while cooler water is drawn to the upwind side. When water temperature is an important factor in bass location or activity, prevailing wind directions can help anglers locate warmer (downwind) or cooler (upwind) surface water.

After winds drop, wind-generated currents continue for a while due to momentum and gradually slow, unless a new strong wind forces a more rapid change. Currents produced by inflowing and outflowing water may overpower and modify wind-generated currents, so wind effects on rivers and riverine reservoirs are less distinct than on lakes.

Current Direction

Steady wind from one direction establishes a surface current moving toward shore. The shore diverts the flow downward and back across the lake in the opposite direction.

If the surface current is strong, it may continue to circulate near shore in a circular gyre. Plankton may collect in this current. Schools of baitfish often congregate here, and predators follow.

Warm circulating water erodes the upper portion of the metalimnion. During summer, calm warm days restore this layer. In fall, circulating water hastens turnover.

Waves are usually more important products of wind than currents are. In clear reservoirs, waves on downwind shores can increase dissolved oxygen, reduce visibility and light penetration, and increase the feeding efficiency of bass. When skies are bright, bass on downwind shores are more likely to be active than bass in calmer, clearer locations. In typically murky impoundments, where waves murk the downwind shoreline even more, bass may evacuate wave-tossed shorelines. Waves produce background noise that may interfere with hearing and lateral-line senses. That's why bass feeding in murky water or at night usually select calm water.

Those are just a few useful observations—but it's worthwhile here to focus more closely on the principles and details of how wind affects water. Few fishermen know enough about wind; examine what you already know from a new perspective, and you'll pose more sophisticated questions and achieve more consistent fishing.

WIND CURRENTS

After wind has blown steadily for several hours, the tug-of-war between wind and gravity creates near-surface currents that move slowly, even in a strong wind. Current is only 2 percent of wind speed in strong winds, 1.3 percent in weaker winds. (A 30-mph wind creates a 0.5-mph current; a 10-mph wind creates almost imperceptible current.) Watch, for example, the movement of neutrally buoyant debris—a piece of vegetation, perhaps—suspended just below the surface; its very slow drift contrasts with that of a floating object—a discarded Styrofoam worm box—which catches the wind and may move faster than 10 mph in a stiff breeze.

This surface movement, contrasting with the "stationary" water below, is why drift socks can be used to slow boats that are being blown across the surface of the water. A sock is a parachute anchored in the relatively stationary water below. Drift speed can be cut by 10 to 90 percent, depending on the size of the drift sock (or socks) and the size of the opening in it.

CORIOLIS FORCE AND CURRENTS

The sun ultimately is responsible for currents in bodies of water. Temperature variation in different levels of the atmosphere causes winds. The interactions of the earth's rotation on its axis, its revolution around the sun, and the movement of our solar system produce global wind patterns.

On either side of the equator, winds typically blow from east to west—the trade winds that powered the mercantile fleets under sail. North of the Fortieth Parallel (which runs roughly through Philadelphia, Indianapolis, Denver, and Redding, California), winds blow predominately from west to east—the westerlies. These are the winds that whip the western plains and sweep past the Great Lakes toward the East.

Add to this mix the *Coriolis force,* generated by the rotation of the earth, which causes air and water to deflect to the right in the northern hemisphere (left in the southern hemisphere). The intensity of the Coriolis force is zero at the equator and increases toward the poles. Wind affects bass, so the Coriolis force affects your fishing.

Angle of currents—Say you assume, as many good fishermen do, that a half day or more of wind from a consistent direction creates a current moving toward structural elements on the windward side of the lake. You're approximately correct, but Coriolis force bends these water currents to the right of the wind direction. In large lakes like Ontario and Superior, the current bends as much as 45 degrees. In smaller and shallower waters, the angle of deflection is less;

limnologists studying 9,600-acre, 80-foot-deep Lake Mendota in Wisconsin, for example, found currents deflected about 20 degrees to the right of the wind. Assume, then, that even in small lakes the deflection is at least slightly to the right of the wind.

Subsurface reverse currents—Opposite currents are created as wind-blown water piles up against shorelines and the weight of the water forces deep water back underneath the surface flow. These currents also are modified by Coriolis force and by friction with surface currents, so their direction is difficult to ascertain from the surface. First figure the deflection of the surface current; then note that below this a reverse current rebounds—10 to 20 to perhaps 30 degrees farther to the right of the surface current, like a pool ball bouncing off a cushion. This often overlooked current affects fish position near middepth structural elements.

Coriolis Force

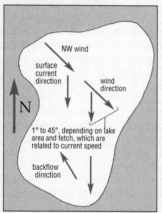

The surface of the earth spins at about 66,600 miles per hour. (Gravity keeps us from flying off the face of the earth.) This velocity affects the direction in movement for all objects. Drain a bathtub in the northern hemisphere, and the water swishes down in a clockwise direction (reversed on the other side of the equator). Winds and water currents tend to circle in the same direction.

In the northern hemisphere, wind-caused currents move to the right of wind direction. The amount of deflection is related to the size of the lake. Maximum deflection of 45° occurs only in the ocean or the world's largest lakes.

Degree of deflection increases with current speed, which is affected by wind speed only up to a critical point of 14 to 18 mph. Stronger winds don't speed currents or increase the angle of Coriolis deflection.

Currents rebound after contacting shorelines and are again deflected in a clockwise direction in the northern hemisphere. In a huge lake, the result often is one or more vast circular currents flowing clockwise.

Rebound Current

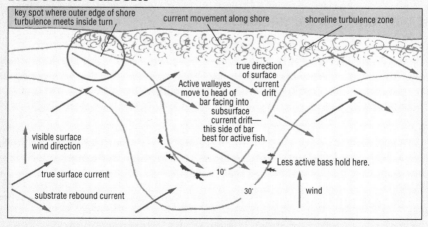

Fish in shallow water usually face into shallow surface current. But fish holding deeper than about 5 feet often face the opposite direction into a reverse current.

The direction fish face affects presentation. In general, presentations should move toward or quarter in front of bass, instead of sneaking up on them from the rear. When fish face the rebound current moving in the opposite direction from the wind, retrieving baits offshore will be more productive.

Currents that hit shorelines—When they contact the shore, currents are also deflected clockwise along the shore. Say you're fishing a plateau reservoir, and wind blowing into shore produces a right-moving current. Follow the shoreline drop-off to the right until you meet a bar. The side of the bar that meets the current is likely to hold active fish. Concentrate on the tip of the point or inside turns. In early spring or late fall, however, when the water's cold and the fish aren't active, the back side of the point (a bit removed from the current) is more likely to hold fish. Try the tip of the point or inside turns but away from the wind-generated current.

Presentation should be based on current direction and speed. Preyfish, and the bass that eat them, orient to current. Baits moving with current often produce more strikes because they remain in the predator's strike zone longer.

Suppose you're casting jigs to bass positioned near the tip of the 10-foot drop-off. Consider their position—probably facing into a rebounding current caused by the wind. You want to cast past the fish and bring the bait toward them. Hold off the point in deep water and cast into the shallows, bringing the jig from the flat toward deeper water. For fish up off bottom, cast crankbaits or spinnerbaits, retrieving with the subsurface current.

If these scenarios confuse you at first, sketch a lake. Draw the wind direction. Add arrows slightly to the right to depict the general direction that surface water flows. Where this current contacts a shallow bar or bank, draw surface current channeled to the right along the shore or bar. Now add arrows to depict a rebound current deflected almost in the opposite direction—again, this current is deflected clockwise and runs deeper. Now draw bass facing this deeper lying current. Also draw fish facing the surface current, particularly where it contacts sharp breaking structural elements. For most fishermen, factoring in the potential effects of Coriolis force and rebound currents provides a new view of the real world of fish.

WAVES AND SURFACE TURBULENCE

What follows has never been a secret and it has a major effect on fishing. Yet it remains a mystery to most anglers: although wind causes the surface of the water to roll into traveling surface waves, very little water actually moves laterally. Instead, the wind raises water, which then curls in a circular pattern as gravity pulls the molecules downward, like a wave traveling along a jump rope.

Turbulence edges—The rolling action of waves creates surface turbulence, but only *to a depth about twice the height of the waves.* If waves crest at 3 feet, then water at 6 feet is only slightly affected, although slow-riding currents may move through those depths. This wave-caused zone of turbulence offers an important edge that focuses the activity of prey and predators—when moving through open water, they may travel just below this edge. When waves increase, prey like shad or bluegills, which hold near the surface in calm conditions, are forced deeper. Predators attack from below, forcing prey upward against the edge of turbulence, where they lose equilibrium. Schools break into disarray, and baitfish drop back into the stable water below, slightly disoriented and vulnerable to attack.

Wave length is the distance between successive wave crests. It affects the amount of turbulence. The typical ratio of wave height to wave length ranges from 1:100 to 1:10. A low ratio (1:100) causes swells typical of calm days on the ocean. When wave height increases toward a ratio of 1:10 (choppy waves), whitecaps form as each wave collapses and its crest blows off as foam.

In small lakes, wave height at a given wind speed isn't related to lake depth. But in large lakes, wave height and wave length increase with depth. The maximum wave height is a factor of the distance the wind blows without interruption (fetch). Waves may reach 8 or even 10 feet on Oahe Reservoir (South Dakota) or on Winnebago (Wisconsin); Lake Superior's vast area and depths to 1,300 feet produce the largest inland waves on the continent, up to 35 feet, the kind of waves that capsized and sank the *Edmund Fitzgerald* in a November gale.

As waves approach shallow water, their velocity and wave length decrease because of the resistance of land. The circular motion of waves changes to an oval movement and then to a back-and-forth slosh when waves crash as breakers.

Waves

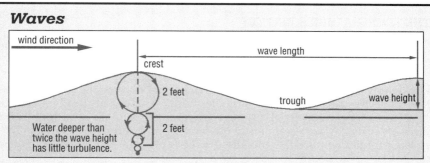

A series of circular currents of decreasing size occurs below a wave, each with a diameter equal to half the one above. Water deeper than twice the wave height has little turbulence. When the ratio of wave height to wave length decreases, whitecaps form as gravity pulls over the crest of the wave and wind blows off water as spray.

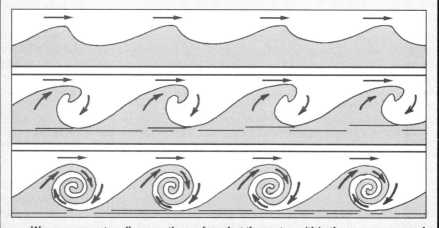

Waves appear to roll across the surface, but the water within them moves up and around without shifting position horizontally.

Across shallow flats or rockbars, wind-induced turbulence may extend all the way to the bottom, sloshing crayfish, larval insects, and bottom-dwelling baitfish from shelter.

This shoreline turbulence creates important fishing patterns. Mudlines that form in reservoirs with clay or shale banks attract bass during the day. The best areas are on or near major structural elements—bars or creek channels—that hold bass in deeper water when the wind isn't blowing. Bass may also follow the rebound current back out to flats and feed near the turbulence there if the flat is deep enough to allow them to move in without being buffeted by the waves.

Another overlooked pattern for bass in summer occurs when wind sweeps weed-choked bars where baitfish usually lie hidden. In lakes, most of these bars run 8 to 15 feet deep at the outside edge, where a weedwall rises almost to the surface to meet open water. Once surface current bends the tops of the weedwall, it flattens weeds on shallower parts of the bar. If the directional wind continues into the evening, predators roam these bars at night, holding just below the zone of turbulence.

THE TEMPERATURE EQUATION

The surface flows and rebound currents that we've described occur during all seasons. Combine these movements with the different densities of water at different temperatures, and the effects of wind become even more significant.

Water is densest at 39°F, so at ice-out (surface temperature 34°F to 36°F), water readily mixes in moderate winds. As surface water becomes heated by the sun, it becomes less dense and floats on cooler water. This density gradient reduces circulation between layers of different temperature. Summer stratification into three layers is the large-scale result of warming and density differences. Even strong summer winds fail to mix these layers, although smaller-scale temperature variances do occur.

On a sunny summer day, the top 3 inches of water may be several degrees warmer than water a foot down—any swimmer will notice that, as well as encounter cold pockets. These same pockets may eventually be moved by wind-caused currents to areas that attract or repel bass.

A strong directional wind, for example, can pile a layer of warm surface water against a bank. Due to gravity, this bulk of warm water squeezes out a mass of cooler, denser water lying just above the thermocline. The colder water sets in motion a rebound current that may concentrate coolwater preyfish like alewives or smelt. Picture pockets of warmer or colder water as drops of oil in water. Colder, denser pockets tend to sink through warmer water; warmer, less dense pockets float on colder water. Both warm and cold pockets can be moved by surface or subsurface current.

A cold rebound current eventually may be forced toward the surface by an offshore bar, forming a cold pocket of surface water surrounded by warmth. With or without an influx of prey, this new water may stimulate predators' activity. Due to its greater density, this cool pocket will again drift downward, but it may be renewed over hours or days by continuing cool currents.

Langmuir circulation—At wind speeds between about 5 and 15 mph, a phenomenon called *Langmuir circulation* may also occur. Currents near the surface form columns of convection when surface water is pushed over slightly cooler water below. The surface water turns downward, forcing cooler water up. Langmuir currents are visible as streaks on the surface that align slightly to the right of the wind direction (again, due to the Coriolis force).

These streaks contain floating debris, including algae, pollen, and invertebrates. Between the streaks are zones of upwelling where cooler water from the depths has been forced to the surface. In oceans and the Great Lakes, upwelling areas are among the most productive fisheries; they are also productive on smaller lakes and reservoirs. Concentrations of microorganisms in the streaks draw baitfish that attract bass.

WATER CLARITY AND COLOR

Water clarity and color are determined by plankton, dissolved organic matter, and suspended particles. In long reservoirs, inflowing water may be turbid and stained, while downstream water is clear.

Langmuir Streaks

streaks of organic material including invertebrates, algae, pollen

wind direction 5 to 15 mph
surface current

5' deep

Currents near surface move in helical pattern.

"tubes" of surface water, drawn to illustrate effects of Langmuir circulation

Small upwellings of cooler water occur between Langmuir streaks.

Adapted from R. Wetzel, *Limnology* (1983).

Water clarity gradients often alter fishing conditions over the length of reservoirs and long reservoir arms. Spring and fall rains may make otherwise clear waters very muddy.

Water clarity determines the maximum depth bass use. Bass usually occupy depths between the surface and the point at which light is too faint for them to see prey. The depth reached by faint light is roughly estimated by measuring the maximum depth at which contrasting objects can be seen from the surface at noon and then multiplying that depth by 4 or 5.

Lakes produce more plankton and become greener when inflows bring nutrients like phosphorus and nitrogen. Reduced water clarity brings bass closer to the surface. Decreased inflows typical of midsummer tend to clear water and allow bass to move deeper. Aquatic vegetation thrives in clear water and also helps to clear the water as it grows, since plants absorb nutrients and thus reduce the amount available to plankton.

Long-term murkiness forces bass to feed by ambush and short-range attacks. Bass can't use their more effective hunt-and-flush and schooling tactics unless they can see at least a foot or two. Constantly murky water in reservoirs or sections of reservoirs usually means bass stay shallow. Muddy reservoirs also tend to have poor bass reproduction.

Bass that live in clear water may stop feeding during periods of muddy water. When faced with sudden murk, bass may move short distances to stay on the clear side of advancing clarity-clines or mudlines. Rather than move far from their home range, however, territorial bass will often stop feeding and wait out brief periods of muddy water. Bass can and frequently do go without food for several weeks without ill effects.

When you're faced with suddenly muddy water, fish the clearest water you can find, usually near the dam or clear inflows. Or else try typically murky headwaters, because bass that live there are accustomed to poor visibility. If the murkiness is extreme, really thick mud, bass try to move away from it, just as they move away from a pH below 6, oxygen below 3 ppm, areas containing no catchable prey, and any other intolerable condition.

Plankton blooms or muddy water that lasts several months can kill underwater vegetation by shading it. The recent history of water color and clarity can be an aid to locating underwater vegetation or predicting its absence. Once it's killed, vegetation may take weeks or years to return, depending on weed species and water conditions. Nutrients released by rotting plants may foster plankton blooms. Waves no longer dampened by surface weedbeds may stir shoreline silt and prevent the light penetration that plants require.

WATER COLOR AFFECTS LURE COLOR CHOICE

Organic stains and particles in water reflect some colors while absorbing others. This limits the depths different wavelengths of light can penetrate, and

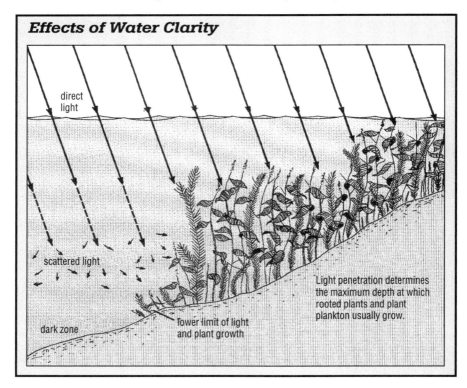

Effects of Water Clarity

direct light

scattered light

dark zone

lower limit of light and plant growth

Light penetration determines the maximum depth at which rooted plants and plant plankton usually grow.

therefore determines the visibility of various colors of lures at different depths. Water in lakes or reservoirs appears blue in the absence of stains or suspended particles. As light penetrates the depths, the red-through-green parts of the spectrum are absorbed, while blue is reflected back to the surface. Water is green when green light is reflected while reds and dark blues are absorbed, as is the case when green plankton is abundant.

Lure colors similar to the colors of water catch and reflect scattered light; they appear brighter than lure colors that reflect absorbed wavelengths. Absorbed colors, on the other hand, may contrast more against a light water background than matching colors. To increase lure visibility in stained water, use baits that contain both the color of the water and a contrasting, dark absorbed color. Fluorescent lures are most visible but may seem unnatural to wary bass.

Fish Vision as We Understand It

Tests of color vision in freshwater sportfish have frequently included only the light spectrum visible to man. We now have evidence that some fish may see spectral ranges humans can't see and that some fish may integrate polarized light detection into their perceptions of color.

When light is reflected, it sometimes polarizes, and UV rays are usually present. Did the largemouth bass tested by Dr. Frank Brown in the 1930s or by Dr. Don McCoy and Dr. Loren Hill in more recent separate experiments see red reflected with or without the aid of polarization or UV light?

Dr. Hill has reported that in murky water, the largemouth bass he tested seemed to see colored targets much farther away than humans can see the same targets. Anglers often note that visual predators like bass track and strike lures accurately at night or in muddy water. Is this because bass see polarized light reflecting from targets or prey? If so, it helps to explain how bass sight-feed in adverse conditions. In water clouded by plankton or silt, fish may see objects up to three times farther away if they are sensitive to polarized light. In addition, polarized light could help bass orient to the sun on partly cloudy days. Direct navigation across open water by black bass, yellow perch, trout, and salmon has caused speculation that these species see polarized light and use it for navigation.

When we buy lures, we know what colors we see but not what colors fish see. Lures with striations aligned across flat surfaces, perhaps simulating scales, may reflect more polarized light than lures without parallel hatching or with curved sides. A chartreuse crankbait that reflects polarized or UV light may look to fish totally different from a nonreflective chartreuse lure.

Valid tests of the ability of fish to see and react to colors, UV, or polarized light are extremely difficult to design and execute. We don't expect soon to have clear scientific evidence of what specific gamefish species see or do not see.

That doesn't mean enterprising lure manufacturers won't claim that their baits are effective because they reflect UV or polarized light. Still, until valid scientific evidence is in of the full range of color vision of bass and other gamefish, we will have to go on selecting lure colors based on trial and error, past successes, and hunches.

When water is murky, noisy lures tell bass something is approaching and prepare them to strike when the lure comes within visible range. Unnatural noises may alarm bass, however. Noise generally seems less effective in clear water where bass have longer to study approaching lures. Different lure colors and types work best in different lakes, or portions of reservoirs. Spinnerbaits, big noisy topwaters, and large rattling crankbaits, for example, often work better in murky or stained water where bass commit to attack before they clearly see targets. Smaller, subtle, natural-colored crankbaits, topwaters, slim minnows, tube lures, and worms and jigs often work best when lures can be seen clearly.

FIELD REPORT: FISHING MUDDY WATER BASS

The techniques for catching bass from muddy water are similar, North or South. Bill Dance is one of North America's best and most famous fishermen, a tournament competitor turned popular TV fishing personality who says, "I don't just tolerate muddy water, I prefer it."

Here is his advice as he told it to fellow Tennessean Don Wirth, a frequent In-Fisherman *contributor.*

"I've fished muddy Pickwick Reservoir and its tailrace during late spring following several days of heavy rain, when fields had recently been plowed, contributing to muddy run-off. Yet in a day's fishing I've caught and released so many largemouth and smallmouth bass between 3 and 6½ pounds that I lost count. I've had many days when I've caught many 4-, 5-, and 6-pound bass from water that would make a hog-wallow look clear. And as I released them, I always marveled at how muddy water had kept other anglers from even trying to fish."

WHEN TO FISH MUDDY WATERS

"Reservoirs and rivers with a perpetually muddy look usually have silty bottoms, lie in lowland areas, and contain little aquatic vegetation. They lack extensive rock, gravel, or sand. Wind roils those waters. Other waters are clear but turn muddy after heavy rain when run-off enters from feeder creeks. Highland reservoirs with rocky bottoms, like Bull Shoals in Arkansas and Dale Hollow in Tennessee-Kentucky, clear quickly. Their rocky limestone and shale basins buffer muddy conditions. The tributaries usually clear a day or so after heavy rain. Weeds also filter suspended particles and clarify water. Still other waters are gin-clear except for periods during winter and spring.

"Bass from clear water are harder to catch when their habitat turns muddy than are bass from typically stained water. Bass accustomed to clear water feed almost entirely by sight. The best times to fish a muddy environment that's usually clear is after conditions have stabilized for three or four days. By then, bass have adapted to reduced visibility and established predictable patterns. Bass accustomed to murky environments seem to rely more on their other senses to cope with reduced visibility. You can fish them in the muddiest conditions; in fact, mud makes the bass more predictable.

I've had better luck fishing in muddy water on sunny days during the brightest part of the day, 9:00 a.m. to 3:00 p.m. Still, when cloud cover and muddy water combine to reduce light penetration, wait for the sun."

AUXILIARY FACTORS

Muddy water usually is accompanied by other factors that affect fishing:

Higher water—When a flood of water enters, water levels rise, flooding shoreline features.

Increased current—I've tried to fish in water racing at 15 mph following a flash flood, but that's too much current. I've found the most productive fishing in water flowing 7 to 10 mph.

Floating debris—Boating can be hazardous when logs and trees float downstream, but fishing in debris-choked pockets and bends can be great.

Increased oxygen—Oxygen may increase as flow increases.

Water temperature—On a sunny day, brown surface water warms faster than clear water, an important factor in late winter and spring.

Forage—Crayfish, insects, worms, and baitfish are dislodged from cover or carried from feeder creeks.

Changes in cover and structure—Some changes take place immediately, such as a new tree entering the reservoir. Over time, seasonal flooding sculpts a reservoir or river, eliminating old bass hangouts and creating new ones.

HOW BASS REACT TO MUDDY WATER

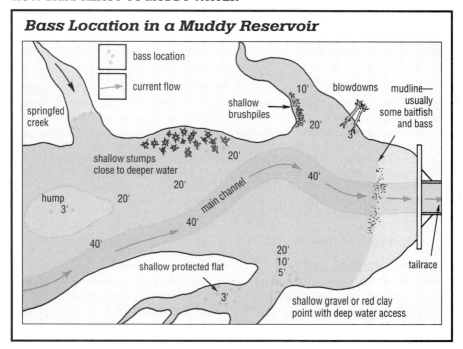

Bass Location in a Muddy Reservoir

"As successful predators, bass have learned to adapt and survive in a variety of conditions, including muddy water. One of many bass myths is that bass leave a muddy environment to find clear water. This implies a mass migration to a clear-running tributary. But bass generally don't move far in clear water; when visibility is limited, they move even less.

"When water turns muddy, bass can do any of these things:

They move shallower—Fish see better in shallow water. I've caught bass with their backs out of water during super-muddy conditions; 1 to 3 feet isn't too shallow when the water looks like chocolate milk.

They move closer to objects—When visibility is reduced, bass seek the security of a dock, brushpile, or boulder, perhaps using the object as a reference point. Present lures as close as possible to cover.

They move out of increased current—Muddy water and high flow usually coincide. Largemouths in particular don't like fast water. They hold in slack-water pockets, backflows, or behind objects that break current. Smallmouths are at home in rivers, but they also avoid heavy current and will be in moderate current in sloughs or downstream from cover objects.

They use other senses in addition to sight—A bass has to see a lure before striking it; even in muddy water, vision is their primary sense. But as visual range is reduced, the lateral line, which can sense vibrations several feet away, becomes more important. Bass also use their inner ear to sense sound produced even farther away. And I think smell is more important in muddy water, so I always use a fish-attracting scent."

BAITFISH MOVEMENT

"Muddy conditions affect the location of forage fish. Most waters I fish have a threadfin and gizzard shad forage base. High muddy water pushes these baitfish toward the shoreline. Shad often seek plankton that accumulates in shoreline eddies. They feed more effectively in the thin band of clearer water that typically forms along the shoreline of a muddy river or reservoir. Target the bass that move to shallow cover away from fast current.

"I like to fish protected areas of muddy water that are warmer than the main reservoir or river. Water temperatures often rise fast in winter and early spring. One of my best fishing days was in January in a reservoir so muddy it looked like I could walk on it. The two days prior to the trip, air temperatures had been in the low 60s with a warming trend. Surface temperature of the main body of the reservoir rose from 40°F to 43°F. I began to search for warmer water in protected areas. A narrow creek mouth measured 43°F. As I moved up the creek several hundred yards, it opened into a wide shallow flat. The surface temperature was 52°F. Visibility was nil, but shad were flipping everywhere and bass were busting them on top, a pattern you'd expect in late June. In 90 minutes, I caught and released 28 bass from 1½ to 6½ pounds.

"Spring is the most dependable time to catch big bass from muddy water. In spring, they shake the winter doldrums and enter a prespawn feeding spree."

PINPOINTING TARGETS

In clear water, bass move several feet to strike a lure, but in muddy water, you should define your targets and place lures accurately. Try these areas:

Shallow points—Reservoirs have many shallow points, but in muddy conditions, look for points far from the main river channel, yet close to deep water. The best ones often have bottom composed of pea gravel, shale, slate, chunk rock, or red clay.

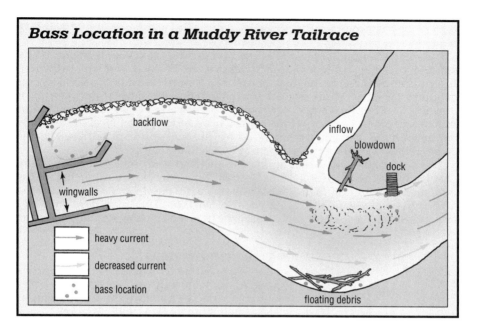

Bass Location in a Muddy River Tailrace

Springs—Clear and muddy waters mix wherever springs enter a river or reservoir. The area around the spring is clearer, so it draws baitfish and bass—but don't expect a mass migration of fish to clearer water.

Shallow flats—An expanse of shallow muddy water warms quickly on a sunny day. During spring, look for creek arms protected from current and wind.

Shoreline objects—Bass hold close to stumps, rocks, brushpiles, or boat docks.

RIVER HOT SPOTS

Rocky banks—Fish gravel bars, riprap banks, and chunk rock in current. Large rocks deflect current and provide holding spots for bass. Smaller rocks also filter sediment from the water, causing it to clear quickly.

Pockets—Current flow is reduced along banks, no matter how shallow. Stumps or logs make spots even better.

Eddies—Forage fish concentrate near structure. Spots where current changes speed or direction are particularly good for smallmouths.

Shoals—Largemouths concentrate along the lower ends of shoals where current is reduced. Look for smallies at the upper end.

Floating debris—Logs and debris are deposited in river bends and behind wing dams—check these spots for largemouths.

Manmade structures—Wing dams and dikes concentrate baitfish and bass, especially where structure is adjacent to shallow slackwater. In muddy water, bass often hold in shallow spots near a current edge or object.

LURES AND PRESENTATIONS

"When visibility is greatly reduced, choose big lures since they're easier for bass to see and catch. Bass seem reluctant to move far from a holding spot, so you want their first swipe at the lure to hook 'em. Big spinnerbaits are my first choice in mud. A big crankbait with a diving lip is deadly, too, even in very shallow water. I use hot colors and a slow retrieve. I'll also use jigs or plastic lizards in black and hot secondary colors like chartreuse and orange.

"If spinnerbaits and crankbaits aren't producing, slow your retrieve. If you still aren't catching fish, change lure styles or sizes. Position your boat away from fast current. Sometimes moving a couple feet toward the bank or behind a point produces effective fishing instead of having to fight the current with your boat and lure. I fish shallow and close to objects in muddy water, so I often use a short underhand pitch. Long casts aren't effective because you can't feel strikes when current pulls on your line. I point the nose of my boat upstream, retrieve with the current flow, and move along slowly as I pitch to the bank.

"Crystal-clear water is beautiful, but those tough and cagey bass are far more predictable in muddy water. And to an ol' Tennessee boy like me, that makes mud mighty beautiful. So next time you pull up to the water's edge and see the lake or river brown, follow my advice and fish. You'll probably have the water to yourself, and reduced fishing pressure can mean catching lunkers as well as lots of fish."

WATER TEMPERATURE

Bass—and some bass fishermen— tolerate a wide range of temperatures. Normally the large-mouth is considered a warmwater fish, thriving at water temperature from the mid-60s to low 80s. In some regions, it's even a hot-water fish; anglers from Arizona to Georgia sometimes catch bass in water close to 100°F or even hotter where power plants release thermal effluent. In Minnesota or Canada on the other hand, lakes rarely reach 80°F, and bass occupy water in the 30s longer than water at 70°, yet folks there enjoy super bass fishing. Adaptable anglers learn to understand and make use of this wide temperature range and the thermal variation within a body of water.

TAKING STOCK OF BASS POPULATIONS

The main reason for such variability, according to Dr. Dave Philipp of the Illinois Natural History Survey, is not the adaptability of any one fish or group of fish, but of the species over time. "We now know," he says, "that a species is not a group of interbreeding animals, but rather a collection of discrete stocks of fish." And in the case of largemouth bass, these stocks vary greatly in their adaptations to diverse environments.

Experiments compared groups of bass from Minnesota, Illinois, Florida, and Texas to see how well each group fared in each environment. For each, the fitness—survival, growth, and reproductive ability—was optimal in home waters and much reduced in alien environments. In fact, the only bass to survive in Minnesota were those from that region—even those from Illinois perished. And Minnesota bass couldn't survive conditions in Texas or Florida.

Philipp points out the bad effects of introducing stocks of bass outside their native range. Not only do introduced stocks often not survive long, but the crosses between native stocks and introduced stocks can weaken the fitness of the native

Bass stocks have unique characteristics that suit them to their particular environment. Minnesota bass, for example, cannot tolerate conditions in central Illinois, and vice versa.

bass and ultimately cause decline in bass populations and fishing success. Even stocks that are closely related geographically may produce less fit offspring. Bass taken from a river drainage in Wisconsin and stocked in a Minnesota lake will interbreed with the native fish and are likely to produce offspring with reduced spawning success, poor recruitment, and lower resistance to disease. His message to managers is clear: "Don't mix stocks. Introduce only fish from within a genetically defined region."

There's a message for anglers, too—expand your own range of bass fishing. Learn to fish in extremes of heat and cold. Bass can be taken in hot conditions, if you know how. Winter bass can be caught in Georgia at 40°F, and in Minnesota, under the ice. Some studies suggest they may not be feeding at all, but they aren't the lethargic creatures described in some popular and scientific reports; underwater cameras catch them meandering along weedlines or peering into the camera lens. To the northern stocks, life under the ice is normal, and if you locate a high concentration of them, you can tempt them to bite.

THERMOCLINES AND OTHER CLINES

Technically speaking, *clines* are slanting areas on graphs, but to bassers, clines are areas where some characteristic of the water changes rapidly. When temperatures at various depths are graphed, temperatures that change rapidly plot as slanted lines. Scientists and fishermen call areas of rapid temperature change *thermoclines.* Similar interfaces between waters with different pH, oxygen, clarity, or chemical properties are called *pH-clines, oxyclines, clarity-clines,* and *chemoclines.*

Currents mix water both horizontally and vertically. The temperature and chemical content of mixed waters becomes fairly uniform, resulting in no clines.

Warm water, however, is lighter than cool water, and the uppermost layer of water absorbs the sun's heat. Unless the heated water is forced down, deep waters stay cold. Thermoclines form at depths where wind or currents aren't strong enough to mix warm, light surface water with heavier, cooler deep water. Sheltered, murky ponds may form midsummer thermoclines at 3 to 6 feet when heat is absorbed in the top few inches and little downward mixing occurs. Clearer waters, which receive deeper light and deeper heat penetration, form thermoclines between 18 and 35 feet, the exact depth often depending on wind. Warm, expansive reservoirs may have even deeper thermoclines.

Strong winds can destroy shallow thermoclines and form new, deeper clines; calm warm periods can form shallower thermoclines above those formed earlier. Seasonal wind shifts, combined with deepwater releases, can create stair-step temperature profiles: multiple thermoclines.

Oxygen is absorbed into surface waters from the atmosphere, generated by plant photosynthesis near the surface, or carried in by inflows. Once thermoclines form, deeper water receives no new oxygen from the surface until fall turnover. Living animals and decomposing matter below the thermocline use up available oxygen in deep water. Oxyclines then form. Bass require 5 parts per million (ppm) or more of dissolved oxygen to stay in good health, and a drop much below that level may stimulate movement to better conditions. Hypolimnions in many reservoirs contain less than 3 ppm oxygen by midsummer, but this usually doesn't affect shallow-water fish like largemouth bass.

In some reservoirs, buoyant decomposing particles suspend in or slightly above thermoclines. Decomposition reduces dissolved oxygen and creates an oxycline far above bottom. Ample oxygen may exist above and below such low-oxygen zones, but few bass live below thermoclines or oxyclines unless they move into deep habitat before clines form in early summer.

Other kinds of clines also can be important to bass and are influenced by wind and currents. When waters with different chemical qualities meet but don't mix completely, chemoclines form. Salt water, for example, is heavier than fresh water and may flow under or lie under fresh water and form a *halocline* (salt-cline).

Food Versus Temperature

Although largemouth bass and other black bass have reported optimum temperature range of 78°F to 86°F, other factors, such as light intensity, oxygen level, cover availability, and food abundance make temperature relatively unimportant in locating bass. A study published in the *Journal of the Environmental Biology of Fish* by John Janssen and John Giesy at Par Pond, a heated impoundment in South Carolina illustrates this.

1. Bass briefly moved into water over 110°F to feed, even though the water temperatures would have been lethal if they remained for long.

2. Many bass congregated near abundant prey, even if water temperatures were not ideal.

3. In summer, bass held in stratified, 72°F to 81°F water, but fed briefly in water up to 114°F. In winter, some bass fed in surface waters up to 60°F, but they held in 50°F to 68°F water—the same water temperatures used by bass in the unheated portion of the pond.

4. When blueback herring concentrated at the warmwater inflow, 70 to 87 percent of the nearby bass had prey in their stomachs. When herring moved into open water, where they were harder to catch, only 15 to 18 percent of the bass contained prey.

5. Herring approached the heated discharge only when plankton were abundant there. Many bass seemed to move in and out with the herring.

Forage abundance is a primary clue to the location of bass . To find preyfish, and thus gamefish, look for plankton concentrations. Both prey and predators seek these areas, even if the temperature, pH, water color, cover, or light levels are not ideal.

Reservoirs may contain distinct chemoclines when watersheds of feeder creeks vary chemically. Bass may prefer one side of these chemoclines over the other.

Rotting matter also creates acidic pH layers and pH-clines near oxyclines; given a choice, bass avoid a pH of less than 6 or more than 9. Masses of water with different clarities or chemi-

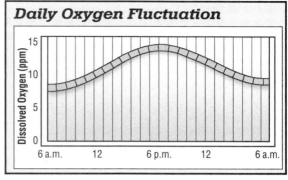

cal composition form clarity-clines or chemoclines where they meet and only partially mix. Clines form semi-impermeable barriers to vertical and horizontal bass movement. When bass stop and concentrate near clines, good fishing is likely.

A temperature gauge is an important fishing tool. Meters are also available to measure dissolved oxygen, pH, and light levels. These devices provide significant information. Changes usually are gradual, so once you've charted a reservoir's temperature, oxygen, and pH profiles, you usually need to measure again only when weather changes dramatically. If you don't repeatedly measure water quality, sonar can provide important information. With the gain set high, it may show clines as distinct lines. Fish sightings indicate conditions are acceptable there, while absence of fish suggests unacceptable conditions.

SOLUNAR EFFECTS

In-Fisherman editors will never forget when Doug Hannon's "Best Fishing Times" was inadvertently omitted from an issue of the magazine. Phones rang for days after readers flipped to the accustomed place and missed this monthly moon chart. Fans of the *Moon Times* and other solunar tables fervently believe that these tables are guides to better fishing; other anglers call the whole thing fantasy and wishful thinking. Both groups cite their own fishing trips in evidence. Many reserve their opinion, unsure why the moon should have such influence or how much it has, or how accurate are the perceptions of lunar enthusiasts.

SOLUNAR THEORY

Solunar tables were first devised by John Alden Knight in the 1920s. His tables are still published, but since then many imitators and innovators have expanded his basic concepts and included new theories. There are many different forms of tables, computer programs, and a watch that compute solunar majors and minors, predicting the best fishing days and best times of day.

Full and new moons rank highest, with days of decreasing fishing strength on either side. The specific hours of predicted good fishing cycle through the clock, regular as the tides.

The moon changes position in the sky at predictable rates that vary with the moon's position in its orbit and its altitude (declination) relative to Earth. Solunar forces are at their strongest (majors) twice a day, when the sun and moon are closest to perpendicular with a particular longitude on earth—that is, when the moon is directly overhead or beneath that longitude. (That's when tidal forces are strongest, although actual tides may be delayed.) Minor activity periods theoretically occur when the moon is positioned at 90 degrees to a particular longitude, and tidal forces are weakest. Computers at the U.S. Naval Observatory calculate these times for reference longitudes; solunar calendar makers center their solunar peaks around them, two majors and two minors every 24 hours and 50 minutes.

Of course folklore, literature, and police records suggest that phases of the moon influence the activity levels of werewolves, lovers, and criminals. Why not bass? Science also shows plenty of evidence of specific lunar effects on sea turtles, oysters, worms, crustaceans. (Mollusks moved from the Atlantic to Chicago, for example, reset their biological clocks in two weeks and started opening and closing to the schedule of a Chicago's tidal cycle—if Chicago had tides.)

Consider that the moon exerts about ⅙ as much gravitational pull as Earth, and that, as it orbits us, its pull causes tides that can raise oceans up to 50 feet twice a day, as occurs in the Bay of Fundy. Solunar theorists propose that freshwater fish retain a primal memory of tidal effects, since their ancestors evolved in marine waters. We do know that tides strongly affect the movements and spawning of invertebrates, preyfish, and other marine species.

But it's complex—marine fish are extremely variable in feeding patterns; water depth and current strength, not tides, usually determine feeding times. Different species feed at high tide, low tide, or in the faster currents in between; furthermore, in estuaries and tidal rivers, the flow of water is impeded so that actual peak tide occurs many hours after peak solunar influence.

If freshwater gamefish retain any ancestral memory of tidal feeding, it isn't likely that they feed around majors and minors. More likely, fish have inherited abilities to use a biological clock (internal timing mechanism) to predict feeding opportunities in their environment. Lunar forces have been suggested as one kind of *zeitgeber*, a term for events that resynchronize the biological clocks of organisms. In response to a zeitgeber, an organism will start or stop bodily functions and behaviors to stay in synch with the environment and be ready for optimal conditions for laying eggs, feeding, or migration. Sunrise and sunset can also be zeitgebers, as they are for many gamefish, which have morning and evening activity peaks synchronized to reduced light periods.

Predatory gamefish become active in response to activity cycles of prey that produce improved feeding opportunities; preyfish in turn respond to the activity cycles of simpler organisms. Since many invertebrates use the moon to time behaviors, intermediate predators that eat them might use solunar forces as a feeding cue.

Most gamefish are several steps up the food ladder from the simple organisms most likely to react directly to solunar force, suggesting that they will react to solunar force with discretion.

If few prey become available on solunar peaks, these peaks won't be optimal fishing periods, regardless of the strength of the lunar force. Whenever events such as sudden cloudiness, increased current, or wave action create a feeding opportunity, predators try to feed. If bass feed successfully, they may be inactive at the next routine feeding period, like sunset or a major. Predators won't ignore a chance to feed just because a major or minor period hasn't arrived.

Many types of research have demonstrated how lunar forces affect a variety of animals, including humans. But in many cases, behavioral changes may be due to changes in light, day length, angle of the sun's rays, or tides, rather than gravitational or electromagnetic forces of the moon and sun.

EVALUATING SOLUNAR EFFECTS

Whatever the theoretical basis for solunar tables, what most anglers want to know is simple—do they work? Evaluation is not easy. *In-Fisherman* researcher Ralph Manns is a trained scientist, one of the foremost experts on solunar effects on fish. He's skeptical about most angler beliefs, even those of acknowledged fishing experts.

"Humans are poor observers of detail," he says. "We instinctively emphasize some experiences and de-emphasize others. This trait allows us to focus on important information while ignoring the apparently unimportant. But it also results in incomplete counts and inaccurate assessments. Without accurate records and careful analysis, we ignore relevant facts, jump to false conclusions, and indulge personal biases."

Manns points out that many anglers who record their own fishing results are dealing with too small a sample to have statistical significance. Some researchers make invalid assumptions—in comparing fish caught during good solunar times and nonsolunar times, they may assume fishing effort is equal, which is seldom the case. Many anglers plan trips around lunar periods; walleye fishermen plan trips around full moons, catfishermen go out on moonlit nights, and fishermen using solunar tables fish through the major hours before quitting. And few people are sophisticated in their use of statistics.

Manns undertook a detailed analysis of several records to determine how much correlation exists between solunar peaks and good catches. Most analyses of solar effects have concentrated on bass, presumably because of their popularity and the many theories explaining their behavior. Without getting into too many fine points, and with much abbreviation, here's his report.

Doug Hannon was one of the first to demonstrate solunar effects on fishing success by analyzing catch data collected over a long period. Counting only bass over 5 pounds, he found that catch rates during majors averaged 0.92 fish per hour. Hannon's catch rate was 0.56 bass per hour during minors and averaged 0.36 over the entire study period. Hannon's use of averages, rather than number of fish caught, reduced chances that unequal fishing effort biased his results. Had he applied statistical tests to his data and the apparent differences proved statistically significant, we'd have scientifically acceptable evidence that solunar forces can influence catch rates.

MASTER ANGLER ANALYSIS

Again concentrating on big fish, Manns analyzed the Master Angler Award applications submitted to *In-Fisherman* from 1987 through 1990. Because times of day weren't available, he identified the lunar day of each catch and tabulated the number of each species of fish caught on each day of the lunar month.

Anglers submitted applications for 1,884 trophy-sized fish of 24 species, caught on 736 different days. Anglers caught trophy fish on every day of the lunar month, which indicates that weak solunar forces didn't prevent good catches. The days of the new and full moon had fewer catches than the immediately preceding days, and the best days were the three days before the full moon. Days of half moons produced poorly. He analyzed these catches with statistical tests to see if apparent differences were significant, based on scientific criteria, and found too much variation among days to come to strong conclusions that solunar influences affected daily catches. Even the average catch on solunar and nonsolunar days wasn't significant; the difference could be due to random chance.

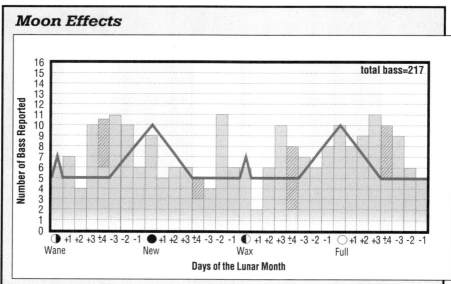

Moon Effects

The number of trophy bass taken on each day of the lunar month (29.5 calendar days), including partial days created by uneven lunar movement. The dark gray line shows the approximate profile when bass are taken according to Doug Hannon's best-day calendars. The "better" solunar days correspond to the peaks in the dark gray line. Days ±4 are partial days, and diagonal barring shows where values have been corrected to compensate for partial days.

BASS CATCH RECORDS

Manns has kept records of his fishing trips since 1975, including times of catches in relation to solunar times. He analyzed the data for 1985 through 1991 with a statistical computer program to see if catch rates for bass on different solunar hours were significantly different.

The data base includes 2,360 bass over 12 inches long, including 96 over five pounds caught in central Texas reservoirs, plus a few trips to New Mexico and Florida. The bass were primarily largemouths, with a few smallmouths and Guadalupes in the sample. This effort included about 250 trips throughout the seasons.

The most noticeable peaks occurred on the major hour and one hour after the minor. Two distinct periods of poor fishing were evident: the hours between minors and majors, and the hour after majors.

He found, however, that even with this much data and apparently large differences, catch rates among solunar hours did not vary significantly according to strict scientific criteria (95 percent confidence intervals). Although the catch data followed patterns predicted by solunar theories, hourly catch rates were too variable to demonstrate scientifically that solunar effects were potent. His mean catch rate during majors was 14 percent higher than the overall average catch rate and 32 percent better than the poorest hourly rate.

"I recommend that bass anglers continue to selectively fish majors," he concluded. "It seems, however, that minor hours are nearly as productive as majors, and that solunar theorists have grossly underestimated these periods. My data showed minors often are far more productive of average size bass than majors."

Bass Catch Rates

	Sunrise	Sunset	Noon	Midnight	Other Periods	
	1.20 10	**1.69** 17	**1.48** 25	**2.00** 4	**1.22** 194	Majors
	1.50 6	**1.15** 13	**1.25** 16	**6.00*** 1	**1.18** 180	Minors
	1.05 43	**1.49** 151	**1.10** 189	**1.51** 23	**1.08** 2196	Other Periods

*This mean was obtained from an insufficient sample. It likely exaggerates the actual mean.

Mean catch rates for black bass of all sizes taken in central Texas, 1985 through 1991, during key hours. Catch rates in bass per hour are in red if considered excellent and blue if better than average. Small numbers in the box are the number of hours fished.

Solunar Hours

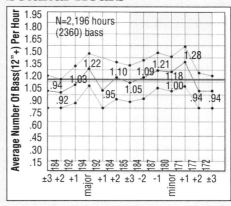

Mean catch rates of bass at least 12 inches long during each hour of the solunar cycle. Means are connected in red; 95 percent confidence intervals are outlined in green. The overall average is in blue. The number of cases (hours of fishing) are shown at the bottom of each solunar hour. Note that the first and last hours on the graph (±3) are the same.

Celestial Positioning

During the moon's 27.3-day revolution around the earth, it makes one complete rotation on its axis. The same side of the moon always faces the earth. Only the half facing the sun is illuminated, so we see the apparent shape of the round moon change as the sunlight moves from one side to the other.

A full moon occurs when the earth is between the sun and the moon. We see the shaded side, or new moon, when the moon is between the earth and the sun. A cycle from full moon to full moon takes an average of 29.5 days.

According to traditional solunar theorists, major activity periods occur near times when the moon is directly over (at zenith) or beneath (at nadir) each longitude. These are the traditional moon-up and moon-down times. Tidal forces are strongest then, although actual tides may be delayed by restrictions of current flow.

Minor activity periods theoretically occur at the time the moon is 90 degrees from a longitude and tidal forces are weakest.

The strength of tidal forces varies with the distance between the moon and earth, the moon's declination (its angle above or below the equator), and the relative position of the sun. Combinations of these factors affect daily and monthly tidal forces.

Some solunar theorists believe that times when tidal forces are

Monthly Lunar Cycle

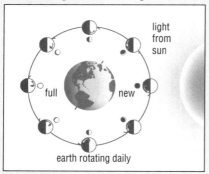

The rotation of the moon around the earth changes the moon's appearance from full to new and back to full. The outer circle of moons illustrates how the sun's light illuminates the moon. The inner circle depicts moon phases as seen from earth. The dots and small arrows on the outer circle illustrate a single rotation of the moon on its axis. This occurs over a 27.3-day period; the same side of the moon always faces the earth.

Tidal Activity

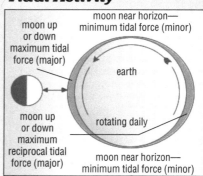

Peaks in tidal force (major activity periods) resulting in exaggerated increases in ocean depth occur as each longitude rotates under the moon. Reciprocal forces create similar peaks on the opposite side of the earth. Minimum tidal forces (minors) are found at longitudes 90 degrees from the moon. As the earth rotates, each longitude experiences two major and two minor solunar forces approximately every 24 hours and 50 minutes, with slightly more than 6 hours and 12 minutes between events.

strongest produce more activity (and thus better fishing) than times when they're weak. Ralph Manns suggests that strong solunar forces provide precise timing signals and concentrate activity within specific periods, thereby providing fast fishing for short periods. In contrast, weak nonsolunar forces spread a similar amount of activity over a longer period, making concentrated catches more difficult.

Effects of Elliptical Orbit

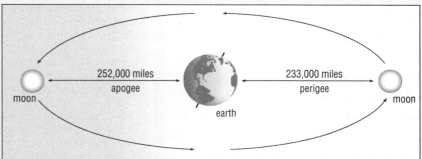

The 27.3-day orbit of the moon is elliptical, not round. At its most distant point (apogee), the moon is about 252,000 miles from the earth. At its closest (perigee), it's about 233,000 miles away. Tidal force is strongest when the moon is at perigee.

Sun–Moon Interaction

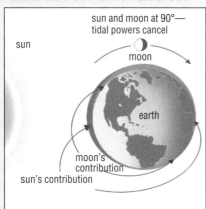 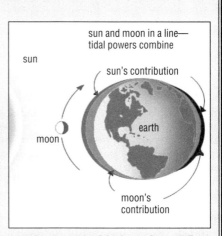

The sun creates a tidal force about 46 percent the strength of the lunar force. When the sun and moon are aligned, the two forces combine to produce highest and lowest tides. When they are at right angles, the sun's force tends to cancel the moon's, reducing tidal forces and tidal fluctuations.

The relative positions of the sun and moon, their declinations, and their distance from the earth combine to vary solunar influence. In most cases, the influence of the moon is stronger than that of the sun.

BIG BASS

Doug Hannon cautions, "little fish lie a lot." That is, they provide erroneous information about lifestyle patterns because they haven't been around long enough to learn which behaviors are most important. Manns' analysis of catches of 5-pound-plus fish in Texas tended to support that contention. Catch rates for big bass showed much greater differences among majors, minors, and poor times. During majors, the mean catch rate for large bass (.082 fish per hour) was twice the overall average (.043 bass per hour), and nearly seven times as high as the lowest hour.

The catch of big bass was much higher during major hours than during minors, but large bass seemed even more likely than smaller ones to stretch feeding efforts around minors. Further analysis indicated good fishing several hours around minors that occurred near noon and midnight.

THE NIGHT BITE

Data on night fishing were limited. Catches were highly variable. The hours on both sides of the minor out produced majors and provided clues: minors produce good catches when they're near noon or midnight, and during fall—at this time of year, majors often occur near sunrise and sunset. Bass with daytime feeding habits likely reference sunrise or sunset to set biological clocks or trigger feeding. Bass that habitually feed during night or at midday might reference the weaker minor solunar force rather than time events with biological clocks reset hours before on majors.

CONCLUSIONS

Ralph Manns says, "Following this research, I've continued to plot catch times and have found that in some waters, particularly ponds, catch rates often peak around majors and minors.

"Solunar effects can be less obvious in larger waters where baitfish movements and feeding opportunities vary more over the course of the day. Solunar theorists were correct when they identified a detectable solunar force that can affect fish behavior and angling catch rates. But they've apparently become so enraptured by these effects that they've become overconfident in predicting the best times to fish. Solunar force routinely motivates only a small portion of predator populations. Its effect is erratic because the solunar cycle isn't a controlling influence. It's only one of many environmental factors that may influence feeding."

"To get the most from solunar tables: (1) be on the water at least an hour before a predicted solunar period; (2) experiment with various locations and presentations appropriate to the body of water, species sought, and Calendar Period; (3) understand how solunar forces and other environmental and weather factors affect fish; and (4) don't leave until at least two hours after the last major or minor you intend to fish."

Chapter 7

Tracking Bass

WHAT TELEMETRY TELLS US

In-Fisherman has long believed that blending science with everyday fishing theory and observation is one of the best ways to solve fishing problems. *In-Fisherman* magazine was the first to employ a certified fishery scientist as a staff editor and to write reviews of ultrasonic tracking studies and other scientific research.

Since the 1950s, when transmitters were first used to follow fish, dozens of studies have followed the movements of bass, and previous chapters have included much information based on these studies. In this chapter we'll summarize some of the major findings, provide a more detailed look at how several of these studies were carried out, and summarize results of several other tracking studies.

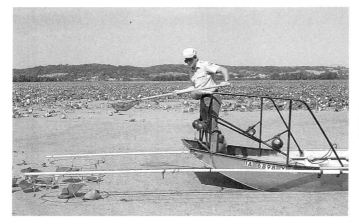

DNR researchers use an electrofishing boat to capture bass.

TRACKING STUDIES: GENERAL OBSERVATIONS

Because of the diverse environments that bass occupy and their various adaptations, results of one study don't necessarily apply to bass from other waters. Still, we can make some noteworthy generalizations based on what the researchers have found:

• Some bass rarely leave the shallows, while others occupy mid-depth or deep water. Bright sunlight or heavy wave action usually does not cause bass to leave shallow water; bass do, however, switch preferred locations for unknown reasons.

Biologist John Pitlo, Jr. holds a suitable specimen. Bass must weigh over 2 pounds to carry the transmitter.

• Several studies indicate that there often are at least two distinct groups of bass in a population. One group occupies a definite home area they rarely leave, while the other group regularly changes locales or wanders.

• Bass become active and hunt prey at a wide range of temperatures.

• Bass rest most of the time, becoming active and seeking food at regular intervals, often around dusk and dawn. Bass in shallow water feed primarily during low-light periods. Bass at greater depths are active later in the day.

• Bass sometimes are active at night, although they don't continually move and feed then.

• Resting bass aren't always in cover but usually spend time near small openings in cover or where two cover types meet. Active bass often cruise the outer edge of cover and sometimes cruise along drop-off breaklines. Bass may also suspend at middepths and may feed on the surface in open water.

A bow-mounted boom antenna is used to locate bass at a distance. It can turned to determine fish location.

• Most bass movements are parallel to cover and involve minor depth changes. When bass move over deep water, they typically hold at a constant depth rather than follow a bottom contour.

• Some bass seem to know their way around a large body of water. Other bass become disoriented and can't find their way back when removed from their home area. Bass in rivers or chains of lakes seem most accustomed to long travel and often return if displaced.

• Bass generally favor shallow water and heavy cover. Several studies found that they rarely went deeper than 15 feet. Yet where oxygen and baitfish are present, bass use depths to 80 feet or more.

• Bass react to changing water quality involving oxygen, temperature, and salinity by moving.

• As spawning approaches, largemouths move to traditional bedding sites—shallow protected bays and canals, preferably with wood or weed cover. Cues causing this movement include changes in length of daylight and water temperature.

• Bass often act like individuals, exhibiting varying activity cycles, cover preferences, and feeding habits. Some bass avoid boats and human activity. Others flock to busy marinas and may become "pets."

• Trophy-sized bass may behave differently than smaller bass, often occupying middepth habitat or suspending.

Bass are anesthetized and opened with a scalpel. The radio tag is then inserted. Each transmitter has a unique frequency that identifies the fish. Sutures close the incisions.

VARIABILITY IN BASS MOVEMENTS

Largemouth and smallmouth bass are products of their environment. Depending on where you find them, they behave similarly or differently, for a variety of reasons. Comparing a Lake Mead largemouth to an Okeechobee bigmouth is like comparing an Iowa corn farmer to a California valley girl or a New York City banker. Same species, different behavior.

Radio telemetry, sometimes augmented by observations of divers, is our best way of learning about these regional variations in behavior and what they mean, as is shown by comparing these four major tracking studies.

TRACKING TEXAS LUNKERS

John Hope is a big-bass fanatic living in a big-bass wonderland—Texas. Hope implanted radio tags in trophy-sized largemouth bass, fish weighing over 8 pounds. While tracking them for 20 months, sometimes all night and at other times during the day, Hope discovered that Texas lunkers are loners. This antisocial behavior may be what allows the fish to reach such prodigious proportions. For when a bass acts like a typical bass—feeding in shallow water during the day—it dramatically reduces its chances of surviving to old age and grand size.

Hope's bass also were creatures of habit, usually to the extreme. Many showed regular daily as well as seasonal patterns and behavior. Like deer that typically frequent small home ranges, Hope's bass knew their woods inside and out. They didn't frequent the whole reservoir but were so intimately aware of their local environment that they didn't need to follow underwater highways to move from their daytime resting areas to their nighttime feeding sites. They moved purposefully in the same direct lines, night after night.

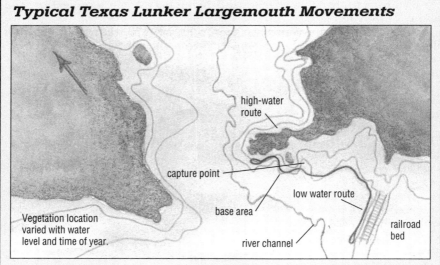

Typical Texas Lunker Largemouth Movements

high-water
route

capture point

low water route

Vegetation location
varied with water
level and time of year.

base area

railroad
bed

river channel

Samantha weighed 10 pounds, 13 ounces when John hope caught her in February at Sam Rayburn, holding in a prespawn location in 10 feet of water. After her release, she spawned and spent the next year nearby, patrolling 5- to 10-foot edges to feed. She altered feeding routes, however, when water levels fluctuated dramatically.

Hope's lunker largemouths selected relatively small home areas that provided all their needs: ideal spawning sites, large, shallow feeding flats, and deep water.

In summer, Hope's giant bass fed only at night. In winter, key feeding periods were dawn and dusk. The rest of the day, regardless of season, the bass held offshore, suspending in 10 feet of water, often over much greater depths. When they rested, they were uncatchable.

During feeding periods, however, the largemouths slowly cruised the outer edges of weedbeds, typically remaining near the same 10-foot level. Like neighborhood cops on a downtown beat, they constantly moved, stopping to poke their heads into dense cover, ever alert for a panicking baitfish trying to make a run for it.

Hope's tracking research is a masterpiece of insight into the habits of trophy-sized largemouth bass in Texas reservoirs. But what does it tell us about bass in general? Do Iowan, Mexican, or Canadian bigmouths behave the same way? Do smallmouth bass exhibit any or all of the same characteristics? The answers to those questions and more become apparent when we examine other tracking studies from different parts of the continent.

PITLO'S POOL

At first glance, the best candidates to contrast with Hope's Texas bass seem to be the 86 largemouth tracked for five years by Iowa fishery biologist John Pitlo, Jr.

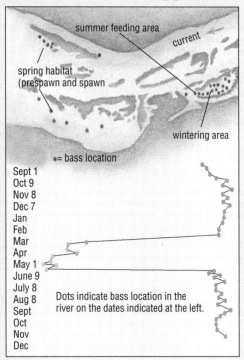

Seasonal Shifts of Largemouth Bass in the Mississippi River

summer feeding area

current

spring habitat
(prespawn and spawn

wintering area

•= bass location

Sept 1
Oct 9
Nov 8
Dec 7
Jan
Feb
Mar
Apr
May 1
June 9
July 8
Aug 8   Dots indicate bass location in the
Sept   river on the dates indicated at the left.
Oct
Nov
Dec

John Pitlo's bass #1416 was captured and tagged at the downstream end of a Mississippi River backwater in 1987. It moved up the slough in late summer, occupied several locations, then settled into an overwintering spot nearby.

Water depth and current were reduced by subnormal rainfall in 1987. In previous years, bass had overwintered in the upper end of the slough with no current but adequate depth and oxygen.

In 1987, the upper end was abnormally shallow. Thick weeds that choked it in summer contributed to low oxygen when they decayed under ice. radio-tagged bass and presumably many others overwintered in the deeper middle of the slough, where oxygen was higher and current absent because of low water. Prior to ice-out, #1416 moved downstream toward what's through to be a spawning location. After spawning, it returned to its home area.

Pitlo's study area was Pools 12 and 13 of the Mississippi River. His fish differed from Hope's in several significant ways.

For starters, they were not giants but averaged about 3 pounds—large adults for that region. Their environment was different, too. Hope tracked his fish in manmade Texas reservoirs, while Pitlo's study area was a pool of the Mississippi River, far enough north (Iowa-Illinois) that the water froze in winter.

Those were the obvious differences, but there were more subtle factors—dissolved oxygen levels, current, fluctuating water temperature, cover, baitfish—that Pitlo found important in locating and positioning bass. They were also closely associated with vegetation. In summer, Pitlo found his bass in underwater vegetation three out of every four times he went looking for them.

Hope's fish occupied a single year-round home range, but the Mississippi River bass often had seasonal sites—one for spawning, another for summer feeding, and a third for winter. And while the fish were faithful to these ranges, returning year after year, the sites were often located miles apart. So while Hope's bass were couch potatoes, Pitlo's fish were far more migratory.

Pitlo's river bass also had to contend with current. Largemouths generally shied away from current if oxygen levels in quiet backwaters were adequate. But in winter, when dissolved oxygen levels fell, they pulled out of shallow back bays and edged closer to moving water that contained more oxygen.

Upon initial review, we find few similarities between Pitlo's Mississippi River bass and Hope's Lone Star largemouths. But when we overlay two other important tracking studies with smallmouth bass, the puzzle starts to come together.

RIDGWAY'S TRAPLINERS

Dr. Mark Ridgway is a research scientist with the Ontario Ministry of Natural Resources at Harknesss Fisheries Research Laboratory in Algonquin Provincial Park. His radio tracking of smallmouth bass in Lake Opeongo has contributed significantly to the longest continuous census of any animal population.

In addition to using sophisticated radio tags, sonar, and listening devices, Ridgway and his colleagues donned scuba gear to spy on their subjects. They discovered that fewer than 30 percent of mature male smallmouth bass living at the northern edge of their range spawn each spring. More amazing, through some complex decision-making process, these few breeding fish are predetermined a year in advance. This means that if any are removed from their nests, no other smallmouth replaces them.

Ridgway also discovered, as had Pitlo, that bass repeatedly homed to specific nesting sites. When Ridgway compared his maps of spawning sites with the maps made by researchers in earlier years, he found remarkable similarities. His bass were using the identical nesting sites that bass used in the 1950s and 1960s.

He also found that once smallmouths completed their bedding chores in Lake Opeongo, they left the nursery areas and swam to distinct summer home ranges in completely different sections of the lake. And they moved quickly and directly, as they did again in fall when they moved to their deep winter domains.

In the cold, crystal-clear water of Lake Opeongo, Ridgway found that a typical summer home range covered 250 to 750 acres. The bass used their entire home range every day, cruising it repeatedly. Indeed, Ridgway's smallmouths swam 1 to 8 miles a day hunting for crayfish. Ridgway referred to this movement as *traplining*.

In many respects, Ridgway's smallmouths behaved like Pitlo's largemouths. In both cases, the fish established seasonal (summer and winter) home ranges in totally different parts of the lake and river, to which they returned season after season. And prey, crayfish in Ridgway's case, shad in Pitlo's—played a key role in where bass lived and how they behaved. Yet Ridgway's smallmouths also showed behavior patterns strikingly similar to Hope's largemouths. Both knew their relatively tiny slice of the watery environment like the back of their fins.

CORBETT'S CLOSERS

The puzzle comes together when we add another tracking study example conducted by Ontario Ministry of Natural Resources biologist Barry Corbett, who for six years replicated Ridgway's work on Lake of the Woods, a much larger and more diverse body of water on the Ontario-Minnesota border. Corbett implanted radio tags in two dozen 3- to 3½-pound smallmouth bass inhabiting discrete sectors of the million-acre lake, including habitats rich in food and sectors not so productive.

When Corbett started his work, he monitored the bass in a rocky, food-rich sector throughout the spring spawn. He expected the males to dash to their summer home ranges as the Lake Opeongo smallmouths had done, but they didn't move. In fact, by July, the fish were so sluggish—shifting only a foot or two a day—that Corbett scuba dived down to see if they were still alive. He need not have worried. He found so many crayfish scurrying across the bottom of the lake that his fat bass were content to spend summer in the same areas where they'd spawned earlier—no reason to move. Indeed, despite attractive structure, often within a few hundreds yards, Corbett's smallmouths rarely changed positions.

A few bass in this food-rich area were more adventurous, however. Off and on throughout the summer, they'd make a brief foray or two around the block. When they went shopping, they moved in direct straight lines, and they returned the same way.

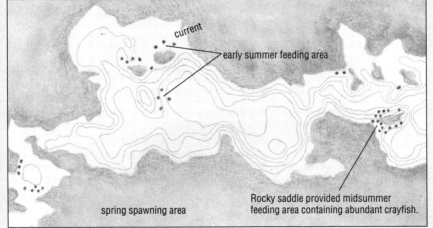

Movements of a Smallmouth Bass in a Moderately Fertile lake

current

early summer feeding area

Rocky saddle provided midsummer feeding area containing abundant crayfish.

spring spawning area

This smallmouth bass studied by Barry Colbert moved from spawning areas to summer ranges as Ridgway's smallmouths and Pitlo's Mississippi largemouths had, but they didn't leave as quickly or roam as extensively.

Bass Behavior After Weed Control

After grass carp eliminated the exotic weed hydrilla, which had covered approximately 80 percent of 148-acre Lake Baldwin, Florida researchers* monitored 16 radio-tagged largemouth bass in 148-acre Lake Baldwin, Florida. Largemouths used three depth zones: (A) inshore (0 to 7 feet), (B) middepth (7 to 11 feet), and (C) offshore (11 feet or deeper).

Inshore bass were most active around dawn and dusk, but some movement was seen throughout the day and night. Middepth bass were most active from midmorning to midafternoon, with a second peak after midnight. Offshore bass were active throughout the entire day, with a major peak at sunset.

Bass in each depth range used different types of cover and hunting tactics. Inshore bass usually stayed near shoreline trees and roots; one stayed near piers. In contrast, four of five middepth bass were near or under piers 39 percent of the time. These bass moved from pier to pier and were more likely to aggregate with other middepth bass than with inshore bass. Offshore areas were devoid to distinct underwater structures and cover. Bass there apparently related to bare bottom and suspended to feed on shad.

The study suggests how bass function after underwater vegetation is removed (in the absence of open-water predators). It also helps explain poor fishing after weeds are removed: bass suspended away from cover are difficult to locate and catch. Use of piers by bass is widely recognized by anglers.

This report confirms information from other tracking studies showing that healthy bass (and other gamefish with large ductless gas bladders) tend to stay in the same depth range day after day. Bass move to feed in local home ranges but seldom shift in depth more than a few feet. Deep bass stay in deep water and their activity periods are established by conditions there. Shallower fish stay put, too, and have activity periods based on conditions there. Depth and time of activity are key variables in pattern fishing.

*Colle, D. E., R. L. Cailteux, and J.V. Shireman. 1989. Distribution of Florida largemouth bass in a lake after elimination of all submersed aquatic vegetation. *N. Amer. J. Fish. Mngt.* 9(2):213-218.

When Corbett later monitored smallmouths in a moderately food-rich portion of the lake, an area less productive than his crayfish-filled zone but more fertile than sterile Lake Opeongo, bass behaved in an intermediate fashion. They vacated their spawning areas and moved to distinct summer ranges as Ridgway's fish had done, but they didn't leave as quickly and sometimes returned to their nesting areas. In addition, once they settled into their summer quarters, they didn't roam nearly as extensively as Lake Opeongo bass. Their traplines, in effect, were far shorter.

COMMON THREADS

In each of these four tracking studies, bass established home ranges. Sometimes, as Pitlo, Ridgway, and Corbett discovered, the fish had discrete seasonal confines. Hope's largemouths, on the other hand, enjoyed one year-round home. Whether the fish used a single home range or multiple ranges, they were faithful to the sites year after year. (As an interesting side note, muskie researchers are discovering the same phenomenon.)

None of the bass in any of the tracking studies wandered aimlessly around the lake, river, or reservoir. Regardless of location, type of body of water, or species of bass, the fish were acutely aware of their surroundings. They staked out a relatively small amount of water or seasonal waters and confined their activities to these areas.

John Hope's trophy largemouths and Corbett's crayfish-gorging smallmouths were remarkably similar in behavior. Pitlo's river fish and Ridgway's trapliners also exhibited similar characteristics. Indeed, despite the widely held belief among anglers that smallmouth bass and largemouth bass behave in a totally different manner, these tracking studies suggest that their seasonal and daily movement patterns may be similar.

Why? Corbett believes it's as fundamental as food resources and energy demands. As he puts it, "When fish don't have to expend energy searching for food, they don't. If they just have to open their mouths and eat because so much food is available, they stay put for the summer." Of course, the opposite is also true. So Ridgway's smallmouths, living in a tough environment, were forced to graze upon a number of spots within large, well-defined summer traplines.

So, is a bass a bass wherever you find it? You decide. What these tracking studies tell us, though, is that smallmouth and largemouth bass are remarkably adaptive. They are magnificently fine-tuned products of their environment.

Bass will do whatever they must to survive. If water temperatures, oxygen levels, cover, and food resources are adequate, the fish move little. If one or more of those factors change, the fish are forced to adjust, their degree of adjustment being relative to the change. That single lesson—and all that it entails—leads to a better understanding of your quarry.

TRACKING TALES OF LUNKER BASS—
MORE ABOUT JOHN HOPE'S RESEARCH

Anglers have long wondered whether those elusive giant bass behave differently than smaller specimens. Thanks to John Hope, whose research was cited briefly above, we now have definitive clues about when and where they're most catchable.

Tracking Research Synopsis

Researcher	Hope	Pitlo	Ridgway	Corbett
Species	Largemouth	Largemouth	Smallmouth	Smallmouth
Body of Water	Reservoirs	Mississippi River	Lake Opeongo	Lake of the Woods
Creatures of Habit	Yes	Yes	Yes	Yes
Home Ranges	One year-round seasonal range	Distinct seasonal ranges	Distinct seasonal ranges	Distinct seasonal ranges
Faithful to Home Ranges	Yes	Yes	Yes	Yes
Reliance on Underwater Highways	No—often moving in direct, straight lines	No	No—routinely crossing deep water to reach specific sites	No

John Hope dived below the surface to check on radio tagged bass.

Unlike most researchers, Hope isn't a trained scientist; he's a fishing guide, a careful observer of bass who turned to tracking, diving, writing, lecturing, and making bass videos. Here's a more detailed look at his methods.

Hope tagged bass in Houston County Lake, a small Texas impoundment, and followed individual bass to identify daily movement patterns and activity periods. He used a chart recorder to describe bottom features and the depths where fish were holding. He monitored each fish 5 to 6 days a week for the first 30 days, then checked each fish 3 or 4 times a week for the next 3 months. For the rest of the year, he monitored them once or twice a week.

A FISH CALLED WANDA

To consider just one example, here's some of what Hope learned from Wanda, a bass he tracked intensively for over a year and frequently tempted with lures and livebait.

Wanda weighed 10½ pounds on March 8, 1986, when she hit a black-and-red metalflake 6-inch curly-tail plastic worm cast into a nest in a cove at Houston County Lake. She was 7 years old, based on growth rings in one of her scales. Hope surgically implanted a small but long-lived ultrasonic transmitter into her abdomen. After a few days of recovery in a holding tank, he released her where she'd been caught.

Wanda's movement pattern remained consistent over the next 13 months. When inactive, she suspended between 8 and 12 feet near the few remaining branches of a rotting stump, over a sloping bottom 14 to 16 feet deep. She held slightly shallower in summer but stayed in the same spot through all four seasons.

Wanda made one or two sorties a day into shallower water, apparently to feed. She'd swim toward shore until she reached a depth of 10 to 12 feet, then turn parallel to shore to patrol. Her cruising depth was between 5 and 12 feet deep, except during infrequent dashes to chase baitfish at the surface or near the bank. When she reached the small cove where she'd been caught, she'd swim back and forth or around and across an indentation in the middle of the cove.

She hunted by flushing and chasing prey, and when active, she moved almost constantly, averaging about 1 mile per hour (about the speed of a 12-volt electric motor on medium), pausing seldom, never more than a minute or two. She traveled slightly faster during major and minor solunar periods and at dusk and dawn.

In 1986, the 10-foot depth contour was the outer edge of a continuous hydrilla bed. Wanda followed this weededge and didn't move into or under the matted vegetation, although she occasionally moved over the hydrilla and swirled at the surface while chasing baitfish.

In January 1987, the vegetation in Houston County Lake was chemically killed. Wanda still moved along the same route at similar depths, following the now barren ledge at a depth of 10 feet. Hope placed several small cedar trees along the ledge, but Wanda didn't stop at this cover. Death of the vegetation didn't alter Wanda's choice of spawning sites, either. In 1987, she spawned only a few feet from her 1986 nesting site.

10-pound Wanda tagged and ready for release—and subsequent revelations about the lives of big largemouth bass.

On a few occasions, when she reached the 10-foot depth, Wanda turned left instead of right. This led her to the mouth of another small cove with a few submerged stumps. She also moved back and forth there. Wanda once moved westward across the cove and patrolled the opposite shore, reversing direction near a weedy point.

Her location, depth, and feeding tactics didn't vary with weather fronts or seasons, but her hours varied by season. From October to May, Wanda used two separate feeding periods, each lasting about 5 hours. One started about an hour before dawn, the other an hour before sunset. From May (postspawn) to October, however, she was inactive all day and moved all night. About an hour before nightfall, she would leave her resting spot, returning shortly after sunrise.

In August 1986, three nights before the full moon, Wanda moved offshore from her feeding position in the cove to where moonlight had apparently caused shad to aggregate. Wanda circled under them, periodically dashing to the surface in obvious feeding attempts. That night, all seven bass being tracked in Houston County Lake were circling and feeding offshore in different spots. None hit lures. This was the only time Hope observed this behavior. He called it "crazy night."

Although Wanda avoided boat noises and lure splashes, Hope hooked and released her three times while she fed in the cove mouth at night. She hit a surface buzzer, a jig, and a plastic worm.

A weather front altered her timing in early March. On March 4, 1987, surface temperature was 58°F while Wanda followed her regular feeding routine. The next day, she didn't return to her stump at dawn but cruised the cove all day. A cold front dropped surface temperatures to 54°F by dawn of the 6th, and she returned to her stump. But water warmed to 58°F by evening, and she fed that night.

On March 7th, the surface temperature held near 60°F. Wanda constantly moved around the cove mouth at 4 or 5 feet, too fast to allow a lure presentation. On the 8th, she joined a male on a nest but was scared off when a homeowner walked onto a nearby dock. That midnight, Hope caught her on a live waterdog, replaced her transmitter (the units last 13 to 19 months and a new one was needed), noted she'd grown to 12½ pounds, and released her in the nest area. She returned to her base area for several days, cruising and apparently feeding in the cove after dark. Then she resumed spawning in her usual feeding area.

At dawn on March 20th, she was on a new nest, slightly outside the point of her cove. She appeared to have a patch of fungus. Hope caught her again on a waterdog. This time she weighed less than 11 pounds, 1.5 pounds below her prespawn weight. He carried her to a nearby marina for observation and treatment in a holding tank.

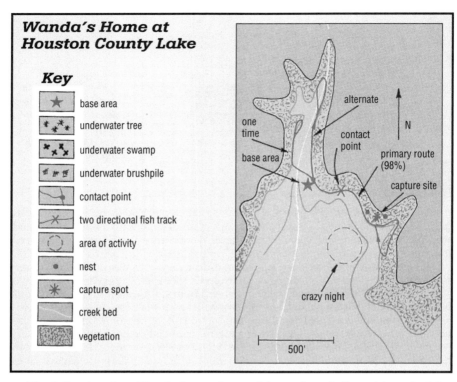

Wanda's Home at Houston County Lake

Key

★	base area
	underwater tree
	underwater swamp
	underwater brushpile
	contact point
✕	two directional fish track
	area of activity
•	nest
✳	capture spot
	creek bed
	vegetation

one time

alternate

contact point

base area

N

primary route (98%)

capture site

crazy night

500'

The following day, Wanda jumped out of the tank and slipped into the lake through a hole in the dock floor. Hope found her on a midlake breakline at about 20 feet, where she remained for three days, apparently recovering from the stress of her ordeals. She returned home on the fourth night, suspended over the same stump at 10 feet, and resumed her daily routine.

On April 9th, Wanda erred again and hit another lure; Hope wasn't there to intercede. Wanda's final trip was to a taxidermist.

Meanwhile, Hope was also tracking other bass who showed many similar patterns, especially in their feeding schedules. A bass named Tina had both a winter and a summer base, the latter adjacent to Wanda's range; they fed in the same cove. The two big females followed the same schedule and sometimes came nose to nose, but each turned back when they met. On crazy night, Tina was near Wanda, but deeper; she sometimes cruised at greater depth, too.

Tina (8.0 Pounds)
Houston County Lake

Lee (8.6 Pounds)
Houston County Lake

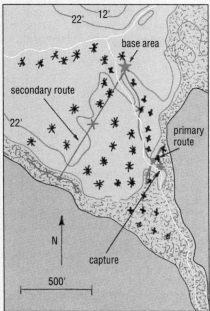

INTERPRETATIONS

Hope says wariness isn't the reason some bass get huge. Lunkers are easy to catch at the right place at the right time, especially off spawning nests. Nevertheless, taking giant bass consistently requires knowing basic facts about how big bass behave. They're creatures of instinct and habit—predictable. Hope's results show that big dominant bass often establish territories close to flats that offer the most food and best spawning opportunities. They don't move far from their spawning areas unless they're forced away by changing water levels, lack of prey, or poor water quality.

Of the small bass found at all depths in most lakes, only a few avoid harvest and reach lunker size. Those that feed near cover typically targeted by anglers are soon caught and killed. The few that feed by moving constantly at night and refuse to bite while suspended near cover are far safer. Hope believes that as a result, these bass are the ones most likely to grow huge.

In the Texas reservoirs John Hope studied (including Lake Fork and Sam Rayburn), 10 feet was the magic depth for lunkers, apparently because this is the deepest a large bass can hold and easily feed at the surface. The surface blocks one escape dimension and greatly increases the ability of predators to corner prey. Otherwise, it's much harder for the solitary big bass to get enough food to continue to grow.

Anglers should concentrate on places where lunkers most likely are at the times they'll be ready to bite. Hope recommends fishing 10-foot breaklines around spawning time and when bass are feeding at night or during the hour and a half near dawn and dusk, times a majority of lunkers are routinely active. Cast parallel to the 10-foot contour to keep lures in the narrow corridor where a cruising bass can see them.

Hope repeatedly tried to catch tagged bass while they were inactive in their holding spots. None ever hit, even though he knew their precise locations. Big bass are virtually uncatchable when they're inactive in offshore base areas and nearly uncatchable while en route to and from feeding areas. Lunkers are almost as easy to hook as smaller adult bass, however, if baits are presented in their strike window while they're actively feeding.

FURTHER STUDIES

After studying big female bass in Houston County Lake, Hope expanded his project, placing ultrasonic transmitters in male bass, smaller females, and lunkers in other waters, looking for similar or different behavior.

Jonathan (17.8 inches, 3 pounds, 5 ounces, and at least 8 years old), was caught while defending his nest (the same one where Wanda's spawning had been interrupted five days earlier); within 30 minutes after release, he was back on the nest, and remained in the 3-foot-deep water for 21 days, guarding eggs and fry. For the next few days, he escorted a school of fry far back in the cove. He and several other male bass were seen chasing bass fry there on several occasions during the next 30 days.

Big Louise on Lake Fork and Samantha in Sam Rayburn Lake helped Hope prove his theories to local guides and at angling seminars. An underwater video Hope made features Amistad Annie.

In general, largemouths over 8 pounds behaved like Wanda. Only Tina and Amistad Annie were deep-dwelling fish, migrating shallow to spawn but staying deeper much of the year. All the others held about 10 feet all year, and all of the largest bass used cruising and flushing tactics rather than ambush. A few smaller fish that Hope tracked stayed shallow, but no fish larger than 8 pounds stayed shallower than 8 feet.

FURTHER CONCLUSIONS

In Texas reservoirs, some bass remain shallow all year, some live deep except during the spawn, and some live around the 10-foot midlayer. Fish in each zone feed opportunistically on a variety of prey. But some individuals seem to specialize in stationary tactics (ambush, habituation, and stalking), while others flush prey along cover edges. Bass that live in shallow areas are heavily harvested when anglers hammer the banks. The bass most likely to reach lunker proportions live in places and behave in ways that give them a chance to escape capture and grow larger.

Hope calls the areas where bass funnel in and out from the 10-foot breakline *funnel points*. Bass move across these spots on their daily patrol routes. Thus they're the highest-percentage areas to hook a giant bass. To locate funnel points, look for places where

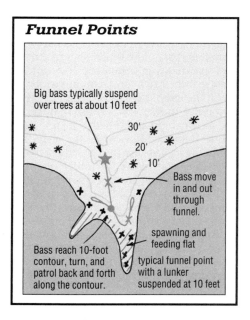

Funnel Points

Big bass typically suspend over trees at about 10 feet

30'
20'
10'

Bass move in and out through funnel.

spawning and feeding flat

typical funnel point with a lunker suspended at 10 feet

Bass reach 10-foot contour, turn, and patrol back and forth along the contour.

bottom contour lines form a funnel aiming into a feeding and spawning area. Best spots are where distinct structural features or lines of cover define the 10-foot cruising lane. Offshore trees in deeper water with their tops near 10 feet further enhance a spot's potential.

Hope recommends not moving back and forth casting baits along contour lines. Experienced bass usually flee a moving boat. Instead, hold near a likely route and quietly wait for bass to come to you. Giant bass avoid lure splashes, boat noises, and trolling motors. Even the noise and high-frequency vibrations of sonar units alert bass to the presence of anglers. Turn off electronics and be prepared to wait until lunkers pass by. Tie to a nearby tree or bush, or troll steadily at minimum power. Hope feels anchors scare giant bass and cause tangles when lunkers are hooked.

Don't let postfrontal conditions or cold water keep you off the water. Big fish in middepth or deep habitat are relatively immune to weather changes and seasonal shifts. Fish more at night during summer, and in winter, fish during early morning and before dusk. "Go early and stay late," Hope recommends.

Hope readily admits that different habitats foster different behaviors in lunker bass. Without fishing pressure, big bass can prosper in the shallows and may feed differently than the fish he tracked. Hope notes, however, that despite his continuing search, he has yet to find a reservoir where lunker largemouths consistently behave differently.

COMPARATIVE STUDIES ON THE DAILY LIVES OF BASS

John Hope's findings generally agree with black bass tracking and diving studies conducted by Bob Knopf, Ralph Manns, and Mike Lembeck, all avid bass anglers. While over 40 researchers have used telemetry to study bass, most haven't reported following individual bass daily for long periods. Therefore the results of these four studies are more useful to anglers. Knopf tracked 2- to 5-pound largemouths and observed fish underwater in Lake Isabella, a 632-acre reservoir in Michigan. Manns tracked and dived to monitor 12- to 16-inch Guadalupe and largemouth bass in Lake Travis, a 19,000-acre Texas reservoir. Lembeck tracked over 200 various-sized largemouths in El Capitan and five other small southern California reservoirs.

Results of Selected Black Bass Tracking Studies

Researcher (Pub. Year)	Bass Species	Number of Bass	Major Daily Depth Changes	Rapid Vertical Feeding	Offshore Suspension	Movements Parallel To Contours-Breaklines	Feeding Movements To and From Deep Water	Lake(s) Location State
Lembeck (Circle 76, Williams 79)	LMB	12	No	Yes	Yes	Yes	No	4 San Diego Lakes, CA
Hope 92	LMB	13	No	Yes	Yes	Yes	No	Houston Co., Fork, TX
Knopf 81 Knopf & Lenon 81	LMB	8	Yes			Yes	Yes	Isabella, MI
Manns 81	GB	14	No	Yes	Yes	Yes	No	Travis, TX
Fish & Savitz 83	LMB	10				**	No	Cedar L., IL
Wanjala et al. 86	LMB	28		Inferred	No	Inferred	No	Alamo, AZ
Cole 95	SMB	38	Yes		Inferred	Yes	Yes	Green L., ME
Ridgway & Shuter 96	SMB	32				Yes	Yes	Opeongo, ON
Langhurst & Schoenike 90	SMB	10	No	No	No		No	Embarrass R., WI

Legend: LMB = Largemouth bass SMB = Smallmouth Bass GB = Guadalupe Bass

Knopf, Manns, and Lembeck located bass at various depths without noting any concentrations of fish around 10 feet. Like Hope, though, they noted a tendency for individual bass to stay at fairly constant depths. Knopf's biggest bass apparently moved up at least 10 feet to feed, a larger daily shift than Hope's giant largemouths or Manns' small Guadalupe bass.

The tendency of bass to hold at a constant depth is probably related to a need to maintain their gas bladders at constant pressure. Because tissues, including the walls of their gas bladders, become proportionally weaker as fish grow larger, lunker bass may be more restricted in vertical movement than smaller bass.

The tendency of big bass to suspend offshore, as Hope's fish did, may be reduced if offshore cover is limited, or if competitive offshore predators like striped bass are present. The biggest largemouth Knopf tracked (about 5 pounds) held in an offshore treetop and hunted over an inshore flat at night. It moved continuously when feeding, a pattern identical to many of Hope's big bass. Lembeck also found many bass suspended offshore. He tracked one that stayed far offshore, feeding on shad attracted to the bubbles of an artificial aerator.

The Guadalupe bass Manns studied in Lake Travis hunted randomly offshore, much as Hope's lunkers did on the "crazy night" when shad schooled under a bright moon. After feeding, small bass didn't stay offshore away from cover. They did, however, frequently suspend 3 to 10 feet away from cover. Hope's lunkers tended to move continuously while hunting, but Manns' Guadalupes moved in stops and starts, frequently pausing as they moved along rock slides.

Some bass monitored by Hope and Knopf moved directly to feeding areas without following lines of structure or cover. Manns recorded movements directly across Lake Travis, and Lembeck watched some bass move up and down the middle of a California reservoir. While some bass may move along "underwater highways" created by cover or structure, clearly these reference points aren't necessary.

Knopf, Manns, and Hope found that feeding bass moved along contours parallel to shorelines. Other studies have reported that bass usually hunt more efficiently by using flushing than ambushing tactics.

All four researchers found that bass are highly sensitive to noises and react by moving away or ignoring lures. Some of Lembeck's fish moved to sanctuary areas where fishing was prohibited. All researchers noted that inactive bass often were uncatchable, even when their exact positions were known.

Hope's observations provide conclusive evidence that large bass aren't significantly affected by the weight of small transmitters. They spawned and grew substantially after transmitters were surgically implanted. The small adult bass in Manns' study were distinctly handicapped by the weight of tracking devices. And Knopf noted that intermediate-sized bass were hampered by his radio units. Results of other tracking studies on average-sized bass may be misleading if effects of the transmitters on behavior weren't acknowledged.

Several conflicts exist among these studies. In contrast to studies by both Manns and Hope, Lembeck reported major seasonal depth shifts and differences in movement patterns among years. He also noted differences among bass populations in different reservoirs.

Not all lunkers share a tendency to feed only at night or during morning and evening. Lembeck's California bass moved little at night. Evidently, local conditions modify bass behavior. Even though big bass tend to hold at Hope's "magic" 10-foot depth and feed at night, lunkers in other lakes may not do so. And, of course, some trophy bass are always shallow because the lakes and rivers they inhabit are less than 10 feet deep. Catches of lunkers during midday throughout

---

their range prove that some giant bass are active then, but giant bass are less likely to feed actively during the day when fishing pressure is high.

BACKWATER BASS—PAST, PRESENT, FUTURE: A CLOSER LOOK AT JOHN PITLO'S RESEARCH

Some scientific studies may not seem to address the immediate concerns of anglers but certainly increase our understanding of fish. Other studies have a direct impact on sportfish populations. John Pitlo's Mississippi River study can affect fishing success for most North American anglers. Largemouth bass aren't often thought of as river fish, although many of North America's best largemouth bass fisheries are rivers. The mighty Mississippi offers prime bass water for anglers in nine states, and most of its features have counterparts in other rivers from coast to coast.

One of Pitlo study objectives was to follow bass to spawning sites, describe preferred habitat, and evaluate effects of water level fluctuations on spawning. Water in the Mississippi is turbid in spring due to suspended sediment and is worsened by rooting carp. The murkiness restricted spotting bass on nests, but radio signals indicated bass holding within restricted areas near protected shorelines during the typical late-May-to-early-June spawning season; schools of tiny bass fry were noted several days later.

While effects of water level and flow on spawning still aren't clear, Pitlo's study revealed other types of habitat critical for largemouth bass survival. During five years of tracking, researchers gathered data on seasonal movements, habitat preference, and specific bass locations that can help river anglers catch bass.

TRACKING TECHNIQUES

The telemetry study involved 86 bass collected by electrofishing. Battery life allowed transmitter operation for about a year, but Pitlo was able to recapture bass just before battery failure and implant new transmitters. One bass carried three transmitters for 700 days before the bass was harvested by an angler.

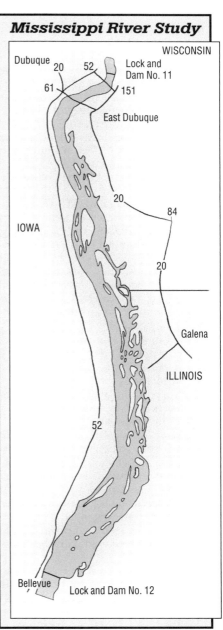

Mississippi River Study

It's time-consuming work. "We begin searching for bass at the point we last located them," Pitlo says. "During winter and summer, they're usually near where we left them. If they're gone, we patrol a mile upstream and downstream, rotating the boat-mounted boom antenna. If we still haven't found them, we search the pool from one dam to the other on the Iowa and Illinois sides.

"When we 'hear' a bass (each one has a different radio frequency), we rotate the boom antenna to check direction. We close in, then switch to a diamond-shaped, handheld loop antenna. When we're very close, we replace the loop antenna with a small wire and can locate a bass in a 2-foot-square area."

Pitlo demonstrates by tracking a largemouth to a fallen log. "He's under that branch," he announces. Pitching jigs and worms to the spot produced no reaction. Had the bass moved? When the shocking boat came by, they sent several hundred volts into the spot. The big bass boiled out furiously and escaped the electric field before it could be netted. The precision of the telemetry location was remarkable, and it was clear that correct location and precise presentation don't guarantee a strike. Electrofishing proves there are nearly uncatchable bass. Anglers who make statements like, "Yup, we fished that bank; no bass there,"show a useful self-confidence but may be dead wrong in biological reasoning.

SEASONAL MOVEMENTS OF RIVER BASS

Five years of tracking indicated that river largemouth bass location is affected by five primary factors: dissolved oxygen, current, water temperature, cover, and presence of baitfish.

Winter—"As the year begins, all bass are in specific wintering areas," Pitlo notes. "Requirements seem to be adequate oxygen, no current, and at least 5 feet of water." Backwater lakes provide this habitat. Water temperature in backwaters is also 2 to 4 degrees warmer than in the river channel. There's a lot of dead organic matter, so during winter, oxygen levels drop steadily. If, as often happens, they get below 2 parts per million, bass seek better water, closer to current but not in it. In low-water winters, current in backwaters is reduced. Bass shift from the upper end of sloughs to lower reaches they wouldn't have used in high-water years. Their previous overwintering spots hold insufficient oxygen and are too shallow.

"Appropriate overwintering spots are scarce; only three seem to exist in a 15-mile section of Pool 12," says Pitlo. "This may be a limiting factor on the number of bass the river can support."

Spring—From ice-out through June, bass use diverse habitats depending on water levels. When spring floods inundate bottomland timber adjacent to the riverbank, bass enter this new habitat. During low water, they move into stumps, brush, or logs soon after ice-out. When flood waters recede and weeds begin growing, bass move into weedbeds and along weededges.

Some bass seem to spawn near overwintering spots. Others move several miles to specific spawning sites. They remain there until early June, then move miles to summer areas. Bass appear to spawn in 1½- to 3-foot depths where hard-pan sand or clay is covered with about 4 to 6 inches of silt. Males sweep off silt, exposing a firm bed.

Summer—Nearly 75 percent of bass summer locations are in weeds, either emergent or submerged types. Water depth in beds of emergent weeds is often just 1 to 2 feet, and water temperature exceeds 80°F. Bass move into side channels and cuts that connect backwaters with the river. They hold behind or in cover objects like weedbeds or fallen trees or stumps near current. Wood and weeds hold larval

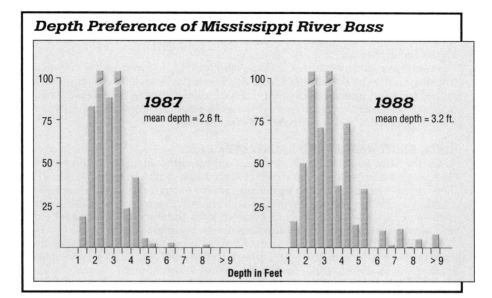

Depth Preference of Mississippi River Bass

1987
mean depth = 2.6 ft.

1988
mean depth = 3.2 ft.

Depth in Feet

insects and aquatic invertebrates that feed on algae and tiny organisms.

Baitfish feed near cover, providing bass with abundant prey. Young gizzard shad are the most important prey species in the Mississippi River and many rivers nationwide. If a shad spawn is poor, bass can switch to 30 other species of preyfish found in the Mississippi.

Fall—As weeds die, bass occupy woodcover. Submerged weedbeds are abandoned first; some bass remain in the bare stalks of emergent weeds until late fall. Some bass leave summer areas and move to the vicinity of their overwintering site in early fall but remain active. Bass usually move back into the upper end of overwintering areas in December, just before ice-up.

These seasonal shifts often cover long distances. For two consecutive years, one bass moved 9 river miles upstream from a summer location to an overwintering slough. It bypassed two spots used by other bass in winter. To reach its preferred summer location, it spurned miles of apparently excellent summer habitat.

"I feel extensive travel indicates how critical the overwintering spots are to largemouth bass," says Pitlo. "It also suggests that bass know large areas of the backwaters they inhabit. Bass in this murky environment return to the same stump after several months' absence and many miles of travel. Their orientation mechanisms remain unknown."

PRACTICAL APPLICATIONS

It's reassuring that Pitlo's research won't just be filed on a shelf for scientific review. Clearly, knowing the location of bass is a great help to anglers, but this study may also aid efforts to improve bass habitat.

The Iowa Department of Natural Resources has gained the cooperation of the Corps of Engineers in an Environmental Management Program to create new overwintering areas, since lack of appropriate winter habitat may limit the size of the Mississippi River bass population, and large winterkills of bass have occurred when oxygen in backwaters has fallen below 2 parts per million throughout a large area.

Bass react to low oxygen by evacuating the area. They don't seem to "know" where oxygen is higher, so they can't move directly toward better water. They seem to instinctively seek deeper downstream spots, but if oxygen isn't much higher there, they die.

A similar pattern occurs on Florida's St. Johns River in summer. In several tracking studies by the Florida Game and Fresh Water Fish Commission, radio-tagged bass and thousands of other fish have died due to oxygen depletion after heavy rains. Organic runoff due to decades of pollution and wetland destruction robs oxygen from backwater bass and other species.

RIVER RESTORATION AND BACKWATER BASS

On the Mississippi River, backwaters can provide winter refuge for bass, but the lock and dam systems have collected so much sediment over the years that these refuges have been filled in, causing severe oxygen declines during winter. The first backwater restoration project was done on the upper and lower sections of 453-acre Brown's Lake in Pool 13, between Iowa and Illinois. This area provided critical winter refuge to largemouth bass until it became silted in.

In 1988, a deflection levy was constructed to divert the main channel flow away from Brown's Lake, effectively shielding it from added silt. Earth-moving equipment also was used to dig 8-foot deep, 60-foot wide channels, flow regulators, and deep holes. To test the effectiveness of the alterations, researchers with the Iowa Department of Natural Resources* radio tagged 20 largemouth bass weighing 2.2 pounds or more and monitored their responses to changes in water temperature, oxygen content, and current velocity from September 1990 through March 1991.

By late December 1990, Brown's Lake was iced over, except for the canals that provided the only suitable bass habitat. Water control gates were kept closed until dissolved oxygen (DO) concentrations dropped to 3 parts per million (ppm) in mid-January. A gate was then opened to add oxygenated water. After five days, DO levels reached 10 ppm in the top 2 feet of surface water throughout the dredged canal system. The inflow was then reduced to the minimum necessary to maintain DO levels above 5 ppm near the surface. This procedure greatly reduced sediment inflow into Brown's Lake at times when heavy rains made the main river channel turbid.

Fourteen radio-tagged bass used the Brown's Lake complex as overwintering habitat. (Six others either were harvested by anglers or were relocated during fishing tournaments.) Tagged bass remained in the Brown's Lake complex throughout December, but began leaving in early January as DO levels declined below 6 ppm.

By January 16, DO had dropped to 2 to 3 ppm in some parts of the canal system, and nine tagged bass had left the complex, leaving only five fish near the mouth of lower Brown's Lake. Five days after water flows raised DO to acceptable levels, six tagged bass were in lower Brown's Lake and several others had moved farther into the canal system, returning to areas that had been too low in oxygen a few days before. By January 28, 10 bass were back in the canals; and a month later, all 14 of the remaining tagged bass had returned.

As is typical of iced-over lakes, the coldest water was at the surface, the warmest in the depths. From mid-January on, oxygen levels were high in only the surface two feet, where incoming currents increased DO from 7 to 13 ppm. The temperatures within this level were 32°F to 33°F. From 2 feet to 6 feet deep, current was zero, DO ranged from 2 to 7 ppm, and water temperature was 34°F to 38°F. Below 6 feet, DO was 0.1 to 2.0 ppm, and the temperature ranged from 36°F to 38°F.

Other observations:
• The tracking equipment used did not allow researchers to determine the depth of the bass, but angler reports confirmed the assumption that bass were suspending to avoid water low in oxygen.
• The deep holes created by dredging lacked oxygen, and tagged bass did not use them. Apparently, this form of habitat enhancement was of little use to bass over-wintering in heavily silted backwaters with ice cover.
• Although over-wintering largemouth bass are known to avoid moderate currents, they remained near the mild surface inflows to obtain adequate oxygen, and they were willing to enter the stronger currents in the main river, when DO dropped below 3 ppm.
The research team concluded that the overall rehabilitation effort at Browns Lake was successful. They say dredging alone won't do the job, suggesting that flow controls also are necessary.

*Gent, R., J. Pitlo Jr. and T. Boland. 1995. Largemouth bass response to habitat and water quality rehabilitation in a backwater of the Upper Mississippi River. *N. Am. J. Fish Mngt.* 15(4):784-793.

DIVING WITH THE BASS: AN ANGLER'S PERSONAL RESEARCH

What researchers have learned through telemetry is useful to anglers, and it's not surprising that most of these researchers are anglers themselves. Typically, though, the main objective of government-sponsored studies is information on environmental issues, or data relevant to management of fisheries. Stan Gerzsenyi is a professional bass angler who conducts his research specifically to get an edge on the tournament circuit, although what he learns also helps biologists complete their picture of the lives of bass.

Gerzsenyi studies bass by scuba diving, a techniques others also use to supplement telemetry. As a young tournament competitor, Gerzsenyi started diving in the deep clear western lakes like Mead, Mojave,

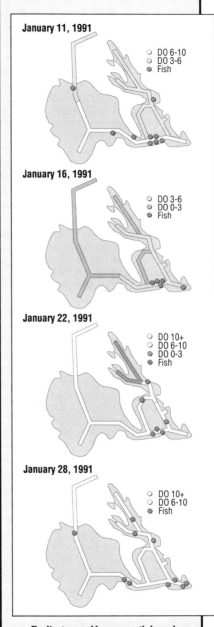

Radio-tagged largemouth bass locations and dissolved oxygen (DO) concentrations in Brown's Lake dredge canals, upper Mississippi River, Pool 13.

Winter Bass Movements, North Carolina

Dr. Rich Noble and Karle Woodward of North Carolina State University tagged 11 adult largemouths in E.B. Jordan Reservoir in the Piedmont region of North Carolina, and followed them from late October into the following May.

All bass were captured in a 23-foot deep bay formed by a tributary creek. Ten bass remained there throughout the study, though seven made occasional forays outside the bay. Water temperature ranged from 69°F in late October to 42° F in late December, before warming to 71° F by late April. At normal pool the bay has scanty cover consisting of sparse vegetation, small stickups, tree roots, and undercut banks.

As water cooled in the fall, largemouths reduced the size of their home ranges. One bass showed no detectable movement from early January through the end of March. It wintered in tree roots at the base of an undercut bank. Most bass shifted farther offshore during the coldest period, which ended in mid-February. When water temperatures climbed, the fish abruptly moved close to the bank. Once water temperatures rose in spring, the bass stayed near shore day and night.

When water levels rose 6 inches or more, bass entered areas with flooded shoreline bushes and trees, some moving at water temperature as low as 43° F.

Several of the largemouths established separate home ranges in winter, returning to the home ranges they'd used in the fall when the water warmed. As other studies have shown, individual bass chose home ranges and faithfully returned to them, though one bass was a wanderer and didn't establish a home range at any point. Late in the tracking period, several fish moved to suspected spawning locations and remained there.

The trackers followed the signal of one bass to an angler's livewell, where the sublegal fish (under 16 inches) was residing. As the researcher approached, the angler released the bass.

*Woodward, K.O. and R.L. Noble. 1997. Over-winter movements of adult largemouth bass in a North Carolina reservoir. *Proc. Annu. Conf. Southeast. Assoc. Fish and Wildl. Agencies* 51:113-122.

Havasu, and Powell. More recently he's observed bass in clear eastern waters, like the Great Lakes. When he's caught a few bass, he'll mark the site and dive to watch them; then he'll surface, cast to them, and submerge again to watch their reactions. Lately he's been experimenting with an underwater camera and video recorder, helpful in observing bass in murkier waters.

What he's learned has placed him repeatedly among the top anglers in the Anglers' Choice Pro-Am events and BASSMASTER events.

Finding Active Bass— Is finding bass difficult? Not really. Gerzsenyi observes lots of bass spread over any productive waters—the problem is that only about 10 percent of them are interested in biting. At times, just one or two percent are active, or as much as 30 percent when vulnerable prey get within reach of hungry bass. Usually, as in a special tree he visits in Lake Mohave, the only bass biting are those who leave their "resting" tree

and come out of cover. (John Hope's Texas bass behaved this way.) Neutral bass can sometimes be triggered to bite, but it's usually more productive to find more active bass.

Are bass cover-oriented?—Gerzsenyi, like many other observers, sees bass suspended near, but not in, cover, or even in open water. In the Great Lakes he's seen them holding on cracks in rock—just these darker lines satisfy their need for concealment. Cover is perhaps more useful to anglers as targets than it is necessary for bass.

Spawning depth—Like other observers, Gerzsenyi has found bass spawning as deep as direct sunlight can penetrate— at 20 to 25 feet in Lake Havasu.

Bass depth and movement—There are two tactics: they cruise along shorelines and contours at a constant depth, or move directly across open water, also at a constant depth. Others, too, have found individual bass holding at the same depth for hours, even days and weeks; different bass, however, are at different depths.

Schooling behavior—When smaller bass are feeding at the surface, larger fish trail behind them, and remain 5 to 10 feet deeper, without joining the surface action. Anglers looking for lunkers should forgo topwaters, and cast sinking lures a few feet behind the surface action, moving them with minimal action to imitate preyfish injured in the commotion above.

Lure action and striking range—Minimal lure action isn't always the answer; Gerzsenyi often jiggles his rod tip to make short jerky lure motions. He watches bass ignore many lures, and attack only those within easy range. Each fish seems to have a strike window, larger in front, smaller to the rear; the size of the window depends on the activity level of the bass. Prey and lures outside this window are generally ignored.

Bass are not all the same—Bass are individuals, some aggressive, some timid; they prefer different feeding times. Some feed alone, others in groups. All are opportunistic, ready to take advantage of any easy meal that comes along.

Gerzsenyi's observations were of bass in water with visibility at least 10 feet. Bass in murky water often avoid potential threats like divers before they can be seen. The behavior of inactive bass in murky water will remain a mystery until some biologist, tracker, or diver finds a way to observe and document it.

Chapter 8

Conservation Know-How

"But now the sport is marred, and wott ye why? Fishes decrease, and fishers multiply."
—Thomas Bastard, 1599

Bass Management Today

KEYSTONES TO BETTER FISHING

Anglers have always looked longingly back to earlier times when fish were larger, more abundant, more eager to bite. Fishing pressure isn't new, but the scale of the problem is radically different. On one hand, today's managers have the benefit of enormous amounts of accumulated research, improved technology, and increased manpower and funding. On the other hand, today's growing legions of anglers are armed with an enormous amount of knowledge and sophisticated fishing aids. Modern management is better than anything that has gone before, but it has to be.

This chapter looks at several key management areas—habitat improvement, stocking and fish genetics, and fishing regulations—and at some of the enormous changes, issues, and controversies in each area. Two critical tools in fish management, catch-and-release fishing and selective harvest, will be discussed in more detail in Chapter 11.

CONSTRAINTS ON MANAGEMENT

The future of fishing depends on more than the public fishery agencies charged with regulating fishermen and managing fish. It depends on the cooperative efforts of diverse groups—the angling public that enjoys recreation; commercial fishermen dependent on abundant edible fish for their livelihood; biologists employed by private and public institutions to study aspects of our environment; manufacturers of fishing equipment who rely on good fishing to sell gear; the outdoor press, which needs not only to entertain but to educate and keep communication open among all factions.

Anglers need to be aware of ways that managing agencies are limited in their attempts to sustain or restore fishing.

• Inadequate funding limits every fishery agency. Despite budget increases, there's never enough money to buy equipment and hire staff to conduct needed studies.

• Political pressures, including those from angler groups, sometimes force managers to make decisions that aren't justifiable on the basis of biological evidence.

• Bureaucratic inefficiency and inertia sometimes stymie sound management, although managers don't readily admit this. Progressive managers are too often forced by their superiors to execute and defend outdated policies.

• The best regulations can be so difficult to enforce that managers sometimes have to settle for policies they consider second best.

• Social traditions mold angler attitudes, and it's often difficult to change the way anglers think and behave. In fact, fish often respond to new management programs better than fishermen do.

There are three basic areas in which managers can work to influence fishing quality: environmental or habitat manipulation, stocking, and fishing restrictions. In each area, having enough knowledge is only part of the problem and solution.

HABITAT MANAGEMENT

Clearly, the best route to good fishing is to have healthy fish habitat where bass and other species can naturally reproduce and thrive. While it's relatively easy to improve fishing by manipulating habitat in small waters, it's difficult and unpredictable in large lakes and reservoirs. Money isn't the only problem. Modern managers also recognize that environmental alteration involves thorny political problems. What's good for bass might not benefit other species.

Theoretically, an infertile lake could be fertilized to promote growth rates, but fertilizing a single large lake, let alone treating many lakes, would be prohibitively expensive, and results are not predictable. Intensive weed management might benefit some lakes, but again the cost would be high. Severe water-level fluctuations hurt bass populations, but fishery managers have limited influence on the agencies that control dam functions. Nor can they prevent the wholesale destruction of fish by power plants.

No environmental manipulation has benefited bass fishing as much as the great boom in pond and reservoir construction during the mid-20th century. Such radical increases in the amount of fishing water won't happen again, so we need to learn to take care of the waters we have.

Ultimately, the safest and most realistic habitat program is protecting water quality and habitat that bass and other species require. Rather than managing waters intensively for maximum production of bass, agencies today are challenged to maintain basic environmental quality, to manage for the benefit of an entire ecosystem.

Anglers and angling groups can work with landowners on small-scale habitat improvements, such as managing ponds, restoring streams, and improving lakeshores. They can also become informed and vocal on the politics of environmental protection.

STOCKING AND FISH GENETICS

The more managers understand about stocking, the more they see limitations and errors that have thwarted management objectives in the past. Putting more fish in does not necessarily lead to more catchable fish. Former stocking

Too Much Emphasis on Hatcheries?

A fishery manager watched an irate resort owner drive away. The resorter wanted fish stocked in his lake after hearing complaints about poor fishing. The manager's efforts to explain natural reproduction, exploitation, harvest, year-class variability, and recruitment had fallen on deaf ears. The resorter had stormed out, threatening to call the governor.

The manager wondered at the lack of progress fishery professionals have made in communicating sound fisheries principles to the public. Meanwhile, the assistant manager was beginning his third hatchery tour of the day for a school group. The jars of eggs and big brood fish intrigue the youngsters.

Fishery professionals need to realistically assess the long-term costs of the way we do business. When the most significant public relations effort is a hatchery tour, the fishery manager has probably conveyed these messages: (1) fish come from hatcheries; (2) habitat degradation is so severe that naturally spawning populations are inadequate or no longer exist; and (3) long-term health of fisheries depends on hatchery technology.

Fishery professionals are quick to talk about the value of habitat protection, watershed management, and preserving the genetic integrity of native stocks—but when was the last time a school group was given a tour that emphasized habitat and genetic diversity?

It's easy to give hatchery tours. They get great reviews and give a fishery program visibility. The long-term costs, however, far exceed the dollars and cents of a cost-to-benefit analysis. The true costs appear later when the child has taken over his parents' resort, a poor year of fishing cuts profits, and he recalls the field trip to the hatchery. Is it so amazing that the resorter won't accept the fishery manager's reasons for not stocking fish?

Well-managed stocking programs have a place in fishery management, but only when they fit within a sound ecological plan that considers the integrity of the resource. Hatchery programs are not an excuse to accept habitat loss or poor management. They treat symptoms rather than remedy problems. Our resources need cures, not painkillers.

—*Tim Goeman, Minnesota Dept. Nat. Res.*

procedures sometimes wasted public dollars while actually degrading fishing quality. In some cases, few of the introduced fish survived to catchable size. Supplementary stockings have sometimes skewed populations toward too many little bass or have harmed native stocks.

Research has taught managers to consider the genetic impacts of stocking. Native fish are usually the most genetically appropriate fish for a given region, and attempts to improve bass fishing through stocking imported fish may destroy the genetic strength of native populations. Stocking to produce a few spectacular trophies can cause long-term genetic damage.

Is bigger better? Larger size doesn't increase the overall fitness of bass. Fish are compromises of many different selective forces. A 50-pound bass wouldn't have to worry about being eaten by an otter and could produce millions of eggs. But how many shiners would it have to eat each day? Could it catch any in a stumpfield or weedbed? By any standard, the mosquito fish *(Gambusia)* is a successful species—it grows, multiplies, and colonizes new waters—but it's rarely over 1½ inches long. Alabama is known for big bass; yet in the lower Alabama River, there's a population of largemouths that are fat and healthy but don't grow large. These characteristics must be advantageous in that environment, but no one knows why. We probably won't see them stocked anywhere else. Understanding fish genetics is the key to stocking the best possible fish.

Stocking is not a solution to most problems of depleted bass fisheries. It's primarily a tool to introduce bass into new waters or to increase bass populations in specific waters where reproduction is severely limited by environmental problems.

FISHING REGULATIONS

Since fishery managers generally have slight control over environmental factors and since native spawning bass are the most efficient stockers, fishing regulations are often the most effective form of management.

TRADITIONAL AND MODERN MANAGEMENT PERSPECTIVES

Many of today's managers were taught that fish populations are a renewable resource that can and should be exploited. While this concept is basically correct, managers have recognized that even a moderate amount of fishing can damage the structure of bass populations.

Maximum sustainable yield—This was the guiding principle of early managers; this guideline fostered activities to generate the largest harvest a fish population could sustain. In those terms, every harvested fish was evidence that things were going well. Released fish were "wasted" fish, poor use of a renewable resource. Creel surveys, which counted fish removed from the water, were the best measure of a fishery's productivity and therefore of the success of a management program.

The question of quality—As fishing pressure increased, anglers found they had to work harder to catch smaller and smaller bass, and they complained to managers. As managers began to probe the concept of fishing quality, it became clear that many anglers weren't interested in just catching or harvesting fish. They wanted an opportunity to catch big fish or to fish in a wilderness setting. "Quality" is a vague concept, but we'll use a simple definition that most bass fishermen can accept: a fine-quality bass fishery provides a fair chance to catch a number of good-sized bass with the possibility of hooking an occasional lunker.

As managers have accepted the responsibility of creating or restoring fine-quality fishing, they've had to change strategies. Instead of maximum sustainable yield, which emphasized high harvest and often contributed to low-quality fishing, managers began to talk about optimum yield.

Optimum sustainable yield—As visionary biologist Dr. Richard 0. Anderson noted, optimizing yield was a more challenging goal than maximizing yield because it involved social and economic factors as well as biological benefits. Yet today, optimum sustainable yield (sometimes called optimal yield, OY, or OSY) steers most modern inland fishery management programs. Managers and knowledgeable anglers recognize that a healthy fishery contains a balance of predators and prey. Each predator species should be balanced, with an appropriate number of large, intermediate, and small fish. Management for high harvest yielded large numbers of small fish at the expense of a healthy balanced ecosystem, and encouraged the removal of the most desirable and valuable fish. Optimum yield management promotes the health of fish populations, sometimes at the expense of harvest.

The threat of angling pressure—New perspectives were also necessary when managers confronted evidence that modern angling pressure is a major threat to bass populations. One source was In-Fisherman's Perch Lake study conducted in the late 1970s. Perch Lake is a typical bass-panfish lake in the upper Midwest, but it had received limited fishing pressure because of the lack of a good public access. The Minnesota Department of Natural Resources (DNR) granted permission for In-Fisherman staff to fish Perch Lake during the traditional spring closed season that protects prespawn and spawning bass. All fish were to be tagged and carefully released.

The study was to determine whether angling pressure could threaten the bass population in such a lake. By the DNR's estimate, 250-acre Perch Lake contained 1,600 bass over 12 inches. Three In-Fisherman staffers caught about 1,100 of those bass—nearly 70 percent of the lake's entire population of adult bass! Most of the bass were caught during the Prespawn Period. This showed that a handful of skillful anglers could wipe out the bass in a small lake in one season if they kept their fish and if bass in the Prespawn and Spawn period weren't protected.

Other studies confirmed the threat. Missouri fishery biologist Lee Redmond documented the 4-day catch of about 70 percent of the total bass population in a small impoundment. In another Missouri study, 1,550 bass were caught and released from a lake with an estimated population of 1,300 bass.

Some biologists believed these studies weren't pertinent to larger bodies of water, but that myth was soon dismissed. On Missouri's 7,800-acre Pomme de Terre Reservoir, biologists confirmed an annual harvest of 50 percent of the bass population. When West Point Reservoir on the Georgia-Alabama border opened to fishing in 1976, it had an excellent population of young bass. Under liberal fishing regulations, within two years West Point's virgin bass fishery was decimated.

Can modern angling pressure hurt fishing quality? You bet!

Downfishing—Traditionally, *overharvest* has referred to a fish population so badly reduced that the total harvest in pounds of fish drops significantly. *Downfishing* refers to the selective removal of larger fish. Lakes affected by downfishing are said to be *fished down*. Downfishing takes place long before a condition of overharvest can be documented. Overharvest is a term stemming from the strategy of managing for high harvest; downfishing, on the other hand, implies concern for fishing quality.

Habitat Management—Brushpiling

To improve fish habitat, management agencies often sink trees or brushpiles. For bass pro Alton Jones, building brushpiles is a way of life. Indeed, the perennial BASS Masters Classic qualifier from Waco, Texas, spends many a day each year meticulously cultivating subsurface entanglements in his favorite waters, sometimes amassing as many as 75 wooden heaps in one reservoir.

"Brushpiles attract bass because they create feeding opportunities where none previously existed. Baitfish begin using them as shelter soon after I plant them. More bait gathers as plankton growth begins and eventually flourishes."

Supply and demand dictates where Jones sinks his brush. "I put brushpiles in various types of lakes," he says. "The primary characteristic these waters share is their lack of abundant cover. If a lake has considerable cover, I sink brush in areas that lack cover," he says.

Alton Jones's Brushpile System

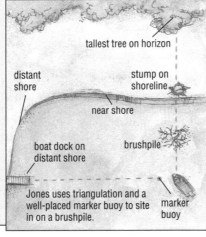

tallest tree on horizon

distant shore

stump on shoreline

near shore

boat dock on distant shore

brushpile

Jones uses triangulation and a well-placed marker buoy to site in on a brushpile.

marker buoy

The System—Jones has devised a system that creates optimal cover with minimal effort. First, he checks the policy of the water's governing body, making sure not to violate any law. If possible, he finds suitable shoreline trees near the spot he wishes to enhance and contacts the landowner, asking permission to thin his timber.

"I want a tree 20 to 30 feet tall, 6 to 10 inches in base diameter, with several thick limbs, so it will sink quickly and last a long time underwater," Jones says. He likes hardwoods—oak, mesquite, and elm. Each sinks unweighted and endures a watery existence well.

After spotting his target brush

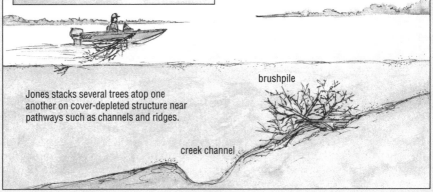

Jones stacks several trees atop one another on cover-depleted structure near pathways such as channels and ridges.

brushpile

creek channel

on the bank—preferably several suitable trees close to one another—Jones beaches his boat and cuts the trees so they fall toward the water. After trimming the trees a bit, he attaches one end of a 5-foot rope to the trunk via a slipknot, the other to the bow cleat of his boat.

Jones next backs his boat away from the bank, dragging the tree into deep water and letting it pendulum beneath as he wheels around and slowly heads out, tugging his take below the surface and alongside his craft. His undertaking is nearly undetectable as he motors toward a preselected drop spot.

"Choose an area along a migration route such as a channel, point, roadbed, or ridge," Jones advises. "Drop the brush on the tip of the point, for example, or right where a channel swings against a ridge."

A buoy placed to the side of his mark allows Jones to stack from three to seven trees atop one another, creating vertical cover that bass often use in many seasons and under various conditions. "If a 20-foot-deep brushpile comes to within 2 feet of the surface, bass can hold at nearly any depth shallower than 21 feet and still be in cover. They have more options and fewer reasons to leave," he says.

Indeed, Jones often must use his loppers to trim surfacing branches from the crowning tree of a new pile. He uses caution not to place high-reaching heaps in popular water-skiing areas.

Jones relies on triangulation—lining up objects along two different angles—as well as his depthfinder, photographs, and notes to locate his brushpiles. "The goal is to pull up, shut down, and reach the pile on the first cast. Idling over a spot before fishing it may spook the bass," he says.

Sow Now, Reap Later—"Bass don't magically detect new brushpiles, flock to them, and lock down immediately," Jones says. "Brushpiles begin holding bass six months after being submerged, reach their peak of production at roughly two years, then require periodic additions of new brush every year or two thereafter."

Jones does most of his work in fall and winter. Cool weather brings fewer inquisitive boaters and prying eyes. And trees that have dropped their leaves create far less drag in the water. Also, after being in the water for approximately one month, brush goes through a sour period of four to six weeks. Heaps made in late season begin holding fish by summer— prime time for brushpile bassin'.

Brushpiling Checklist:

Check local laws.
•
Get permission from landowners to cut.
•
Choose a safe place to pile brush, away from water-skiing areas.
•
Bring a bow saw, loppers, long pants, a long-sleeved shirt, gloves, eye protection, and a rope.
•
Use a depthfinder, marker buoy, GPS, camera, notes, and triangulation to locate and record brushpiles.

Dumb and Smart Bass

When a new water is opened to fishing, black bass usually are naive and easy to catch, but years of exposure to anglers appears to smarten them. Lures that once worked become less effective; innovative techniques and new lures are necessary for decent catches.

Researchers with the Texas Parks and Wildlife Department attempted to document whether some bass were easier to catch than others and whether this tendency was inherited. Project chief Dr. Gary Garrett placed 110 largemouth bass that had never been fished for into a research pond. Biologists then fished the pond, marking and releasing all bass taken.

After a month, the pond was drained and the bass sorted. Eight percent had been caught three or more times and were designated the "naive" or "dumb" group. The 22 percent that had never been caught formed the "smart" group. The groups were separated and allowed to spawn within their group.

Young bass produced by these matings were then tested by anglers. Offspring of difficult-to-catch parents were twice as likely to avoid capture as bass spawned by easily caught fish.

Of the second generation of naive bass, 12 percent were caught several times and only 17 percent avoided capture, a slight increase in the proportion of catchable fish compared to the parent stock. A second year of angling reduced the percentage of uncaught bass to 12.

When offspring of the original batch of "smart" bass produced young, 48 percent of this generation couldn't be caught even once. Breeding less-catchable bass increased the percentage of uncatchable fish more dramatically than breeding "naive" bass increased catchability.

As controls, bass from the same source that hadn't been fished for were allowed to spawn. Catch rates for offspring from these matings fell between the rates for the two extreme test groups.

These experiments support intuitive assumptions that catchability varies among individual bass. They also show that the catchability of fish is at least partly due to genetics.

Harvesting highly catchable bass is likely to reduce the tendency of bass in

Catch-and-Release—The first Catch-and-Release Symposium was held at Humboldt State University in 1977. There, several scientists argued that managers had to address the growing problem of downfishing and proposed catch-and-release regulations. The Bass Anglers Sportsman Society had initiated catch-and-release bass tournaments in 1971, but the success of catch-and-release management of warmwater fish like largemouth bass hadn't been sufficiently demonstrated. The first symposium ended with an urgent call for research. A decade later, at the second Catch-and-Release Symposium, biologists revealed abundant data on the topic.

The first issue was whether fish survived the trauma of being caught, unhooked, and released. Studies showed that bass are hardy: those caught on artificial lures and promptly returned to the water have at least a 95-percent survival rate. Research has also proven that the right catch-and-release policy or size-limit regulation can increase the numbers of catchable bass, boost catch rates, balance preyfish populations, and increase potential for trophy fish. Catch-and-release regulations have been successful on large and small lakes in many regions of North America.

that population to strike lures or bait. Even though catch-and-release is popular or required by special regulations, postrelease mortality of "naive" bass might shift the balance in heavily fished waters to include mostly hard-to-catch bass.

This study demonstrated no difference between sexes in willingness to bite and no indication of specific genetic factors that affect catchability. Catchable bass may be dumber or less likely to learn than uncatchable bass. Or they may have weaker vision or be more aggressive, less wary, or less choosy about food than nonbiters. In natural habitats, aggressive bass probably capture more food, grow faster, and spawn sooner than cautious bass. Catchable bass that we casually label "dumb" may be more successful predators and actually be the "smarter" fish in waters where anglers aren't a major cause of mortality.

Some anglers may be tempted to ask that hatcheries breed only catchable bass. This might improve catch rates initially but could be a serious mistake. Populations of easily caught fish can quickly be overharvested. Waters with naive fish require stricter harvest regulations than waters holding fish that avoid hooks and continue to breed.

Moreover, lunker bass grow large by avoiding capture year after year. It's unlikely that naive bass live long enough to create trophy fisheries. If a strain of easily catchable bass could be isolated and produced in hatcheries, the fish would be suitable only for no-harvest waters or put-and-take fisheries supported by regular stocking.

This study shows that angling harvest can shift the genetic balance in heavily fished populations. It gives us another scientific reason to practice selective harvest.

Voluntary release by anglers has also helped maintain good fishing.

Chapter 10 covers in more detail the politics and practical issues of catch-and-release fishing.

Length limits—Fishing regulations based on concern for maximum yield usually limited the number of bass an angler could take in a day; bag limits were intended to spread available fish among anglers. Concern for angling quality obliged managers to consider fish size as well. Length limits expose some sizes of bass to harvest pressure while protecting others. They have become an effective management tool for maintaining high-quality fisheries.

Length limits can take three forms. A *minimum length limit* means all bass below a designated size must be released. This protects bass populations that have poor recruitment, the process by which fish hatch and grow to catchable size. One example might be a strip pit with ample food, but little spawning habitat. A *maximum length limit* protects trophy fish where angling pressure has targeted them. This regulation, however, has rarely been tried on bass.

Big Bass Mean Big Bucks

Lake Fork in northeast Texas has produced 37 of the 50 biggest largemouth bass ever caught in Texas. Most of these lunkers over 15 pounds have been caught since 1990, due in part to a high and protected slot limit and abundant bass habitat. This productivity has kept Lake Fork a favorite fishing location for Texans and anglers across the continent.

To quantify the value of this fishery, the Texas Parks and Wildlife Department commissioned a study that questioned anglers about their opinions and expenditures. The survey estimated a total of 205,000 fishing trips to Lake Fork between June 1994 and May 1995. Seventy-four percent of the trips were by Texas anglers, who drove an average of 87 miles one way. Ten percent of the anglers were from bordering states, and they drove an average of 245 miles one way.

Expenditures at the 27,000-acre impoundment totaled $27.5 million, not counting economic multipliers that economists often use to estimate total economic impact. Eighty-eight percent of anglers targeted largemouth bass, followed by 9 percent who sought crappies. Forty-four percent of anglers had fished a tournament on Lake Fork, and 83 percent were reportedly seeking a trophy bass.

Fisheries chief Phil Durocher noted, "This study shows a constituency of anglers who want an opportunity to pursue a specific type of fishing experience, are willing to pay for it, and would like certain resources managed accordingly. If we managed this resource for the average angler, we might alienate hardcore anglers who help pay the bills there."

Direct Spending on Lake Fork Fishing Trips

Residence	Est. No. Fishing Trips	$ Spent in Lake Fork Region	$ Spent Elsewhere in Texas	$ Spent Outside of Texas	Total $ Spent
Local	27,953	1,242,790	202,100	-0-	1,444,890
Nonlocal TX	161,948	9,639,145	9,441,568	-0-	19,080,713
AR, OK, LA	11,714	3,422,830	466,100	612,057	4,500,987
Non-res.	3,124	1,479,995	528,800	455,323	2,464,118
Total	204,739	15,784,760	10,638,568	1,067,380	27,490,708

A *protected slot limit* requires releasing certain size ranges of bass. Much research has dealt with slot limits, potentially the most flexible tool for managing bass populations. A commonly chosen slot protects 12- to 15-inchers, but that's not the best regulation for many lakes. In lakes with high recruitment, a protected slot of 11 to 14 inches might be best. On lakes where anglers seem unwilling to harvest small bass, slots protecting 14- to 18-inch fish might work better. For slot limits to work, the bulk of the harvest must be bass below the low end of the slot, since reducing numbers of small fish increases growth rates. Angler reluctance to harvest small bass can turn a slot limit into a functional minimum length limit and make the limit ineffective as a means to produce more trophy-size fish.

Super Bass

"Our goal is to produce a largemouth bass that will exceed the current world-record weight of 22.25 pounds," states Alan Forshage, a biologist with Texas Parks and Wildlife Department. Forshage heads the "Operation World Record" a selective-breeding program being conducted at the Texas Freshwater Fisheries Center in Athens.

The program's origins lie with the ShareLunker Program (formerly Share A Lonestar Lunker), which acquires, for breeding, largemouth bass larger than 13 pounds. The hope is that mating offspring from unusually large bass will result in giant offspring. Now that many adult bass have been produced from the pairings, this genetic theory will be tested.

Forshage and his staff are arranging for private impoundments to house the bass, where harvest will be restricted. For habitat, they have selected nutrient-rich watershed lakes of at least 10 acres in East Texas to provide excellent feeding conditions for the bass.

Landowners must contract with the department for 15 years, allowing biologists to carry out their management plan. During the study, biologists will stock the previously fishless lakes, then regularly sample the fish population and remove some of the bass for research.

The hope is that mating offspring from unusually large bass will result in even larger fish.

In some cases, protected slots also restrict the harvest of fish over a specific large size to one per day. Harvest slots are yet another option, allowing anglers to keep fish only within an intermediate size range. *Harvest slots* have not been widely used in bass management. They may benefit populations with low recruitment and good growth rates, where increased numbers of large fish also are sought.

Selective harvest—Emphasis on catch-and-release doesn't mean only releasing. Fishing has traditionally involved keeping and eating fish, a practice that is entirely appropriate today if anglers make sound decisions about which fish to keep—depending on the species, the size, and the body of water they come from. Keeping smaller bass helps make slot limits work to improve the population. The best policy for the future is a practice we call selective harvest, discussed in Chapter 11.

Pond Angling and Management

Ponds are the most numerous fishing waters in the U. S. and can produce monster bass, as well as tiger muskies, and record crappies, pike, perch, catfish, carp, and buffalo. The key to angling success is good management. Find out how the pond you want to fish is managed, and then cooperate with the management plan.

If you're lucky enough to own a pond or two, or a place to build one, you can try your own hand at fish management. The boom in pond construction began in 1936, when the U.S. Agricultural Conservation Program gave farmers subsidies to build ponds. In 1934, the U.S. had an estimated 20,000 ponds; by 1965, the number had grown to 2 million. Subsidies are now reduced, but pond building goes on, for agricultural, aesthetic, and angling purposes.

Research and recommendations for pond management came from Alabama Polytechnic Institute (later Auburn University), and from the Illinois Natural History Survey—the southeastern and midwestern schools of thought. Dr. Dave Willis at South Dakota State University provides a northern perspective. There are regional differences, but many basics are the same.

You can manage a pond for bass only, a bass-bluegill balance (the goal of most pond owners), panfish, or big bass. Some of the management initiatives are major—stocking a new species or starting a fertilization program—but most routine management involves fishing. Selective harvest is essential to ensure continued good fishing and to prevent collapse of the miniature ecosystem.

TROPHY BASS

One theme in modern bass management is the importance of large fish. Because anglers often target and sometimes selectively harvest large bass, management plans must consider strategies to keep large bass in the water. That's a rather new idea. Managers once encouraged the harvest of trophy bass to prevent wasting the resource by releasing fish near the end of their lifespans. It was also incorrectly assumed that big bass weren't as important to spawning efforts as were midsized bass.

Progressive managers and anglers have a new perspective. Trophy bass have demonstrated exceptional ability to resist disease, avoid predators, and grow. They're fish that have successfully beaten incredible odds, and they're not quickly or easily replaced.

The glamour of big bass has encouraged some states to stock Florida strain bass or even conduct genetic experiments to create a "superbass." These programs aren't necessarily bad, but they represent a quick-fix approach to the challenge of managing for trophy bass. Trophy bass management should never detract attention from the basic need to manage for overall bass fishing quality. And the best way to manage for trophy bass is not to create them artificially, but to improve habitat conditions and protect large bass that develop naturally so they can achieve giant size. These are the true "superbass!"

CUSTOMIZED MANAGEMENT

No single management formula can be applied to every body of water. Regulations ideal for Florida will not necessarily work in Montana. In fact, an ideal management strategy for one lake can be detrimental to a neighboring lake.

Why? In addition to climate, two key variables are recruitment and growth rates. Growth rates are determined by food supply, lake fertility, genetics of the fish population, harvest rates, and the length of the growing season. Recruitment depends on spawning habitat and factors that determine how many young bass survive to adulthood. Factors like soil characteristics, size and shape of the basin, nature of the water supply, types of vegetation, and composition of the fish community all affect growth and recruitment, and vary among waters. Waters with differing rates of growth and recruitment may require different size limits to promote quality fishing.

Progressive management rejects focus on a single species. That is, rather than simply trying to manipulate bass numbers, managers study the whole lake community before attempting to alter the size structure of the population. Management policies that affect one species in a lake affect all other species. Fishing pressure must also be a consideration in management decisions; a lake near a large metropolitan area requires a different management plan than a remote lake.

Each body of water is unique and so presents unique management challenges. In some cases, regulations specifically designed for individual bodies of water maximize angling opportunities while also protecting bass populations. Where they have been used, special limits often have been successful. Communicating with anglers during the planning phases and with law enforcement becomes more challenging, however. And the success of custom management depends on adequate research.

ANGLER DIVERSITY

As managers pondered what their programs should accomplish, they began asking anglers what they expected, and they learned that anglers, of course, don't agree on what they want management to accomplish.

Sociologists and biologists now tend to categorize several groups of anglers. Skilled specialist anglers who prefer fishing for one species of fish often favor catch-and-release and put a high premium on a chance to catch trophy fish. Generalists who fish for several species, and for food, want large catches, prefer liberal limits, and like stocking as a management tool. Casual anglers who value a relaxing, hassle-free trip are the majority; they're typically content to catch small fish and favor liberal bag limits, but they're not likely to take a deep interest in management issues.

Surveys haven't measured the relative catch rates and harvest of these groups. Some managers assume most of the harvest is made by the numerous casual anglers; others assume skilled anglers making multiple trips take far more fish. Certainly skilled anglers, though fewer in number, create much of the fishing pressure and are more likely to try to influence management decisions.

At first, variability of anglers might seem too problematical. But instead of problems, management based on public preferences offers new opportunities. Because different lakes have different qualities, and because different angler groups have different expectations, the future of bass management is sure to involve special regulations that create a variety of angling experiences. Some lakes might be fly-fishing only. Others might be managed for trophy bass. Others might be managed to produce many small bass for fast, easy fishing.

Are Trout and Bass Anglers Different?

University of Massachusetts researchers Dr. Mike Ross and Dr. Dave Loomis* studied Massachusetts anglers to determine differences in attitudes and reasons for fishing. Almost all the anglers questioned fished for several species, though 48 percent favored bass and 33 percent favored trout.

Motivations for fishing were remarkably similar in the two groups. Bass anglers focused a bit more on recreation with friends and family, adventure and excitement, the challenge of catching large fish, developing new skills, and catch-and-release fishing. Trout anglers were more concerned with fish to eat and were more focused on the fish species they caught. Primary motivations were identical for the two groups, however—relaxation and being outdoors in natural surroundings.

Almost all the anglers questioned fished for several species, though 48 percent favored bass and 33 percent favored trout.

Ross and Loomis further divided trout anglers into wild-trout enthusiasts and those who preferred stocked waters. Again, the two groups had similar interests in fishing, although wild-trout specialists were less interested in social factors, instead focusing on challenges in equipment and catching fish, as well as favoring wilder surroundings.

Anglers who fished for stocked trout were only slightly more concerned with harvest than wild-trout enthusiasts, yet this motivation consistently ranked low in importance. The authors suggest that management agencies reexamine stocking rates, since angler interest and participation seem not closely linked to the number of fish stocked or the number caught. But they caution that fishing motivation in put-and-take trout fisheries may vary greatly among waters and regions.

*Ross, M. R., and D. K. Loomis. 2001. Put-and-take fisheries: investigating catch and retention assumptions. *Fisheries* 26(2):13-18.

CONTROVERSIES TODAY

Here's a brief look at the complexity of several issues that currently demand the attention of fishery managers and bass anglers. Solutions require balancing and compromising biological facts, public opinions, and political differences.

SPECIAL LIMITS

Special limits work when biologists tailor them to specific waters. State after state has tried special limits and proven them an excellent management tool whenever overharvest of larger bass is a problem.

In recent years, however, some states have been reluctant to apply tailored limits. Texas, where special limits have created or sustained world-class bass fishing, has only about 40 waters under special limits. The remaining 350-plus

Texas reservoirs have been slightly improved by a statewide 14-inch, 5-bass limit, but few of these waters provide angling as good as that created by more restrictive limits. Many of these waters could be further improved, but expansion of the special limit program has been slow recently, due to public opposition.

When special-limits were a new management technique, opposition came primarily from anglers who thought bragging rights, big stringers, and food were important angling goals. Sport-minded anglers, however, have convinced more and more of this faction that bass have greater value alive than as fillets or trophies.

Anglers who have difficulty understanding, remembering, or obeying complex rules also have resisted the complexities associated with special limits. This faction probably always will want game regulations to be as simple as possible, but many of them, too, have been won over by the improved fishing that special limits can provide. Nevertheless, state fishery agencies will have to compromise for the sake of simplicity. Perhaps, like Texas, they will use a standardized set of tailored limit options rather than giving each lake a unique limit.

The strongest opposition to further use of special limits now comes from some tournament bass anglers, once eager supporters of catch-and-release and special limits. They're an organized and informed lobby and advocate exemptions to length limits for tournaments—obviously a controversial idea, which we'll look at in the next chapter.

No one likes over-regulation—but there are only two alternatives to accepting catch-and-release and biologically beneficial length-limit regulations. The obvious one is to accept a continual decline in fishing quality. If catching bass becomes increasingly difficult, and if the bass caught are too small to be interesting, bass fishing itself will become an endangered sport, because the rewards won't justify the effort. Many people contend that this has already happened in some regions. The other alternative is where it's clear that bass fishing is damaging bass populations, managers might be forced to impose harsh limits on anglers' access. For example, a fishing license in the future might entitle an angler to 15 days of fishing.

We love to fish and encourage others to do so, so we don't want to even contemplate the prospect of limits on fishing opportunity. Ultimately, it seems far more desirable for anglers to accept sound harvest limitations.

WHEN LIMITS DON'T APPEAR TO BE WORKING

Fishery managers have used tailored length and bag limits to create and sustain better bass fishing in many states. But some states have revoked restrictive limits when studies show declining growth rates, reduced recruitment, or bass in poorer condition. Any of these effects sometimes has been used as an indicator that a limit wasn't working.

Modern fishery management aims to improve bass fishing by sustaining larger populations of good-sized fish, usually through the application of appropriately tailored length and bag limits. In the past, fishery biologists had aimed to produce the maximum number of fast-growing recruits. This seemed necessary, because anglers unrestricted by limits quickly removed most of the large bass from fisheries near population centers. Years of managing waters for high production of bass conditioned many fishery managers to believe growth and recruitment were key management factors. They can be, usually when heavy harvest is encouraged.

Although data are limited on unfished natural waters, old fishing photos show that productive waters held mainly large bass and few recruits. Why? Because recruits weren't needed. What's more, the large fish weren't fat. After hundreds of years, unfished natural waters tended to reach equilibrium at carrying capacity. Adult bass and preyfish typically were in balance, although the balance might shift from year to year, when a large excess of prey spurred fast growth and created fat adults. High recruitment of juvenile bass probably was rare. At maximum density of adult bass, little room remained for recruits. The size of the spawn, therefore, was relatively unimportant, and almost all fry and fingerlings produced became fish food for adult bass. Natural mortality, not fishing mortality, set the need for replacements.

When adult mortality is high, an average of one or two fry from each nest must be recruited to adulthood to sustain the population size. But if significant numbers of adults live for 6, 8, 10, or more years, only 1 or 2 fry from their lifetime of spawns need to survive to adulthood.

General rules for fishery managers suggest that abundant prey produces fast growth, fish in good condition (fat fish), and maximum spawning potential. A food shortage yields slow growth, skinny fish (with little stored body fat), and reduced spawning potential. And the more adult fish in a water, the better the fishing. The problem is that the densest populations are near capacity and exhibit slower growth, thinner fish, and low recruitment rates due to heavy predation (although spawns may be large). These waters don't need recruits.

Capacity bass populations don't need numerous recruits and fast growth. Special limits that work usually reduce the growth rate and condition of fish. Occasionally, a biologist recommends removal of the limit because of too many fish, too little food, slow growth, and a worsening fish condition. When the objective of management is to provide good fishing rather than to maximize harvest, a maximum number of good-sized bass must remain in the fishery.

Of course, we don't want fisheries with starved and emaciated fish or fish that are too small. A limit that creates stunted juveniles needs revising. But managers must accept bass in moderate condition, fewer recruits, and slower growth to produce reasonably high catch rates for quality-size bass.

If growing trophy bass is the sole management goal, only bass that surpass 20 inches or more should be protected. Harvest of small bass should be encouraged. Though such a fishery would produce some giants, catch rates would be low and steady recruitment would be needed.

A problem with this management plan is that excess fat and overly rapid growth seem to shorten the life span of bass. The football-shape largemouth bass from Braunig Lake in Texas, where a massive excess of prey exists, die after reaching 21 to 23 inches and 8 to 12 pounds. Braunig produces trophies, but not record-sized fish. Lake Fork, where a 14- to 21-inch slot limit maintains a near-capacity population of slower-growing bass in average condition, cranks out far more giants than any other Texas water.

Most anglers prefer to fish waters holding lots of good-sized bass for plenty of action. The bass should be in average or better condition, which places the population slightly below capacity. But fishing pressure on a good fishery causes a moderate mortality rate due to handling and hooking injuries. This, plus natural mortality, should stabilize the adult population at a level where a few recruits survive and adults aren't too thin.

Biologists must ponder whether or not slow growth rates and reduced condition are appropriate by-products of special limits. The assumption that poor recruitment and slow growth are indications of limit failure should be reexamined. When a water has a capacity population of large adult bass, it doesn't need many recruits. Slow growth and reduced condition aren't necessarily problems. They may be indicators that prey and predator populations are balanced and that the limit is meeting its primary objective—a fishery full of good-sized bass.

SHOULD WE FISH FOR SPAWNING BASS?

Fishing for bass on their spawning beds—the idea makes some anglers' eyes light up; others are repulsed by that idea. The social aspect of this issue involves both personal ethics and strong regional traditions. Anglers in Ontario or Minnesota might oppose opening the bass season as strongly as Floridians would oppose closing it. Even a scientific consensus is lacking: do bass need to be protected during the Prespawn and Spawn periods?

Certainly bass are most vulnerable then. During In-Fisherman's Perch Lake study, two anglers in one boat caught and released 80 prespawn bass in less than three hours. It's common for 50 percent of the annual bass harvest to take place during spring (February through April in the South, March through May farther north).

Large bass are especially vulnerable when they're shallow early in the year. A Texas report of the 50 largest bass ever caught showed that 58 percent were caught in February or March. Florida guides who once guaranteed 10-pound bass by targeting big spawners are all out of business, because they removed too many trophies that require a decade to replace under optimal environmental conditions, even in Florida or California. As the number of big bass rises again in these productive waters, it's hoped that more stringent bag and size limits will be enough to protect them.

Still, even professional fishery managers disagree about the desirability of protecting bass in spring. Some of the differences are regional. Because of the short growing seasons in the North, it may take 12 years to produce a 5-pound bass. Under ideal circumstances, bass can reach that size in 5 or 6 years in southern waters. Competent biologists contend that fast growth rates in the South allow bass to replenish themselves without the protection of a closed season. In Florida, for example, spawning may take place from December into May, while many northern bass populations complete the spawn in a few weeks, making bass there far more vulnerable.

It's not just the impact on adult bass that's at issue. The success of the spawn and recruitment can be affected. Large bass are particularly early and fertile spawners. Big males are the most effective guardians of nests, and although they aren't feeding, they'll often strike anything resembling a nest predator. Catch-and-release isn't an easy answer, either; studies of spawning smallmouths in Ontario show that holding a male away from the nest for even two minutes gives nest predators time to move in and eat eggs and fry. Released males are more

Early Season Bass Fishing in Michigan

Black bass have long been protected by a closed season in New York, Minnesota, Michigan, parts or all of several Canadian provinces, and Pennsylvania (though a catch-and-release spring season has recently been enacted there). In Michigan, the popularity of bass fishing has grown tremendously. At Pontiac Lake, for example, the proportion of anglers targeting bass rose from 7 percent in 1951 to 39 percent in 1980, 67 percent in 1988, and 71 percent in 1990. This trend has led biologists to explore ways of expanding bass opportunities, including early season bass fishing.

Biologists with the Michigan Department of Natural Resources experimentally opened six lakes to catch-and-release fishing from April 1 until the normal bass opener on the Saturday of Memorial Day Weekend.* They conducted surveys of angler opinion about this experimental regulation as well as checked catch rates. Effects of fishing on recruitment also were checked by sampling bass in the fall by electrofishing.

Anglers contacted both during the special early season and the normal bass season were overwhelmingly supportive of the measure. Eighty-two percent of respondents approved of the early season, while 94 to 97 percent of more frequent bass anglers approved. Over 80 percent reported that they released most legal-length bass they caught during the traditional bass season. The questionnaire also revealed that over 40 percent of anglers had targeted bass during the closed season in prior years.

Although spring fishing effort increased by about 40 percent, total annual fishing effort didn't increase during the experiment. And the spring bass catch was modest. Catch rates for largemouth bass were lower than during the traditional open season, while catch rates for smallmouths were considerably higher in 4,150-acre Muskegon Lake, the largest smallmouth fishery in the study.

Electrofishing showed adequate numbers of small bass in fall following the fishing season, and no effects on recruitment were noted. The biologists felt that the catch-and-release spring season could be expanded to more lakes in southern Michigan. To further expand such regulations, however, the legislature would have to grant regulatory power to the Department of Natural Resources, a power the legislature now holds. This shift of power may delay further expansion of the spring catch-and-release season.

*Schneider, J.C., J.R. Waybrant, and R.P. O'Neal. 1991. Results of early season, catch-and-release bass fishing at six lakes. *Michigan Dept. Nat. Res. Tech. Rept.* 91-6, Ann Arbor.

Anglers contacted both during the special early season and the normal bass season were overwhelmingly supportive of the measure.

Closed Bass Seasons

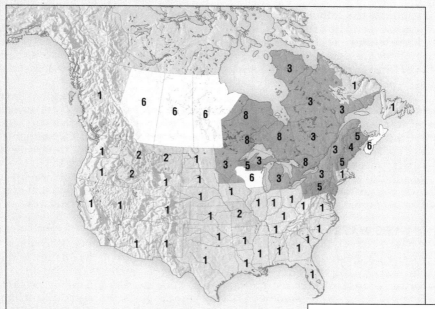

1	year-round bass season
2	year-round bass season with exceptions
3	statewide/provincewide closed season for bass
4	reduced harvest during spring
5	catch-and-release only during spring
6	closed fishing season for all species or for all gamefish
7	season opens in early spring
8	season varies among regions

The seasonal regulations of states and provinces reflect the conservation concerns of their jurisdictions, intertwined with regional traditions and perceptions. The southern United States is solid in allowing year-round bass fishing. In Missouri, a traditional closure is in effect on Ozark streams from March 1 through May 29. Regulations in the West are similar, but with more exceptions. In several states, waters are closed seasonally or are catch-and-release only in spring.

In the Northeast, a diversity of regulations exist, from an extended closed season in New York to year-round fishing in Massachusetts. Pennsylvania recently joined New Jersey, Vermont, New Hampshire, and Maine in imposing a catch-and-release or reduced-harvest regulation in spring.

Canada also presents a patchwork quilt of regulations; four of the eight provinces have closed seasons for all fishing, generally extending from the beginning of April to mid-May. Ontario is divided into 34 Conservation Districts, with regulations that include a long closed season in eastern Ontario, an open season in northwestern Ontario, and catch-and-release regulations on other waters. New Brunswick has a catch-and-release season in spring, and British Columbia allows year-round bass fishing, except on one lake with a catch-and-release season.

In the Midwest, little agreement exists. Minnesota and Michigan have spring closures, while most states allow year-round bass fishing. Northern Wisconsin has a catch-and-release season, while southern Wisconsin has a 2-month closure for all gamefish (March 1 through the Friday before the first Saturday in May).

The topic is receiving more attention from anglers and biologists concerned with maintaining the quality of bass fishing.

likely to abandon the nest as time between capture and release increases. Largemouths haven't been studied as rigorously, but researchers have found that Ontario largemouths react similarly to handling and removal from nests.

It gets even more complex. Closing a season for several months can result in high catch rates once the season opens; strict size and bag limits may be necessary. Evidence seems to indicate that protection of prespawn and spawning bass is warranted in some northern regions, although spring catch-and-release seasons have been tried successfully in several states.

It would be politically impossible to close the bass season in states that have never had a closed season and where spring bass fishing is traditional and brings in big tourism money. It's also possible that a closed season wouldn't help keep big bass abundant and isn't necessary for adequate recruitment. Experimental closed spawning sanctuaries in Florida's Lake George produced no difference in the abundance of young bass compared to areas with year-round fishing.

Ideally, the effects of catching spawning bass, whether for harvest or for release, should be addressed on a lake-by-lake basis. Practically, it's a regional matter, with most protection in eastern Canada, the Northeast, and upper Midwest.

THE WEED WARS

"Weed control is the biggest fishery management problem of the 21st century," say some administrators whose pessimism is in proportion to the amount of the exotic weed hydrilla they have to deal with. Most research has focused on bass fisheries, because of the heavy infestations of exotic hydrilla and milfoil in many reservoirs. No matter what solutions technology develops, the most difficult hurdles will be the conflicts among various user groups, who too often are unwilling to give an inch.

Underwater vegetation provides superb cover for bass. Good bass management requires effort to promote plants but limit their area coverage.

Some bass anglers, for example, feel that underwater vegetation is always good for fishing, and they've organized to fight against plant-control programs. They've made exaggerated claims about the potential harm of chemical treatments to drinking water quality and fish health, the importance of vegetation to fisheries, and the desirability of exotic weeds like hydrilla and Eurasian milfoil. Some anglers have even tried to introduce exotic plants where these weeds are absent.

Unfortunately, the role of water weeds in bass fisheries isn't so simple, and the introduction of hydrilla or Eurasian water milfoil into some waters is a gross mistake, wasting millions of dollars and man-hours in subsequent control efforts. It's also illegal in most areas.

On the other side, state vegetation-control agencies and reservoir and power plant managers sometimes label all exotic plants "infestations" and proceed as if total eradication were the only choice. They may concede that some aquatic plants can improve fisheries, but they insist that all underwater vegetation should be native species. They refuse to consider the possibility that sometimes the benefits of exotic plants might outweigh potential harm through eradication by chemicals or stocking of grass carp.

When using chemicals, some weed-control agencies have ignored the possibility of partial or selective treatments, instead resorting to major herbicide treatments at times of the year when massive weed kills are likely. Homeowners' demands for cleared shorelines, boat lanes, and swimming areas might better be accomplished by periodic mechanical harvesting or limited use of chemicals. More laws may be needed to prevent private, irresponsible use of herbicides or grass carp by lakeshore property owners. Moreover, some state agencies use fishing license funds for weed clearing, when homeowners or the general public should instead pay. The possibility that weeds should be left alone to benefit the greater majority who fish is typically ignored.

The situation is, of course, more complex than partisans in heated controversies admit. In most waters, underwater weeds are a mixed blessing. Plants sometimes benefit bass fisheries and sometimes harm them, particularly when coverage exceeds 30 or 40 percent of the surface area. Moreover, some plant species are more beneficial than others. A desirable plant in one lake may be undesirable in another.

Biologists try to keep vegetation out of small, intensively managed impoundments. These waters, where bass harvest is tightly controlled, are usually more productive and easier to fish without vegetation. In small waters, it's easier for weeds to blanket the lake and damage fish populations. In larger systems, however, weeds protect fry, fingerlings, and juvenile bass and may help prevent a heavy bass harvest.

If few bass are harvested, few recruits are needed, and protective cover isn't as essential. Vegetation monopolizes the nutrients entering a fishery, so the absence of vegetation allows more plankton to grow, shortens the food web, and supports more and faster-growing adult bass at the top of the food pyramid.

Research has shown that public reservoirs in Texas that contain 15 to 30 percent weedcover produce more bass than reservoirs where weeds are scarcer or more abundant. This finding can be misleading, however, for the research involved impoundments at a time when overharvest was encouraged by liberal size and bag limits, and only thick vegetation protected adult bass from overharvest. When vegetation is removed without a change in harvest pressure or stricter regulations, the bass population often declines because it becomes more vulnerable to harvest.

Anglers who insist that hydrilla and other thick weeds create better bass fishing are reporting their experiences accurately. They aren't, however, evaluating the cause-and-effect relationship accurately. If a strict limit prevents overharvest of bass as effectively as does dense vegetation, then reservoir bass populations can be as strong or stronger after vegetation is removed. But if biologists inform anglers that they must learn to fish differently after the weeds are removed, the advice may rankle them.

If, however, a reservoir contains competitive predators like white, hybrid, or striped bass, the increase in pelagic prey and the decrease in sunfish that often accompany vegetation removal may result in a switch to dominance by pelagic predators and a decrease in numbers of black bass. Bass must be both abundant and the dominant predators to make the switch from edge feeding around vegetation to feeding in offshore schools.

The primary reason bass anglers hold exotic vegetation in reverence is the tremendous boost that older reservoir have received when vegetation has taken hold. Fishery managers face major problems as reservoirs age. Here's a typical reservoir evolution: (1) an explosion of fish life takes place in the years following impoundment, (2) woody habitat rots away, and this lack of cover, along with increased turbidity, reduced primary productivity, and perhaps overharvest, causes a slump in bass fishing, (3) reintroducing or establishing vegetation, even an exotic species, may be the best way to rejuvenate these bass fisheries.

Hydrilla and Eurasian water milfoil may not be the most desirable plant species, but they're here to stay, and sometimes they are better than nothing. When turbidity limits the establishment and growth of native plants, these exotics may survive. Native species can then sometimes be reintroduced after exotic plants have reduced wave action, controlled excess silt, and increased water clarity.

In reservoirs that still have substantial wood cover, or a healthy bass population due to length limits, exotic weeds offer no advantage and are soon a substantial nuisance to other users of shallow water. When hydrilla was found in Lake Walter F. George (Lake Eufaula) or John H. Kerr (Buggs Island), cooperative efforts were sought to eradicate it. Biologists and ecologists agree that annihilation of large growths of vegetation is not a good practice, whether as a result of herbicides, grass carp, or natural conditions like floods. Rapid change affects water quality and is a shock to the aquatic ecosystem.

States that have separate weed- control and fishery management agencies should unite them or better coordinate their programs so that vegetation control doesn't conflict with fishery management. Perhaps the key need is for agencies that control vegetation to realize that eradication of exotic weeds is extremely costly, politically dangerous, and likely damaging to the fishery. And in most cases, the vegetation returns quickly. They should refocus efforts on programs that manage and control problems

Angling Pressure Makes a Difference

The overharvest of adult fish ruins fishing quality. But is harvest the only problem? Or is high fishing pressure a concern even when anglers don't kill many fish?

Fishing pressure apparently does reduce fishing success even if the fish are released. A study done at the University of Illinois* compared catch rates from identical ponds containing the same number of adult largemouth bass but subjected to different amounts of fishing pressure. The catch rate dropped from 2.99 bass per hour in the pond under light pressure to 0.35 bass per hour in the pond under heavy pressure. The bass became harder to catch as they learned to avoid fishermen's offerings.

Researchers also compared the catch rates in ponds subjected to the same amount of pressure but containing different densities (numbers) of bass. As expected, the catch rate increased from 0.11 bass per hour in the pond with the least bass to 1.61 bass per hour in the pond with the most bass. It takes a lot of bass in the water to provide good-quality fishing.

Light pressure and dense fish populations combine to provide good fishing. Heavy pressure and low fish populations provide poor angling. Fishermen, of course, like going where fish are dense and "naive" and fishing is fast, but they are working against themselves. Pressure then increases and fishing declines, particularly if harvest thins the population.

Fishery managers thus face a paradox. If they make fishing better, a body of water draws more pressure and fishing quality declines. Each body of water can eventually reach a point where population density and pressure are balanced. Further management efforts may not produce obvious improved results. Don't expect more than is possible, given the productivity of the water and the number of anglers who use it.

*Mankin, P.C., D.P. Burkett, P.R. Beaty, W.E. Childers, and D.P. Philipp. 1984. Effects on population density and fishing pressure on hook-and-line vulnerability of largemouth bass. *Trans. Ill. Acad. Sci.* 77(3-4):229-240.

---

created by excessive vegetation, rather than waging war on all exotic weeds regardless of their role in fish habitat. They should acknowledge and appreciate exotic vegetation when it's beneficial.

More cooperation and understanding among all parties would be helpful. When weed-control advocates disparage the claims of anglers that hydrilla improved their favorite bass fishery, they deny what bass anglers "know" is true. They would create less animosity if they acknowledged these claims, while urging more protective harvest limits to protect bass exposed to overharvest when large amounts of weeds are removed.

Bassers don't like the way vegetation-control agencies overtreat vegetation.

They want to see restraint and a balanced ecosystem approach to aquatic management. But similar restraint should be used by anglers who promote hydrilla and other exotic vegetation as bass habitat and attack any use of herbicides.

Chemicals are effective and can be safely used if properly applied. Mechanical weed harvesting has often been expensive and inefficient in controlling dense growths. Grass carp, on the other hand, are so effective that weed control can become weed eradication. Perhaps new technologies will help. Biologists at the Corps of Engineers' Waterways Experiment Station in Vickburg are even experimenting with injecting rotenone pellets into grass carp to program them to die in four years, leaving, say, 20 or 30 percent vegetation. It's not yet known if that idea is practical. The station is a think tank for weed control and tries to stay out of controversies among user groups.

Exotic weeds offer benefits and drawbacks. This is a situation that calls for compromises and carefully worked solutions, rather than a political face-off. There is no one clear, right answer to all vegetation-control problems and needs.

BASS MANAGEMENT IN A NEW MILLENNIUM
BLACK BASS 2000

Black Bass 2000, a four-day symposium convened in St. Louis in conjunction with the 130th annual meeting of the American Fisheries Society, was the first major meeting to examine the biology and management of black bass since the one held in Tulsa in 1975. Organized by fishery geneticist Dr. Dave Philipp of the Illinois Natural History Survey and bass researcher Dr. Mark Ridgway of the Ontario Ministry of Natural Resources, it attracted hundred of biologists who study and manage bass in North America. The proceedings were published by the American Fisheries Society in 2002 in a massive volume that provides diverse looks at the world of bass management.

"Genetic conservation" seeks to preserve the genetic background of native fish.

Just a few of the topics included:

• the negative effects that bass introductions can have on native species. We bass fans tend to think our favorite fish can do no wrong, but it's an aggressive and opportunistic predator that can markedly alter entire ecosystems. There is more management emphasis on protecting native species.

• we are able to obtain a much clearer understanding from examining ecosystems for decades, rather than for just a few years. New techniques for studying microhabitats important to bass will also be important.

• the need for genetic conservation in bass management.

• biological and social aspects of bass tournaments.

Given the substantial changes in philosophy and knowledge since 1975, we probably won't have to wait another 25 years for an update.

BENCHMARKS IN BASS MANAGEMENT

A look at the evolution in bass management since the 1970s shows rapid changes in policies and procedures. To summarize some of the major achievements:

Stricter harvest regulations—Liberal size and bag limits encouraged maximum harvest of bass. During the 1970s, studies showed that fine-quality bass fishing was best produced not by heavy spawns or stocking but by dense populations of adult bass. Stricter limits were enacted to prevent overharvest of adult bass.

Voluntary catch-and-release—Scientific studies suggesting that release could sustain good fishing were popularized in magazines and at conferences and contributed to a new conservation ethic. Bass anglers began to release most of the fish they caught—in fact, today managers must educate anglers on the need to selectively harvest bass in some situations.

Federal aid in sportfish restoration—2000 marked the 50th anniversary of passage of the Dingell-Johnson Act, a self-imposed excise tax heralded as the best example of a user pays-user benefits program in U.S. history. In 1984, the Wallop-Breaux Amendment expanded the "Sport Fish Restoration Act," with new excise taxes on tackle, equipment, and fuel, and since then over $5 billion has been spent on fishery programs, enabling more research, public education, management, and access development.

More science in management—Decades ago, scientific study of fish, fishery management, and predator-prey relationships was mostly limited to universities. Meanwhile, the heads of fishery agencies often were political appointees; biological staffs were small and decisions often politically inspired. Today, agency staffs have increased, and research findings usually are the basis for management decisions. Social science has also begun to play a role in decision making.

The future—There's much unfinished business. We need to learn to sustain the productivity of impoundments. Management for trophy-sized bass raises questions. Habitat remains the key to bass population success, but we lag in ability to manage habitat. Fishery managers must be accomplished politicians as well as scientists, able to balance interests of diverse groups. We need to inspire today's youth with a love of the outdoors and fishing. Finally, we need to find ways to make nonfishermen pay their share of water management costs.

A trend that must continue if managers are to meet the challenges of providing fine-quality fishing in the future is the increase in cooperation among fishery managers, other regulatory authorities, and angler groups. For example, although managers can't force the Corps of Engineers or other agencies to regulate water flows to enhance fisheries, respectful communication has increased voluntary cooperation. Many cooperative projects have been launched between fishery managers and fishing clubs, national fishing organizations, community groups, and private businesses to improve fishing. We need more of this. The Fish America Foundation, associated with the American Sportfishing Association, has spearheaded countless projects beneficial to sport fisheries and habitat by coordinating local organizations, state agencies, and volunteers.

Achieving better mutual respect and communication between anglers and managers is one of the most urgent missions of In-Fisherman. The progress we've already seen is one of the most promising indications that good bass fishing will be available for future generations.

Bass Tournaments

TAKING IT TO A NEW LEVEL

Bass are popular just because of the kind of fish they are—sporty, challenging, and widely available. Yet there's no doubt that the bass's popularity is also dependent on its status as a tournament fish. Tournaments have influenced bass fishing by:

- popularizing bass fishing and making the bass a media star.
- creating pro bass anglers. In their roles as educators, professional athletes, researchers, and tackle promoters, they have exerted a powerful influence on American fishing.
- advancing the art of bass angling by bringing the most skillful bass anglers in the world to events where they can continue to learn from one another.

• advancing development of new designs and technologies for rods, reels, lines, lures, boats, and more.

• educating thousands of anglers in advanced bass fishing techniques.

• promoting conservation, including catch-and-release and better management of bass stocks.

At the same time, tournaments are a sensitive topic and sometimes inspire controversy. Because of this, the impact of tournaments on the quality of bass fishing is well researched. This chapter looks at both the contributions of tournament angling and the controversies around it.

A HISTORY OF BASS TOURNAMENTS

The bass evolved into a tournament fish largely through the work of Ray Scott, the founder of Bass Anglers Sportsman Society (B.A.S.S.), probably the most influential person in the history of bass fishing.

There were a few organized tournaments before Scott's. The first in our records, an invitational at Lake Whitney, Texas, was held in 1955, organized by angler and outdoor writer Earl Golding. The event was transformed into the State Bass Tournament of Texas in 1956 and has been held every year since then. The first interstate bass tournament was apparently held in 1957; Hy Peskin, a sports photographer, initiated the World Series of Sport Fishing. Competitors had to prove their skill in

The First Bass Tournaments

Legendary angler Virgil Ward won the 1962 World Series of Sport Fishing held on Fort Gibson Lake in Oklahoma.

Ray Scott emcees the 1968 Lake Eufaula National.

lesser tournaments or qualify as "pros," a category that included outdoor writers, lure manufacturers, and fishing tackle representatives. The championships were held on mid-American reservoirs, which favored bass anglers, although other species were eligible. Legendary angler Virgil Ward won the 1962 World Series of Sport Fishing held on Fort Gibson Lake in Oklahoma. A dozen women fished in the 1962 finals, with guides provided to drive them about in small aluminum boats with vintage kickers. In the finals, 70 anglers vied for the title from 6:30 a.m. to 5:00 p.m. As in the earliest tourneys of the Bass Anglers Sportsman Society, no attempt was made to release fish alive. Instead, they were donated to charities.

Ray Scott, a young Alabama insurance salesman, organized B.A.S.S. in 1967; boldness and entrepreneurial flair characterized his organization. Scott saw the potential popularity of a circuit of bass tournaments that would be above scandal. He also saw the need to go beyond tournaments to build a federation of bass clubs. By the mid-1990s, the B.A.S.S. Federation network had grown to over 2,000 clubs that sponsor tournaments, informational meetings, youth activities, charity events, and conservation work. The net effect is a huge organized interest in bass.

In addition, many clubs not affiliated with B.A.S.S. offer similar programs, and today there are many other well-run circuits and tournaments. Women have their own bass organizations. The original was Bass'n Gal, a tournament circuit, club, and magazine organized in 1976 by Sugar Ferris and no longer active. Their tournaments produced highly skilled anglers who obtained sponsorships and endorsement contracts from manufacturers. Today, the Woman's Bass Fishing Association (WBFA) is the foremost women's bass tournament circuit.

TYPES OF BASS TOURNAMENTS

Tournaments are organized on several different principles. *Club tournaments* are grassroots events providing an opportunity for camaraderie and for less experienced anglers to fish with skilled anglers in a competitive but friendly atmosphere. Competitions leading to formation of a B.A.S.S. State Team use a blind-draw format. Officials even avoid pairing contestants from the same town.

The *draw tournament* pairs two anglers who must share the boat, fishing locations, and time allocations since they are competing between themselves as well as with the rest of the field. Draw tournaments are common in bass clubs, state championship events, and were used through the 2001-2002 season in BASSMASTER Open events held across the United States.

Team tournaments increasingly dominate the competitive fishing scene. In their favor, they are fun, and some raise a lot of money for charity; they let anglers fish with compatible partners, and they keep fishing spots more secret. They are criticized, however, for defeating the purpose of angler education, making it hard for newcomers to do well, and hurting the industry by making it harder for anglers to advance. They also are more susceptible to cheating.

Since their origin in 1987, *pro-am tournaments* have been very popular with amateurs, and some attract far more applications than available spots. Amateurs find the learning experience and the comradeship with top local or national pros very rewarding. Pros have also been enthusiastic, whether at the top level of angling in the CITGO BASSMASTER Tour events and the Forrest L. Wood (FLW) tournaments, or in the Bass Fishing League (BFL; formerly Redman and Golden Blend) and other local and regional circuits. Pros have full control of the boat and location. Usually the pros' and amateurs' catches are kept separate, but in some events such as the Western Outdoor News (WON), their catches are combined in a team total. The number of amateurs who have entered pro ranks proves the educational value of these tournaments; the number who plan to buy a GPS unit after using one with a pro partner shows how they benefit the fishing industry.

Big bass tournaments vary from casual bass derbies sponsored by a local bait shop or chamber of commerce to events drawing thousands of anglers for prize money over $50,000. They frequently raise money for charities and include spectator events. In the case of large weekend events, polygraph tests are often administered, and good livewells and live releases are mandatory.

For the last three decades, biologists and tournament organizers have strived to find ways to ensure successful release of tournament-caught bass.

KEEPING TOURNAMENT BASS ALIVE

The catch-and-release ethic came to North America via trout fisherman Lee Wulff in the 1930s. Fishing pressure was hurting New England trout fishing, and rather than advocate stocking hatchery trout, Wulff separated the idea of catching fish from killing them. "Gamefish are too valuable to be caught only once," he wrote. The idea was slow to catch on outside trout fishing circles. In 1971 Ray Scott attended a trout fishing conference and decided, "If it's that much fun to let a 10-inch trout go, think what a thrill it would be to release a 6-pound bass."

The move to catch-and-release at Scott's tournaments was motivated by political shrewdness as well as conservation ethics. Some local anglers expressed resentment at these groups of hotshot anglers swooping in on their lakes and killing "their" fish. So why not give them their fish back? Scott began rewarding anglers for keeping their fish healthy; aerated livewells began to appear in boats; B.A.S.S. tournaments were scheduled to avoid the hot weather that increased bass mortality.

THE RESEARCH

Dozens of studies have addressed the mortality of bass in tournaments. In general, reported survival rates have increased over time, as anglers have become more aware of the need for good care in livewells and tournament boats have grown in size, with increased livewell capacity and better aeration. Most tournament organizers also have tried to modify weigh-in procedures to reduce stress on bass. Yet even the most recent studies have found tournament mortality over 40 percent in some events, particularly during summer in southern waters.

Gene Gilliland, a research biologist with the Oklahoma Department of Wildlife Conservation, conducted an investigation of factors that cause lethal levels of stress and of ways that anglers can alleviate these problems. Gilliland's familiarity with bass tournaments, gained by his years of competition, produced the most concrete advice to date on keeping a catch alive and healthy.

Gilliland first worked with tournament organizers to standardize weigh-in procedures, which typically vary from event to event. When water temperatures exceeded 72°F, ice blocks were used to cool holding tanks at weigh-in sites by about 10°F. Salt was also added. Standardized procedures then allowed Gilliland to compare how different treatments in boat livewells affected bass survival.

Bass boat livewells vary in design, size, and aeration equipment. In Gilliland's study, a group of participants were instructed to operate their aerators continually or at the maximum setting. Another group treated their livewells with ice and salt, while constantly running their recirculating pumps. Some used livewell treatment chemicals. Preliminary tests had found that adding three 8-pound blocks of ice over the course of a day to a 25- to 30-gallon livewell holding 15 pounds of bass cooled the livewells from 85°F to 75°F. Each time a block was added, half the livewell water was replaced with fresh 85°F water to reduce metabolic wastes. Trace chlorine in the ice blocks had no negative effect on fish and might actually have reduced infections. As a control, biologists collected bass by electrofishing and then subjected them to standard weigh-in procedures.

Initial mortality at spring and summer tournaments was low, averaging 1.6 percent in spring, increasing to 4.1 percent in summer. Delayed mortality told a different tale, however. Total mortality in spring events averaged 2.9 percent with a high of 5.1 percent, while mortality in summer averaged 33.6 percent with a maximum of 43.3 percent. Almost 11 percent of tournament-caught bass showed signs of bacterial or fungal infections after a 6-day holding period, while fewer than 2 percent of the electroshocked bass appeared infected.

Dead-Release Tournaments

Next year? Same time? Same place?

Major tournament promoters have applied the lessons learned from early tournaments and can achieve a high survival rate—90 or even 95 percent for a well-run tournament when water temperatures are cool to moderate. But too many tournaments don't have such acceptable results. In Alabama, researchers placed 242 largemouth bass from eight tournaments at Walter F. George Reservoir in holding tanks, along with 33 control fish collected by electrofishing.

After four days, the control bass experienced only a 3 percent mortality rate, but the bass caught by tournament anglers showed a 25 percent mortality. Add the average death rate of 8 percent before weigh-in, and the total loss was 33 percent.

What went wrong? Studies have long shown that successful live-release events are held when water is cool, not in an Alabama summer. Six of the eight tournaments were held between June 29 and September 8; at four, the air temperature was over 90° F. None of the contests required chemical conditioners in livewells. Two did impose penalties for dead fish, but the many tournament judges fail to penalize anglers for sick fish that were likely to die later.

Events where bass were held in bags for more than 10 minutes had the lowest survival rates, including one with 52 percent mortality. One of the worst events lacked a recovery tank—the fish were presumably released directly into the lake.

What did the fish die of? In this study, a variety of bacterial infections. Almost all had reddish abrasions around their mouths; many also had ragged fins and abrasions on their sides. Much of this obvious damage is attributed to holding cages, but it may also have been caused by landing procedures or fish being bounced into the bottom of a boat. Infections were concentrated on external surfaces. Control fish carried the same common pathogens, but the stressed tournament fish were less able to resist them.

The tournament organizations are not identified in the study, but the descriptions suggest they were local contests rather than events staged by experienced national tournament groups. These contests gave lip service to live release, but the well-known procedures necessary to make release work were not in place. All the research and advice are useless unless they're followed.

Studies of fish physiology have shown that stress is additive. A combination of adverse factors, none sufficient to cause death itself, easily combine to create deadly levels of stress. Stress incapacitates the fish's immune system, leaving it open to various infections.

Dissolved oxygen (DO) levels in livewells at weigh-in time seemed related to bass mortality. Bass from livewells with more than 6 parts per million (ppm) dissolved oxygen suffered 35 percent mortality in summer, but when DO was less than 6 ppm, bass suffered 51 percent mortality. Nearly 60 percent of the boats that ran aerators constantly had more than 6 ppm oxygen. Oxygen levels in boats with recirculating systems averaged 6.7 ppm, while those without averaged 3.9 ppm, a stressful level. The value of constant recirculators became obvious at a tournament where the weigh-in was held 19 miles from the water, with boats trailered. Overall, the best livewell conditions (water temperature and dissolved oxygen level) and the highest survival were from boats using chemicals, constant aeration, and ice. During summer, however, even this group showed an 18 percent total mortality rate.

A surprise was that 53 percent of the bass that died in the holding areas didn't float, as is often supposed. In a natural system, turtles or other scavengers would probably have eaten the dead fish, leaving little surface evidence of mortality.

Summer tournaments in warm weather clearly imperil bass, but anglers using the best equipment in a conscientious manner can lower bass mortality. In Oklahoma, 75 percent of tournaments were held from October through May, keeping the number of summer events low. For summer tournaments, shorter fishing hours or multiple weigh-in sites improve bass survival. An even better choice, however, would be paper tournaments, where fish are measured and immediately released.

Another study was conducted in Alabama by Ken Weathers and Mike Newman in 1997, examining immediate and postrelease mortality during summer tournaments at Lake Eufaula. Mortality rates varied from 9 to 64 percent, and the mortality for the largest bass caught averaged 47percent. Their recommendations to anglers and tournament managers are similar to Gilliland's:

• maintain a low bag limit and impose penalties for dead fish.

• no more than 50 anglers should weigh in during a 30-minute interval.

• hold bass in water-filled plastic bags for no more than 10 minutes before weigh-in.

• holding tanks with sufficient dissolved oxygen and water conditioners should be used to replenish bags while waiting to weigh in, and after weigh-in to hold bass momentarily before release.

• water in holding tanks should be no more than 15 degrees cooler than lake water.

• use rubber nets or tubes with flowing water, and return bass to the lake quickly.

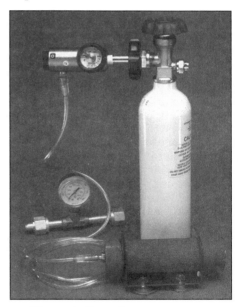

The cost of running pure oxygenation is just a couple pennies per hour, as the small onboard tank will provide supersaturated oxygen for several days and can be easily refilled from a larger tank or at a welding shop, fire station, or hospital.

• air temperature during weigh-in should be less than 85° F.
• boats must have aerated livewells, which should run constantly. Fish should not be crowded. Livewell treatments, including salt and commercial formulas, aid survival.

The latest breakthrough in keeping tournament bass alive is the use of pure oxygen in livewells. Carefully crafted systems use a small tank, oxygen regulators, tubing, and porous stones or micropore tubing to boost dissolved oxygen levels as high as 22 percent. Gene Gilliland tested the Oxy-Edge system designed by David Kinser and found that tournament-related mortality was reduced to 7 percent during blistering hot conditions (108°F air temperature and water temperatures from 82 to 95°F). In comparison, continuous flow-through livewell systems produced 22 percent mortality, and timed aeration had 32 percent mortality. Water must be added periodically to reduce ammonia wastes, but the supersaturated oxygen seems to drastically reduce stress in fish.

RELEASE OF BASS FROM DEEP WATER

Catching bass from deep water presents additional problems. Many experienced bass anglers have seen bass suffer trauma and expanded air bladders when brought to the surface from deep water. Some expect harm to bass only when fish are taken from water 50 feet or deeper, but the greatest pressure changes and much physical harm take place in the top 30 feet of water.

When pulled up from 25 feet or more, some adult largemouth bass of average size show overinflation after a few minutes in a livewell. Larger bass have even less tolerance for pressure change, sometimes showing bladder expansion a few minutes after being hooked at just 15 feet. Bladder expansion is only one symptom of pressure damage. In severe cases, organs rupture, tissues tear, and gills and blood vessels hemorrhage. Deep-caught bass undoubtedly suffer higher postrelease mortality than those taken in shallow water. Interestingly, observations suggest that spotted and smallmouth bass are less prone to decompression problems when caught at intermediate depths, 15 to 40 feet or so.

Damage to deep-water fish wasn't much of a problem in the days of large bag limits and catch-and-keep bassing, but it is an ethical problem now. It isn't ethical or legal to waste bass by releasing them in damaged condition, unable to swim away or unlikely to live. To do so is "wanton waste," an ecological crime in most states. Still, in many states, size limits force release.

Texas had to modify a special crappie limit when anglers fishing deep water in winter were releasing large numbers of small crappies that floated away and died on the surface. It's likely that many bass anglers have watched small (or slot-sized) bass struggle on the surface after mandatory release. Rather than expand the bag or size limit, some states have qualified limits that allow one or two otherwise illegal bass to be kept, hoping anglers will use this permission to keep bass that otherwise would die.

Many states don't have rules preventing continued fishing for catch-and-release purposes or culling after a legal limit accumulates in a livewell. Culling or releasing deep-caught bass without proper treatment wastes fish and could harm populations.

HANDLING DEEP-CAUGHT FISH

Deep-caught bass should be released as rapidly as possible and never held in livewells to be released later, except during tournaments. The longer that depressured bass stay at surface pressure, the more tissue damage they sustain. Held for pictures or weigh-ins, they quickly lose the strength needed to swim back down on their own.

One technique that makes it possible for deep-caught fish to survive a trip to the surface is *fizzing*–depressurizing them by piercing the gas bladder with a small hypodermic needle. In one study, untreated bass released into considerably warmer water suffered 78 percent mortality, while all fish that were fizzed and placed in warm water survived.

For bass that show loss of equilibrium in the livewell, recent observations indicate that clipping a lead ice-fishing "fish finder" on the anal fin or on each pelvic fin helps bass swim normally. Fish can equalize pressure over several hours but will suffer greater stress if they cannot remain upright.

It's asking too much to expect tournament organizers to schedule events only when bass are typically shallow or to limit contestants to fishing shallower than 20 or even 10 feet. These groups can, however, make sure that they are able either to safely deflate all floating bass before release or lower them in cages to be repressurized before release. Tournament organizers should be prepared to fizz bass any time many fish are likely to be caught deeper than 15 to 20 feet

ETHICAL BEHAVIOR

Until state fishery agencies find appropriate and workable solutions, ethical fishing behavior rests with individual anglers. Where legal, sportsmen should keep and eat bass likely to die after release, and release only those fish likely to live. To facilitate healthy releases they should become proficient at "fizzing" bass with a needle or use safe-release cages.

When a bag limit has been harvested, sportsmen should stop fishing deep water. They must not cull smaller, deep-caught fish to make room in a limit for larger fish. While culling is a time-honored practice among tournament bass anglers, it violates both ethical and tournament rules if harvestable fish are wasted by the process.

The few long-term postrelease mortality studies to date haven't examined in detail the mortality of deep-caught bass; we need more data to understand the extent of mortality. If deep-water mortalities are high, we may need to voluntarily limit the depth below which we fish. Enforceable regulations that could protect the resource, allow continued fishing, and satisfy anglers are elusive. How well deep-caught bass are protected is likely to remain a question of personal ethics.

SPECIAL LIMITS AND TOURNAMENT FORMATS

In the early days of modern fishery management, tournament anglers supported catch-and-release fishing and special limits. Now the strongest opposition to further use of special limits comes from some tournament bass fishermen, who see slot limits, small bag limits, and high size limits as hindrances to their competitive sport.

Particularly objectionable are rules that limit the number of large bass held in livewells. To ban holding lunker bass seems incompatible with tournament competition. Also, many competitors feel a bag limit of at least five bass is necessary to demonstrate fishing proficiency and to rank and reward more successful anglers. They feel strict limits de-emphasize skill and can make winning more a matter of luck.

These competitive anglers might reconsider whether keeping existing tournament formats is more important than improved fisheries. Organized bass clubs and national tournament associations have disproportionate power. Participating anglers often are better informed, better organized, and better able to apply political influence than noncompetitors. They also have disproportionate influence on

the media and the opinions of other anglers. Their views and protests can prevent fishery managers from taking needed actions based on biological data and
from being responsive to the needs of all segments of the angling public.

One solution? Change the format of tournaments. Ethical competitors who
want the best possible bass fishing for everyone should petition tournament organizations to use modified formats. For club contests, competitors can adopt a

---

Fizzing Bass

To learn more about the short-term and long-term effects of fizzing on
largemouth bass, researchers at Southern Illinois University pressurized bass in a hyperbaric chamber to pressures equivalent to those at
depths down to 34 feet.* They fizzed some fish with an 18-gauge hypodermic needle, left some untouched, cut ⅛-inch diameter holes in the gas bladders of some, and performed a sham operation on some that replicated the
incision without puncturing the gas bladder.

Some bass were returned to their accustomed experimental temperature
of about 57°F, while others were returned to water more than 20 degrees
warmer, to simulate effects of tournament anglers catching bass in deep,
cool water, then holding them in much warmer livewells.

Bass pressurized to the equivalent of only 11 feet showed signs of positive
buoyancy, swimming at a downward angle when pressure was reduced to
match surface pressure. At pressures equivalent to 18 to 28 feet, increasing
numbers of bass floated on the surface when brought to surface pressure.

Untreated bass released into cool water did not die but remained floating for more than 6 hours. In a lake, many would die from bird or turtle
attacks or from sunburn. Untreated bass released into considerably
warmer water suffered 78 percent mortality. All fish that were fizzed and
placed in warm water survived.

The fizzing was easily accomplished. With some experience, workers
could deflate bass in less than a minute, with no mortality or damage from
incorrect insertion of the needle. They inserted the hypodermic needle 3 to
5 scale rows below the lateral line, on an imaginary line between the spiny
and soft dorsal fins and the anal vent. Angling the needle upward toward
the spine invariably pierced the gas bladder, and bubbles emitting from the
submerged bass indicated relief from pressure.

Observers noted that bass deflated with an 18-gauge hypodermic needle were able to regain neutral buoyancy immediately after fizzing, so the
tiny hole didn't disable the gas bladder. Fish with larger holes cut in the
bladder held on the bottom for the first day and were less affected by pressure changes, indicating that their bladders were dysfunctional, but after a

---

paper-fishing format. Bass clubs with limited monetary prizes have for years
used "fish-for-inches" to benefit from the excellent fishing at special-regulation
lakes and to reduce tournament mortality.

Big money and national tournament groups might experiment with other formats that would allow them to fish lakes with special limits and allow immediate release. Measuring boards and Polaroid cameras with date-time inserts could
be used to document bass caught. Video cameras with live broadcasts to central

Needle Insertion for Relieving Pressure.

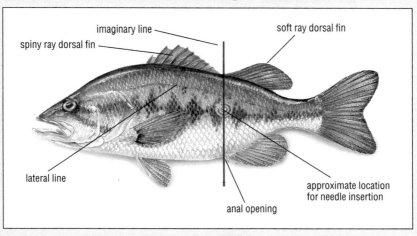

A study at Southern Illinois University suggested that tournament organizers should be prepared to fizz bass if many fish are likely to be caught deeper than 15 feet.

Draw an imaginary line from the notch separating the spinyray and softray portions of the dorsal fin, downward to the anal opening. Insert an 18-gauge hypodermic needle 3 to 5 scale rows below the lateral line along this imaginary line. Angle needle upward toward the spine.

day and a half, they returned to normal behavior. Dissection revealed that their gas bladders had resealed, leaving only a small area of inflammation.

Some fizzed and untreated bass were held for four weeks to check long-term survival and growth. No fish died, and growth of the two groups was nearly identical. The researchers concluded that fizzing was beneficial whenever bass show signs of depressurization problems, particularly in tournaments, where these problems are exacerbated by holding fish in livewells.

While pressurizing largemouth bass for the experiment, researchers found the maximum rate that bass could be pressurized without causing positive buoyancy was 6 inches per hour. This suggests that bass gradually increase internal pressure when moving to deeper habitat. It would take most of a day for bass holding at 10 feet to acclimate to the 20-foot level.

* Shasteen, S.P., and R.J. Sheehan. 1997. Laboratory evaluation of artificial swim bladder deflation in largemouth bass: potential benefits for catch-and-release fisheries. *N. Am. J. Fish. Mngt.* 17 (1):32-37

viewing areas also could document catches and releases, letting spectators watch contests from start to finish, as in other sports. Organizers might even consider having no limit on the number of caught-and-released bass. This format would let the best anglers fully display their skills.

Perhaps the most immediate solution, however, is for tournament associations to ask for and for fishery agencies to grant, permission for competitors using optimum livewell systems to hold live fish for weigh-in and mandatory

Timing the Bass Bite

ADVICE BASED ON COMPUTER ANALYSIS OF 8,000 BASS TOURNAMENTS
Some anglers fish whenever they have a chance; others select times likely to be most successful. Intensive study of tournament fishing provides an opportunity for statistically valid comparisons. Dr. Carl Quertermus, professor of biology at the State University of West Georgia and an avid angler, analyzed data for 8,178 tournaments on eight northern Georgia reservoirs from 1978 to 1998, comparing fishing across the months and between day and night.

All tournaments were club competitions associated with B.A.S.S. and had a 12-inch minimum size limit throughout the study period.

Dr. Carl Quertermus analyzed over 8,000 bass tournaments to define peak fishing periods.

release, even though holding these fish for harvest would be illegal.

Some fishery managers in Texas and other states are afraid such permission will be seen as favoritism, and they anticipate negative public response. They fear that separate catch-and-keep and catch-and-release limits would be almost impossible to enforce. In Florida and California, however, special permits allow competitive anglers to hold more than a harvest limit of large bass for weigh-in and subsequent release, and they seem to be working. No significant public

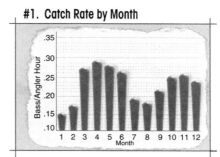

#1. Catch Rate by Month

The catch rate, winning weight, and unsuccessful angler data all suggest that bass are more vulnerable to angling during spring and fall. If fishing success is measured by average bass weight, however, the cold months are best, in all eight lakes studied.

Particularly in summer in the southern states, many bass anglers prefer to fish at night, and many believe night-fishing is better. Quertermus compared fishing success in 677 daytime tournaments with 758 night tournaments during July and August.

#2. Winning Weight by Month

Overall, there was no distinct difference between day- and night-fishing. Some differences appeared in individual lakes: four were equal day and night, two had slightly better catch rates by day, and two were better by night (on the order of one more keeper bass per angler in 10 hours of fishing). Lakes with a large percentage of spotted bass showed another difference: largemouths were easier to catch in daylight, spotted bass at night.

There was no correlation between catch rate and moon phase, but catch rates were slightly higher during apogee—when the earth and moon are farthest apart.

#3. Average Bass Weight by Month

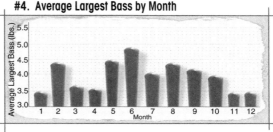

#4. Average Largest Bass by Month

outcry has arisen, and the needs of tournament anglers have been accommodated. Competitors there should no longer have reason to resist additional special limits.

In Texas, however, experimental tournaments at Lake Fork that allowed competitors to hold large, slot-sized bass showed substantial mortality. Outcry from local guides and anglers ended the push for exemptions to length limits, at least at Lake Fork.

THE FUTURE OF TOURNAMENTS

Bass tournaments continue to grow in popularity, with more events attracting more anglers. Some data suggest that the number of bass anglers remains rather constant, so a higher proportion of bass anglers appears to be fishing competitive events.

Even in areas where the bass traditionally wasn't a status fish, like the upper Midwest, New England, western states, and the mid-Atlantic region, the number of bass tournaments has increased. In core bass fishing states, participation is higher than ever. Agencies are now more involved in monitoring tournaments through voluntary report systems or mandatory permits, to assess participation and catch. In Georgia, the number of tournaments under B.A.S.S. Federation auspices grew from 500 in 1982 to about 1,100 in 1997; angler participation rose from 9,100 to 15,700. In Oklahoma, participation hit an all-time high with 45,795 participants and a sharp increase in the number of weekday evening "jackpot" tournaments. In Oklahoma, biologists use tournament data on total weight and average weight of fish caught to rank the health of bass populations in various reservoirs.

Interestingly, all these competitive anglers are not slicing up a finite pie into even smaller pieces; catch rates and bass size have remained rather constant or have increased over the years. This shows that catch-and-release works, and tournament anglers as well as noncompetitive anglers recycle bass over and over.

Clearly, tournaments have changed the nature of bass fishing, with increases in knowledge, efficiency, and gear. They have influenced its whole style. Because successful bass pros are so visible, thousands of other enthusiastic anglers model themselves after them. In some states, one in five bass anglers competes. Others, though they never fish tournaments, still own a collection of graphite rods, a boat that costs as much as a modest house, and plenty of high-tech electronics. Other anglers may resent or misunderstand those no-expense-spared fishermen who roar around lakes, wearing jackets covered with patches.

High-tech anglers aren't the only good bass fishermen. Some top-notch bass anglers spurn the high-tech approach. Betty Thurmond, one of the most accomplished anglers with live shiners, doesn't look like a tournament pro; her boat's not flashy, and she's usually barefoot, but her stillfishing expertise has made her one of the most respected guides for large bass. "Lunker" Bill Murphy, renowned big bass expert from California, favors a small aluminum boat and a relative handful of tackle for his pursuit of giant fish. Doug Hannon, the "Bass Professor," often wears an old campaign hat that looks like it came from a Goodwill shop, and fishes from a small metal johnboat that looks more like a duck

The competition of tournaments has revolutionized boat building technology, along with other aspects of the fishing tackle industry.

New Bass Tournament Format

Despite the successful use of "witnessed measurements and releases" by Bass'n Gal at Lake Fork several years ago, major tournament groups have rejected the idea, claiming that the excitement of weigh-ins is necessary. The immediate-release tournament seemed doomed until recently.

The managers of the *Honey Hole* magazine and tournament organization devised measurement backgrounds that identified the specific day and allowed the measurement of fish to ⅛ inch for subsequent conversion to equivalent weights. In October 2001, participants in a Texas-wide Top-Six Competition were given dated measurement boards and cameras for each day of the tournament at Lake Fork. Fork has a 16- to 24-inch slot limit that forces the immediate release of bass that would be tournament winners at most other lakes.

Anglers weighed in and measured in 1,304 pounds of bass of which 589 pounds were slot bass. Without the measurements and camera verification, the larger fish wouldn't have counted. Texas fishery personnel were pleased with results that showed the photo-measurement system would work on lakes with special limits. Biologists also gained valuable information on bass population structure at Lake Fork.

The reaction of participants was favorable. The conversion of photo images to weight values apparently provided ample excitement at the weigh-in,where under-the-slot and over-the-slot bass were weighed.

Tournament formats could be modified to support immediate capture, evaluation, and release of fish to maximize postrelease survival while presenting television images to viewers. Televising on-board measurements or the conversion process using photos could create national TV interest.

The use of verification photos has an important secondary benefit. Tournament fisherman no longer will need to resist the application of special limits on waters that could be improved by more intensive fishery management.

boat than a bass boat. His low-profile approach has as much to teach as the frenetic high-speed approach of tournament anglers.

Hannon confesses to a certain nostalgia—"I remember the fine feeling of being able to fit all the lures I owned into one tackle box." At some time in the early 1970s, he says, bass fishing began to change. "The proliferation of high-dollar tournaments brought large numbers of relatively expert fishermen to the virtually untapped fish populations of our southern reservoirs. This produced images of sometimes thousands of pounds of bass hung on bragging boards, with the empty-sounding caption that they would be donated to charity."

That stage produced a quick backlash and a rapid change to strict catch-and-release regulations. The no-kill ethic dominated. "The industry succumbed to the stranglehold of the big tournament organizations and stopped directing their

Are Tournament Fishermen Different?

In 1992, Texas researchers* surveyed 95 bass club presidents, 322 licensed freshwater fishing guides, and 1,180 licensed black bass anglers. One of the 47 questions in a self-administered questionnaire was about participation in freshwater fishing tournaments. Of those responding, 18 percent answered yes, while 82 percent said no.

Tournament participants were on average older (44 versus 39 years), more avid (40 versus 19 fishing days per year), and more likely to belong to fishing clubs (35 versus 5 percent). Tournament anglers generally were more supportive of management initiatives like special limits but less likely to support a tournament-permit program (41 versus 64 percent).

Freshwater guides averaged 122 days per year on the water, club presidents 74 days, while "average" anglers fished 23 days. Guides averaged 27 years of experience, while both club presidents and "average" anglers had about 20 years. Guides and club presidents gave stronger support than average anglers to a proposed rule requiring release of some bass over 21 inches long by limiting the number that could be harvested per year.

When asked whether they supported organized bass tournaments in Texas, the general fishing population split 50 percent for and 50 against. About 68 percent of guides and 96 percent of club presidents supported contests. Most bass anglers supported a tournament-permit system and a portion of tournament fees to support the management of bass waters.

advertising toward the casual angler who fishes for reason other than competition.

"When," Hannon asks, "is the last time you saw a full or even half-page ad in a major outdoor magazine for a fish cooker? Make no mistake, I still believe the release of most of our rare outsized fish is necessary to preserve the gene pool and the predator and prey balance. I haven't intentionally killed a bass over 4 pounds since 1973. But the bass world rightly includes many folks who fish with family and friends for the enjoyment of the experience and a satisfying meal of fresh fish."

The everyday angler, however, has not been ignored in another development in bass fishing—the knowledge explosion. The tradition of the In-Fisherman Communications Network has been to bring to readers tournament skills, fishery science, and the practical and theoretical wisdom that improve fishing techniques, knowledge, and ethics. This fosters interest among a wide variety of people who appreciate the sport in many different ways. Anglers today have available not just books and magazines, but videos, radio and TV, the Internet, interactive computer games, and moving 3-D maps. Both technology and communications have mushroomed, and not just to the benefit of any one user group. Bass anglers include the professor fishing inner-city lakes from a canoe, the traveling salesman with a belly boat in the

But 69 percent of club presidents opposed permits and 53 percent opposed mandatory fees for tournaments, even when all fees were targeted for fishery management.

Overall, the preferences of competitive anglers reflected their interest in management measures that increase bass size and number of trophy bass. Noncompetitors preferred more diverse management, based on their more varied use of fisheries and angling expectations.

All surveyed groups favored regulations customized to specific waters instead of standard statewide regulations. All three groups wanted more lakes with 14- to 21-inch slot limits, with guides constituting the strongest supporters. About 39 percent of average anglers reported they were "very" to "extremely" satisfied with black bass fishing in Texas, while 58 percent of the guides and 63 percent of club presidents were highly satisfied.

The survey finds support for stricter limits that improve fisheries, but it reveals considerable diversity among anglers. Some diversity is due to the different ways anglers use fishery resources and to different amounts of information available to various groups. Guides, bass club leaders, and tournament competitors likely read and study more about fisheries management and are more likely to be involved in political issues involving fish. Average anglers, on the other hand, may consider fishing an incidental activity, giving it limited attention.

To gain public acceptance of new management programs, fishery agencies must tailor their public information programs to varying users, just as they tailor management rules to specific fisheries and specific users of those fisheries.

*Reichers, R.K., G.R. Wilde, R.B. Ditton and M. Fisher. 1993. Comparison of demographic characteristics, attitudes, and management preferences of tournament and nontournament black bass anglers in Texas. *Annu. Proc. TX Chapt., Am. Fish. Soc.*, 15:6.

back of his station wagon, the bass fly-fisher, the rancher who dug 32 stock dams and lets polite strangers fish all but one, and the kid who rushes home from school to make a few casts before supper.

"Keeping Bass Alive," published by the Bass Anglers Sportsman Society in 2002, is the most complete reference on safe tournament operations.

BEYOND CATCH AND RELEASE

Fishing has been revolutionized in recent decades, by techniques and fishing ethics. Simple rods and reels, two-tier tackle boxes, and rowboats have yielded to space-age tackle, a mind-numbing variety of lures and gadgets, and boats that almost fly. Fishermen have learned to catch enough fish to make a difference in every environment; they realize it, and some old traditions are disappearing. Stringer shots are no longer acceptable; keeping trophy after trophy has given way to releasing the big ones to thrill other anglers.

Catch-and-release was the watchword of the 1980s and 1990s, a generation's great contribution to conservation. Today, with millions of anglers fishing a finite amount of water, the growing popularity of catch-and-release has maintained or restored bass fisheries by reducing fish mortality, allowing production of more and larger bass. Catch-and-release fishing is good medicine for heavily fished waters, but it can be overdone. Releasing fish sometimes is unnecessary, and in some waters total catch-and-release can actually do more harm than good.

Selective harvest is the concept In-Fisherman has been advocating since the mid-1980s. The object is to release the right fish to sustain good fishing while allowing harvest of others. The tradition of eating fish is worth preserving, for they are nutritious, tasty, and, if harvested wisely, renewable. There is no fundamental conflict between anglers who want to eat fish and those who release them. In fact, harvest of particular species or sizes of fish can be a valuable tool in managing a body of water for sustained good fishing.

Selective harvest is a comprehensive approach—a simple, sensible solution to many of the fishery resource problems that face our maturing and increasingly sophisticated fishing world, a world that faces challenges on many fronts. Not the least of these challenges is teaching the importance of using natural resources wisely in a world where antiharvest groups are becoming more vocal.

Selective harvest, then, is a matter of common sense and finding a balance between release and harvest. It also incorporates many ideas about handling fish correctly, releasing them unharmed, and not wasting those that are kept.

SLOT LIMITS AND THE PROBLEM OF UNDERHARVEST

Black bass have an essential ecological role. As predators, often the top predators, bass are needed to keep populations of preyfish in check. Larger bass can better control preyfish populations; they're also better spawners.

Some important bass fisheries are suffering from too little harvesting. Too many bass for the available food supply leads to slow bass growth and thin fish. Slot limits protect a size range of bass (say, 14 to 18 inches), allowing them to grow

Selective harvest encompasses both catch-and-release and appropriate harvest.

to large size while allowing harvest of many smaller bass, so the remaining fish have a good food supply and can grow faster. When well-meaning anglers fail to harvest bass under the slot—when they treat the upper end of the slot limit as a high minimum-size limit—bass often become too abundant, and the growth rate slows.

Excessive harvest of bass below the slot could, theoretically, leave too few fish protected within the slot, but this situation has never been documented, due to the powerful release ethic among bass specialists. This release ethic, misunderstood, also has caused social problems, such as tournament participants jeering at bank anglers for stringering a few small bass. That's rude and presumptuous, and it may be counterproductive to good fishing.

HOW TO PRACTICE SELECTIVE HARVEST

Selective harvest means an angler takes responsibility for learning more than how to catch fish. Fishery managers, by monitoring bass populations, usually can determine the best harvest strategy or regulation. For most agencies, implementing regulations requires public input. This is the angler's opportunity to ask important questions like "Why?" "What effect will the regulation have?" "How long before we see the desired result?" "Is this the right regulation for this population?"

Regulations set by state agencies partially answer the question: *Which fish should I keep, and which should I release?* But in the absence of regulation, or for the angler who chooses to practice ethical fishing beyond what regulations require, selective harvest is a matter of considering the numbers and size of fish and their place in the food chain.

Selective harvest is an angler's voluntary equivalent of varying regulations for different sportfish populations. Good practice of catch-and-release depends on many factors: it makes a difference how often you fish, and how successfully. The more fish you catch, the more you should be willing to release. What you fish for, and where you fish, should also affect your decisions.

Panfishermen have less need to release their catch than muskie fishermen. Segments of panfish populations, however, are vulnerable, too. The odds of any individual crappie, perch, or muskie getting unusually large are slight. Larger panfish are a valuable resource and should also be candidates for release—a thought that hasn't caught on among many fishermen. Our rule, then, is to (1) keep more numerous panfish before harvesting less-abundant larger predators; and (2) keep smaller, more abundant fish of a species before harvesting larger, less abundant ones.

Anglers fishing a lake that freezes out every fourth year need not release fish, but fishermen targeting popular predatory species on bodies of water that receive heavy fishing pressure need to release all larger fish to help sustain good fishing.

Anglers must wisely select the species, sizes, and number of fish to harvest in many different environments. The best general advice is:
• harvest only those fish you and your family will eat.
• if a slot limit is in effect, harvest fish smaller than the protected size range.
• conservatively harvest fish of the most abundant species and sizes.
• never assume that the "daily limit" is the right number of fish to harvest; if you fish the same water repeatedly, harvest fewer than the daily limit.

If you practice selective harvest, you're doing half your job as an angler. The other half is to encourage your fellow anglers to conserve the resource by practicing selective harvest.

Avoiding Underharvest

Mountain Harbor Resort on Lake Ouachita, Arkansas, was the scene of one of the finest lunches I've enjoyed. After an action-filled morning of bass fishing, we put the electric fillet knife to 25 or so largemouth and spotted bass. The largemouths had eagerly smacked topwaters worked over 70-foot depths; the spots came on live crawdads in the upper end of the reservoir. The fried bass, accompanied by coleslaw, hush puppies, onions, and fried potatoes, made an exquisite meal.

The bass were below Ouachita's protected slot limit of 13 to 16 inches. We caught and released several in the slot and kept limits of small ones—an appropriate action from a conservation standpoint as well as a culinary perspective. Ouachita's length limit was instituted by the Arkansas Fish and Game Commission to boost the harvest of small bass, both increasing their growth rate and protecting the majority of the spawning stock of the lake.

Not overharvest but underharvest has reduced the potential to grow big bass in many reservoirs. Unfortunately, slot limits don't work if anglers refuse to keep and eat small bass. Why are people so reluctant to keep little ones? Walleye anglers don't have a problem keeping fish under the protected slot. A 14-inch walleye is a delicacy, and so is a 12-inch bass from most impoundments. Granted, in some eutrophic waters with dense algae blooms, bass can acquire a muddy flavor, as do catfish, crappies, and sunfish; in that case, smoke the fish or use them in a spicy chowder. In contaminated waters, smaller fish have a lower concentrations of toxins like PCBs or mercury in their bodies than larger fish.

Don't worry about bragging rights. Folks who understand fish populations won't applaud you for taking many large fish; the small ones make an equally fine meal, and releasing large fish maintains the quality of the fishery. Larger black bass also are more prolific spawners, and big females typically spawn earlier in the season than young females, giving their offspring a longer growing season, therefore a jump on life. Larger males typically make more dependable and formidable guardians.

How you apply selective harvest depends on where you fish. In some

SUCCESSFUL RELEASE—CUTTING THROUGH THE CONTROVERSY

A hot round of controversy began in 1991 when we reported that David Campbell, hatchery manager at the Texas Parks and Wildlife Department's Tyler Hatchery, observed that several giant largemouth bass had broken jaws that prevented them from feeding. These bass had been handled frequently during photo sessions or at weigh-ins before they were donated to Operation Share a Lone-Star Lunker. Campbell said these fish would become postrelease mortalities because of the way anglers lifted the bass, even though they thought they were handling them properly.

While lipping bass is the standard way to land and hold them, Campbell suggested that irreparable damage can occur when the lower jaw is rolled downward to lift the fish horizontally. All the weight is on the lower jaw, which systems, like most of Minnesota's natural lakes, bass populations seem to maintain a good balance with no signs of overpopulation and resulting slow growth. In fact, they grow remarkably fast, considering that they live under ice for four to five months. Harvesting small bass usually isn't necessary to maintain good populations, but it's OK for folks who like to eat bass. Selective harvest calls for releasing bigger bass—say, over 15 inches, in Minnesota waters.

In manmade impoundments, however, biological processes often are more complicated. Largemouths may produce too many offspring, creating cohorts of slow-growing bass that compete for food with larger bass or other predators. Stocking of smallmouth bass outside their range also has fostered overpopulation, and spotted bass are notorious overbreeders in their favored reservoir habitats, sometimes crowding out largemouths and smallmouths.

Do yourself and your favorite bass population a favor: harvest selectively. And go farther: spread the word. We anglers who profess such devotion to the sport of bass fishing and to conserving bass are often the cause of declines in fishing quality. Biologists sometimes complain about lack of cooperation from anglers and try in their way to encourage harvest. It's time for serious bass anglers to assume the challenge and inform fellow club members, tournament competitors, and the folks we chat with at the boat ramp. Tell them—eat those little bass.

—Steve Quinn

Harvesting abundant smaller bass enables protected slot limits to function properly.

becomes hyperextended in an unnatural position. Holding bass vertically without the hyperextension apparently causes no problem.

America's most fanatical fishermen were quick to pick up on the potential problem and to call attention to photos they thought indicated damaging holds. Letters to various editors flew. The cover of the May 1991 *Sports Afield* displayed a lip-held largemouth with the jaw somewhat overextended, and the magazine subsequently published letters from readers expressing dismay at the use of a photo showing an "inappropriate" hold. The editor commented, "We are utterly astonished at these letters. Are the animal rightists at work again?" Obviously at least one angling editor was unaware of Campbell's report. Other prominent anglers were aware of the report but didn't fully understand it; one TV angler claimed it only applied to bass over 6 pounds. We, too, received letters, objecting to the way some anglers held fish in articles in *In-Fisherman* magazine.

We're Holding and Releasing Bass Wrong!

David Campbell, biologist in charge of spawning the 13-pound-plus lunkers donated by anglers to the Texas Parks and Wildlife Department's Share a Lone-Star Lunker program, says he's received several bass with damaged jaws. Jaws were broken or cartilage torn so badly that bass couldn't eat. Eventually the fish starved. Damage apparently is due to the way bassers display fish for friends and cameras while holding them by the lower jaw.

The jaw grip immobilizes bass, makes them easier to handle, and doesn't remove protective fish slime. Small bass aren't usually harmed when held by the jaw. But as bass grow, weight increases faster than the strength of the thin jaw tissues. When compared to the strength of jaw bones and muscles, the weight of small fish is proportionally much less than that of larger fish. By the time bass reach lunker size, their weight can damage jaw tissue if they're held horizontally with one hand.

When large bass are lip-landed and held by the jaw, they must be held absolutely vertical until the weight of the tail can be supported by the angler's other hand. The jaw should never be forced into a full open position. It should point forward, not down, when bass are held horizontally for pictures. Anglers must support the weight of the body and tail.

Unfortunately, we've been holding bass wrong for years. Television stars routinely display bass by bending jaws down for prerelease pictures. Outdoor magazines have used many photos showing improper bass holds because we haven't known better. Hopefully, this will end.

You may also see anglers swish fish back and forth in the water before release. Allegedly, this reoxygenates the gills. But gill filaments are designed to stream with a flow from only one direction. Filaments are attached at only the forward end, and backward currents can bend, bruise, or break them. In addition, too much forward movement can force excess water into the fish's stomach. Simply releasing fish is best if they're strong enough to swim away.

The controversy doesn't end there—photos and film footage of muskies and pike also have come under scrutiny. Readers have criticized photos of fish held vertically, claiming that fish held this way suffer damage to the spine or to organs that sag from their normal position, or that inserting fingers into the gill area causes damage or infection that can be fatal.

We're proud that the original source of these objections is information we published. The first comprehensive report concerning mortality involved with catch-and-release fishing was published in *In-Fisherman* in 1980.

The general success of catch-and-release has been documented across North America, where catches can be accurately counted. In some small impoundments, anglers annually have caught two or three times the number of bass estimated to be present. Other studies have shown a 95 percent or higher survival rate of released bass. Still, we need to look seriously at how best to safely unhook, hold, and release fish, especially these hard-to-handle large fish.

Are the most common objections realistic? How should fishermen handle valuable but vulnerable giant fish? Releasing large gamefish is an integral part of our selective harvest philosophy. If released fish don't survive, there's no gain.

HANDLING BASS

Black bass have an ideal handle—their protruding lower jaw. A bass held by the lower jaw should hang vertically or at a slight angle.

When the jaw is held and the bass is forced into a more horizontal position, it doesn't struggle. Hooks are easily removed, and reduced struggling may mean less physiological stress and physical damage. Why do bass stop struggling? Big-bass specialist Doug Hannon guesses, "They seem to instinctively know that if they struggle while their jaw is distended, it could be damaged. Bass are very aware of their jaws. Before they begin active feeding, they stretch their jaws in a yawn, like a runner stretching before a race." Alternatively, pressure on the mouth may touch a nerve that quiets the fish.

As bass grow, their weight increases exponentially. While body length doubles from 12 to 24 inches, most bones roughly double in length and diameter and approximately quadruple in strength. The weight of the bass, however, may increase by a factor of 10. Raising a bass to a horizontal position by rotating the lower jaw downward can be lethal to giant bass and may also damage smaller fish, although studies haven't proven this.

Bob Crupi demonstrates safe handling techniques on this 18.58-pound beauty.

Bob Crupi of Castaic, California, has caught several of the largest bass ever recorded and carefully released most of the giants. "I've learned not to lift huge bass with one hand," he says. "I hold the lower jaw with one hand to control the bass and slide the other hand under the belly to the anal fin. Then I lift the fish with two hands."

Smallmouths, spots, and other black bass have shorter jaws and smaller mouths. They're harder to lip, and they struggle more in a lip hold. Their shorter, stouter bones and ligaments may be more resistant to damage. These species also are smaller, yet the same careful handling should be practiced.

Breaking bad habits takes attention: bug your buddies; write to magazines; call TV stations; teach children respect for the fish they catch. Anglers in the public eye should be overcautious rather than callous. Damage to prize fish resources is needless.

STRESS AND RELEASED FISH

When possible, of course, big fish are best released while they're still in the water. Grasp the hook by hand or with a pliers and back it out. Simply release the fish gently at the surface, supporting it under the belly if it needs time to recuperate.

Each phase of hooking, battling, and landing a fish, and time spent out of water, contributes to the physiological problems a fish may suffer. Perhaps the most critical aspect of physiological stress is the suppression of a fish's immune system. Its ability to fight disease may be impaired for days or even weeks after a stressful experience.

Proper Release

Harvesting bass is a traditional part of the angling experience and doesn't damage populations if practiced in moderation. Yet increasing fishing pressure on bass means most anglers must release most of the legally harvestable bass they catch, most of the time, if fishing quality is to be maintained.

These guidelines help ensure bass survival:
• minimize the time a bass are held out of water.
• grip bass by the lower jaw between your thumb and fingers, which prevents them from struggling and injuring themselves. Do not squeeze fish around the abdomen or gill plates.

• hold heavy bass vertically so their weight doesn't tear jaw tissues.
• there are several options for landing bass: lead them boatside, then grab them by the lower jaw; lift smaller fish directly from the water with the rod; or use a net with a nonabrasive mesh, such as coated nylon or rubber. Don't let the fish bounce on a boat deck.
• carefully remove hooks to avoid unnecessary injury. Cut barbs on large hooks or back out small bait hooks. If you decide to leave a hook embedded, leave an 18-inch length of line attached to help prevent blockage of the gullet.
• a nicked gill may bleed profusely, but fish blood clots quickly following release, and most bass survive such injuries.
• gently release bass at the surface; don't drop fish, particularly large ones.

Levels of Stress

Bass intercept shad school.

Angler spots schooling bass and hooks one.

Scene 1

Catecholamines released along the backbone of the shad are carried in the bloodstream to organs. Blood flow through gill tissues increases; oxygen supplies swimming muscles to aid escape. Blood glucose levels rise to supply extra energy.

Fresh water enters the shad's body fluids, diluting the critical ion concentration. Its immune system shuts down to divert available resources to survival.

If the shad escapes, it moves to a resting position and catecholamine levels drop quickly. Corticosteroids may remain elevated for hours; the immune system gradually returns to normal. Blood flow declines and glucose levels drop to prestress levels. The shad's kidneys produce large volumes of dilute urine. Chloride cells in its gills extract salt from the water to regain osmotic balance.

Scene 2

Bass immediately reacts to hookset, and stress response begins. Stress hormone levels rise and physiological reactions are identical to the shad's, but longer as the bass is battled to the boat and landed. Ion and water balance is shifted farther out of balance.

Its immune system is suppressed, leaving the hook wound open to infection. Immediate release allows the bass to seek shelter in a familiar location and return the salt-water balance to prestress levels.

Kidneys eliminate excess water, and chloride cells increase salt levels in the bass. Immune systems gradually return to normal, and the bass is ready to bite again.

Scene 3

Unlike the immediately released bass, the tanked fish cannot find cover to recuperate from stress. Competition with other fish for available oxygen requires exaggerated gill movements. More salts are lost as fresh water moves through the gills by osmosis.

Higher water temperature causes greater production of stress hormones. The stress response is prolonged and exaggerated. Bouncing in the boat and interacting with other fish cause panic reactions that raise hormone levels and increase oxygen demand.

Release of the bass after photographs or in the process of culling allows it to seek better, though often unfamiliar, conditions. Tournament weigh-in procedures prolong and aggravate the stress response.

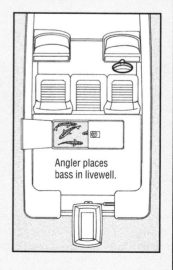

Angler places bass in livewell.

Squeezing can damage the mucus-secreting cells of a fish's skin and injure internal organs. Without the protection of the mucus layer, fish are more susceptible to bacterial and fungal diseases; this problem is compounded by a compromised immune system. Most damage is not through loss of slime but injury to cells that produce the slime. A healthy fish quickly renews mucus if its cells are healthy.

Wounds, of course, provide entries for disease organisms and require extra energy for healing. Gill or eye damage, injuries to the roof of the mouth or esophagus, torn branchiostegals, and distended jaws add strikes against survival. Selective harvest means keeping badly injured fish and minimizing stress whenever possible in handling them.

FISH OUT OF WATER

Air contains 30 times more oxygen than water, but even when gills are kept moist and air is pumped over them, fish suffocate out of water. Their delicate secondary gill lamellae, where oxygen exchange occurs, require water to hold them upright on the gill filaments. In air, they collapse against each other, eliminating this surface and eventually causing brain damage, disease, and death.

To calm me down a bit before you release me, I suggest you put me in with your minnows for a minute or two...

Bob the Bass figures as long as he's up here...

Water and air temperature also are important. In cool water, metabolisms are slowed, so less oxygen is required. The stress response also is suppressed. Fish can therefore survive out of water much longer when the water's cool.

Tolerances among species vary, too. Catfish can survive out of water longer than other fish because the thicker secondary lamellae of their gills provide more support in air, which allows more oxygen intake. Fish that fight actively and strenuously—including many bass—must be released quickly when air and water are warm. Walleyes are more easily stressed than bass, and trout require even more delicate handling.

PHOTOGRAPHING OR WEIGHING YOUR FISH

Anglers who release giant fish often want to preserve the moment on film, something we encourage, but if you try too many different poses and bracket exposures to ensure a good shot, your fish may be in critical condition. Photography can be done safely. For years, we've shot magazine-quality photos of giant fish and then released them. European anglers routinely release giant pike, carp, and catfish after photographs; many are repeatedly caught, suggesting that these basic handling procedures work.

Support the fish carefully. Gripping a fish at the gill opening is common for pike, big walleyes, salmon, catfish, and saltwater species; this does not doom fish. The key is to support the body so delicate tissues of the gill and isthmus (throat area) aren't torn and to grip the inside of the jaw, not the actual gill filaments. Bass should be held with the lip hold suggested above. Control the head and support the abdomen without squeezing.

Have the camera ready as the fish approaches the boat, or hold the fish in water until the photographer's ready. If you take more than a few exposures, soak the

Weighing Fish Without a Scale

We're often asked about estimating fish weights. "How much did that 20-incher weigh that I released last week?" The answer varies, based on how the fish is measured.

If you didn't measure the fish's girth (maximum circumference of the body), try this formula:

$$\text{Weight (pounds)} = \frac{\text{Length (inches)}^3}{1{,}600}$$

A 20-incher weighs about 8,000 (20 x 20 x 20) divided by 1,600, or 5.0 pounds. This formula provides an estimate based on the average proportions of a bass. Adjust up or down slightly for unusually fat or thin fish.

Biologists studying a fish population often calculate a length-weight relationship based on measurements of a large sample of many sizes of fish. They transform the lengths and weights to base-10 logarithms and calculate a regression line. Weights can be estimated from the equation:

$\log W = \log a + b \times \log L$

Where:

$\log W$ = base-10 logarithm of weight
$\log a$ = a population-specific intercept
b = the slope of the regression line
$\log L$ = base-10 logarithm of length

For example, the relationship for a sample of largemouth bass from Clear Lake, Iowa, was

$\log W$ (grams) = -4.999 + 3.091 x $\log L$ (millimeters).

For a 20-inch (508-millimeter) bass, the equation calculates:

$\log W$ = -4.999 + 3.091 x 2.71
$\log W$ = 8.377 - 4.999 = 3.778 = 2,386 grams = 5.26 pounds.

If you measure length and girth, use the general formula:

$$\text{Weight (pounds)} = \frac{\text{Girth (inches)}^2 \times \text{Length (inches)}}{800}$$

A 20-incher with a 14-inch girth weighs 4.9 pounds (14 x 14 x 20, divided by 800). A 20-incher with a 16-inch girth weighs 6.4 pounds.

In 2002, Don Peters published a new set of formulas in the annual edition of "World Record Game Fishes" by the International Game Fish Association (IGFA). In place of the denominator of 800, he suggests a variable number that's based on the geometry of a species shape. For largemouth, 927 works well for trophy-size bass, yielding an estimate of 5.5 pounds.

Useful Equipment for Releasing Fish

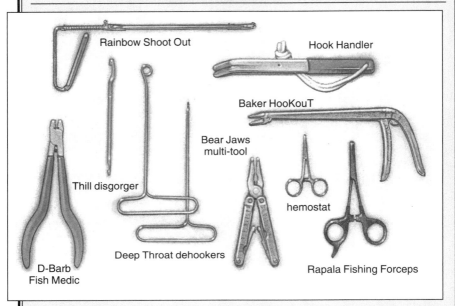

Rainbow Shoot Out

Hook Handler

Baker HooKouT

Bear Jaws multi-tool

Thill disgorger

hemostat

D-Barb Fish Medic

Deep Throat dehookers

Rapala Fishing Forceps

Release cradles—A prototype was devised by Minnesota Department of Natural Resources fishery manager Bob Strand for handling muskies during spawn-stripping procedures in spring. Commercial versions of the net measure 52 to 55 inches; the bag is made of ¼-inch soft-mesh (nonabrasive) nylon netting.

Nets—When choosing a net, consider handle length, hoop diameter, bag depth, mesh size, and material. Fishing from piers and high banks demands the longest handle to reach fish. Great Lakes boats with high gunwales also demand long-handled, large-diameter nets (diameter dictated by fish length). Nets with large hoops have large mesh (1 ½ inches or more) because they're otherwise too difficult to scoop or raise through the water. Large mesh, especially knotted polypropylene or nylon, is more likely to tear fins. When fish are curled in the deep bag of a net and lifted, they often thrash wildly, damaging their fins and tangling hooks. Net a fish, but keep it in the water at boatside for unhooking.

Nets with smaller and more rubbery mesh are heavier in the water, but fine mesh causes less damage to fins, scales, gills, and eyes. For bass, walleyes, and panfish, choose fine mesh of rubber or plastic-coated nylon.

Hook removers—A catch-and-release tool kit helps get fish back in the water with minimal damage. Hook disgorgers are offered commercially in many sizes. Hemostats (available in pharmacies, medical supply stores, and many fishing catalogs) are essential. Large treble-hook plugs are dangerous to fish and anglers. Hold the fish still and grab the hooks with a needlenose pliers or Baker Hookout. Cut stubborn hooks with wire cutting pliers or a tool like the D-Barb Fish Medic. Hooks are easy to replace. Big fish aren't.

fish at boatside or in the livewell. Keep the camera loaded and accessible; rehearse your photography procedures with your fishing partner and know the camera's features, so no one needs a last-minute photography lesson.

Stringer shots are generally a poor practice. Photos of individual, living fish are best. At times, holding a couple of fish from the livewell makes an impressive photo. In some environments, some species including bass are abundant and can stand harvest. An occasional stringer shot of smaller fish is legitimate. The main problem with stringer shots may be the message they convey about what fishermen need to get from a trip. No matter how wonderful the scenery or how companionable your companions, eventually most fishermen must catch some fish to keep fishing. But how many? A limit? On each outing? If your stringer isn't full, have you failed? Or should you revel in each fish, no matter the species, no matter the size, no matter how many?

And what angler isn't curious about the actual length and weight of a giant fish? Fishing buddies won't settle for estimates. Weigh and/or measure big fish quickly if at all, snap a few pictures, then release them. For weighing, we recommend placing fish in an opaque plastic bag that has a grommet at the mouth to accommodate the hook of a scale. Hanging fish from a hook often causes mouth damage and worse, when fish jump off and land on the deck.

Admiring a caught fish fulfills one of the objectives we have in fishing—to look at and learn more about these mysterious creatures that populate our waters. That image can last a lifetime. At times, however, such as with a tired fish or in hot weather, we should moderate our curiosity and desire for memories and release it fast. Once we choose not to harvest a fish, we must ensure that it survives to fulfill its predatory role and perhaps to thrill another angler.

CARING FOR YOUR CATCH

Handle the fish you keep carefully so they aren't wasted. This is a conservation measure as well as a culinary one. A fine meal is the perfect end to most fishing trips. How good they taste, however, depends on how well they're cared for from the time they're caught until they're cooked. Fish flesh is fragile, and it begins to deteriorate if the fish is roughly handled and stressed before it dies. Bruised flesh doesn't taste good. A livewell is far better than a stringer.

The flesh deteriorates even more quickly after a fish dies. Bacterial growth is a principal enemy of fresh fish. Once your fish die, gut them, making sure not to let their sour, bacteria-filled stomach and intestinal juices touch the flesh. Wash fish in cold water to remove bacteria. Then place them on ice to retard bacterial growth.

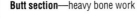

Anatomy of a Knife

Butt section—heavy bone work

Tip section—fine finishing

finish

start

Workload transfer—cutting tasks begin with the butt and transfer to the tip for finishing work.

Middle section—determines the primary purpose of the knife. A knife that tapers quickly and progressively toward a fine point is for general cutting purposes, especially on smaller fish. A knife that doesn't taper progressively but ends quickly with a sharp point is for heavy-duty work.

CLEANING THE CATCH

At the cleaning table: general procedure— Wherever you clean your catch, cleanliness is critical. Be sure to have ice available for fish that have already been chilled and to cool fish that are still alive when they reach the cleaning table.

Let's say you'll be filleting your catch. At the cleaning table, you need:

1. cleaning utensils, including fillet knives and sharpening tools, plus a bowl of cold water (add ice cubes) to soak fillets in briefly to remove blood and bacteria (photo 1).

2. clean paper towels for wiping slime from fish and keeping the fillet board clean. Pat fillets dry after they've soaked if you don't plan to freeze them. (A solution of 1 teaspoon vinegar to 3 quarts water helps cut fish slime.)

3. packing material for freezing or refrigerating fish.

Proceed—1. If fish are alive, dispatch them with a sharp blow to the head, then bleed them (photo 2).

2. Remove the fillets, being careful not to rupture the digestive tract with your knife.

3. Place fillets in cold water to help remove blood and bacteria. With lean fish such as bass, pike, or walleyes, add 1/2 teaspoon salt to help neutralize acids and draw out blood.

4. Discard the carcass, wipe the board and knife clean (photo 3), and start on another fish. Replace the water in the bowl when it begins to thicken with fish juices.

Filleting fish—The butt of a fillet knife blade does the heavy work; the point does the detailed work. The first cut behind the gill covers and down to the bone of a fish on its side is best done with the butt and middle of the knife blade. Don't use the tip.

photo 1

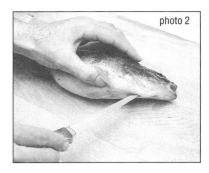

photo 2

photo 3

Likewise, the cut that removes the fillet from the backbone is made most efficiently with the butt of the knife laid close to the dorsal fin on one side and close to the backbone on the other side. The heavy part of the knife is used for cutting through the heaviest flesh and bones.

Now start a rib removal cut with the heavy butt of the knife, but quickly transfer the work to the middle and finally to the tip of the knife.

Fillets can be fried, broiled, poached, baked, steamed, and used in casseroles, stews, and soups. Fillets cook faster and more thoroughly than pan cuts. The result is tastier flesh, in the opinion of most experts.

Basic filleting—Filleting is the most popular method for cleaning most fish. The steps are easy but require practice to master.

Tools for Cleaning Fish

Tools needed to clean fish successfully depend on the cleaning method. Filleting is popular, but so are scaling and dressing or skinning and dressing. One favorite method is scaling and filleting. To enjoy baked and stuffed fish, it's necessary to know how to butterfly fish. Other baking methods call for gilled and gutted whole fish. Poaching and steaming also call for filleted or gilled and gutted whole fish, although steaked fish will work, too. Smoking usually calls for steaked, chunked, or gilled and gutted whole fish. Pan-sized dressed fish or fillets work as well.

Basic tools include a fillet knife, sharpening stone and steel, fish scaler, fillet board, and perhaps a skinning pliers. Or you can go a step farther and include fillet knives with different blade sizes (4-, 6-, and 9-inch blades), a protective fish cleaning glove, electric fish scaler, electric knife, and perhaps a fancy fish-cleaning board.

Knives—If you're buying only one knife, a 6-inch blade is probably best. Knives with different blade sizes are helpful. Match the knife to the task. Many people prefer to use an electric knife to fillet fish, especially for a mess of bigger fish. Fillet knives should have a heavy butt tapering progressively toward a small point. The heavier, thicker butt is designed to handle coarse, heavy work; the smaller, finer tip is for finishing work.

Stone and steel—A stone sharpens blade edges and a steel realigns them. A good knife stays sharp for a long time, but its edge may need realigning during each cleaning session. Sharpen a fillet knife by drawing it at a 10° to 15° angle across a fine-grade oiled honing stone. Realign edges by drawing the knife at the same angle across the steel. Use the same number and type of strokes on each side of the blade.

Scaler—A scaler can be as simple as a spoon or as advanced as a heavy-duty electric scaler. To reduce flying scales, you can scale fish while holding them under water in the sink (not with an electric fish scaler, of course). Or scale fish inside a paper sack or plastic bag. After you've scaled a fish, pinch the top of the sack shut and give the bag a snap so the scales drop to the bottom of the sack.

Fish skinners—With the advent of filleting and the current preference for fillets, fish skinners may seem unnecessary. Plier-style skinners remain the standard for bullheads and catfish.

Cleaning glove—Made from the same material as a bulletproof vest, Kevlar gloves allow you to use a knife without cutting your hand.

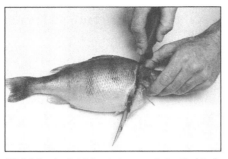 

(1) Make the initial cut at an angle just behind the pectoral fin. Cut with the scales, not through them. Include as much of the loin as possible where the neck meets the back of the head. Cut down to the backbone, lift the dorsal (back) portion of the fish slightly, and turn the knife blade toward the tail of the fish.

(2) Making certain to use the butt section of the knife to cut through the rib cage, slide the knife along the backbone toward the tail. Lead with the butt of the knife, making sure to cut as close as possible to the backbone so little meat is wasted.

 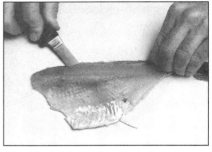

(3) Remove the rib cage by leading with the butt or middle of the knife and finishing with the middle or tip of the knife. The knife blade should slip just below the ribs, cutting through the epipleural ribs in the process.

(4) If the fish hasn't been scaled, remove the skin by sliding the blade of the knife between the skin and the fillet. Again, lead with the butt of the knife, beginning either at the head or tail end of the fillet.

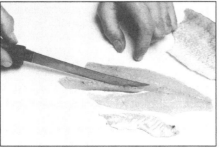

(5) For perfectly boneless fillets from bony fish except pike, trout, and salmon, remove the epipleural ribs. The epipleurals are small rib bones that lie at right angles to the main ribs, along the upper portion of the rib cage. Remove them with a V-cut. Feel for the ribs and then make as fine a cut as possible to remove only the epipleurals.

Pan Dressing

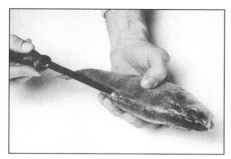

(1) Insert the knife point under the skin at the rear of one side of the dorsal fin. Slide the knife forward just under the skin beyond the front of the dorsal fin.

(2) Make a fillet cut in back of the head. Use the tip of your knife to cut along the ventral (stomach) portion of the fish, around the anal pore, and along the pelvic fin.

(3) Grab the pelvic fin and rip it forward. Remove the offal along with the pelvic fin, and tear the head off the fish.

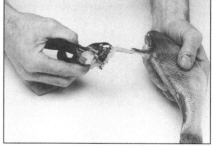

(4) Remove the dorsal fin.

(5) If the fish has been scaled, it is pan ready. If you prefer to skin the fish, peal it with a Townsend skinner.

(6) The skinned, pan-ready fish.

Butterflying Method #1

(1) After scaling the fish, make a fillet cut along one side, taking care not to cut through the belly portion. At this point, remove the fish's intestines and stomach.

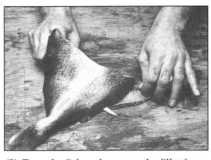

(2) Turn the fish and remove the fillet from the other side.

(3) Remove the primary ribs. The epipleurals can also be removed, but be careful not to cut through the skin.

(4) The final product. The butterfly fillet can be fried and then drizzled with your favorite white sauce.

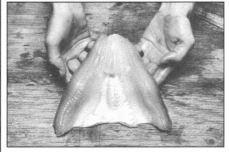

(5) Try stuffing the fillet with your favorite stuffing (even cooked Stove-Top works) or vegetables (precooked). Bake the stuffed fillet after wrapping it with bacon strips.

Butterflying Method #2

(1) After scaling the fish, cut along the backbone and down to the rib cage on one side of the fish.

(2) Work your way along and around the rib cage, taking care not to cut through the skin on the side of or along the stomach of the fish.

(3) Cut along the backbone toward the tail of the fish, again being careful not to cut through the skin beneath the fillet. Repeat this procedure on the other side of the fish.

(4) The final product. Stuff and bake.

Fat Content and Storage Life

SPECIES	STORAGE TIME
lake trout, rainbow trout, whitefish, carp, catfish, ciscoes, smelt, pike	3 to 5 months
suckers, chinook salmon, coho salmon, white bass	5 to 8 months
walleyes, yellow perch, bass, burbot, crappies, bluegills	8 to 12 months

Source: *Fixin' Fish*, University of Minnesota Press.

Fish with high fat content generally become rancid quicker than lean fish when frozen. Exceptions include ciscoes, smelt, and pike, which may not withstand frozen storage as well as other fish of similar fat content. On the other hand, king and coho salmon, with their relatively high fat content, store better than fish with less fat. Always keep your freezer as cold as possible.

Chilling Fish

Method 1—Fill a bowl half full with ice and place the fish on the ice. Cover the fish with more ice and the bowl with cling wrap. Periodically drain the meltwater. Fish stored in crushed ice (32°F) keep longer than fish stored at the usual refrigerator temperature of 40°F.

Method 2—Remove the fillets and pat them dry with a towel. Sprinkle water droplets onto a clean dry towel so it's damp but not wet. Line a bowl with the damp towel and place the fillets on the towel. Use cling wrap to seal the bowl. The fish will keep for up to 3 days.

Chilling fish—Gutting fish bleeds them, and blood left in flesh speeds deterioration. After gutting fish, rinse them in cold water and then surround them with crushed ice. Don't let fish soak in water, even cold water. Crushed ice is best for chilling fish, as it packs closer and cools quicker than large blocks of ice or frozen bottles of water. Crushed ice keeps fish for up to three days, although the table quality of their flesh deteriorates each day. To keep fish on ice longer, use super-chilling.

Super-chilling—Super-chilled fish can be kept on ice for up to 5 and perhaps 7

days. To super-chill, first line the bottom of an insulated cooler with several inches of crushed ice, leaving the drain open. In another container, mix coarse ice-cream salt and crushed ice at a ratio of 1 to 20. For average-sized coolers, that's 1 pound of salt to 20 pounds of ice.

Wrap fillets or pan-dressed fish in plastic wrap. Layer the fish in the ice chest, making sure to surround each fish with plenty of salted ice. Super-chilling lowers the temperature to about 30°F. Replenish salted ice as it melts.

Packaging for the refrigerator—The best way to keep fish in a refrigerator is in crushed ice. Fill a bowl with crushed ice and surround the fish with ice. Cover the bowl with cling wrap (Saran Wrap or something similar). Drain the water occasionally so the fish doesn't sit in water. Keep the fish very cold and nearly dry. The temperature of most refrigerators is near 40°F. To keep fish on ice in a refrigerator, you want to lower the temperature of the fish to about 34°F, which allows several additional days of storage, depending on how fresh the fish were when refrigerated.

Another method works when you don't have ice, although not as well. Pat clean fillets dry with paper towels. Moisten a clean dish towel. Line the bottom of a bowl with the towel and spread the fillets on top. Cover the bowl with cling wrap. This keeps the fillets cold and moist but not sloppy wet. Never keep fish in a plastic bag, soaking in water containing their juices.

Freezing Fish

Packaging materials for freezing that work when used correctly include polyvinylidene chloride cling wraps, aluminum foil, Tupperware-type containers, polyester freezer bags, and wax-coated freezer paper. Wax paper and polyethylene plastic bags (like bread bags) don't lock water vapor in and oxygen out.

One way to freeze fish is to tightly wrap it in cling wrap or aluminum foil. Follow with a secondary wrapping of freezer wrap. Write the contents and date of packaging on the outside.

Place fish into a polyester freezer bag, add a bit of water, and submerge the bag in water to squeeze out the air, or add a small amount of water to the bag to help force out the air. Seal the bag.

FREEZING FISH

Too many fishermen use the wrong type of packaging, keep fish in the freezer too long, and store them at the wrong temperature. Properly frozen fish keep well and hold their flavor for months, although the quality deteriorates through dehydration and oxidation. "Freezer burn" (whitish, leather-tough flesh) is an advanced stage of dehydration; it results from using the wrong wrap or wrapping improperly. When the wrap doesn't seal in moisture effectively, fish flesh loses its moisture and turns tough.

Oxidation is also caused by poor packaging. Using the wrong wrap or failing to remove air from the package before freezing causes oxygen to combine with polyunsaturated fats and oils in the flesh. These fats turn rancid in the presence of oxygen.

Packaging Materials—Seal packaged fish to hold in moisture and lock out oxygen. Be sure to remove any air surrounding the flesh. Some popular materials do a poor job. Polyethylene, the material used in bread wrappers, fails the test. Waxed paper and cellophane are too porous. Aluminum foil works, but it punctures easily. It's best used as a final wrap on top of cling wrap.

Polyvinylidene chloride, from which cling wraps such as Saran Wrap are made, forms good barriers and clings to fish, eliminating air pockets. It's the best initial wrap. Wrap fish in cling wrap, making sure to remove the air from the wrap, then follow with another layer of cling wrap, and finally a layer of wax-coated freezer wrap.

Plastic bags labeled "freezer bags" are good, too, especially as outer bags. They form barriers against the transmission of air or moisture. They're harder to wrap tightly around fillets, however, so to minimize air pockets, plunge the filled bags in water to force air out. Seal the bags underwater—leaving a little water in the bags is better than leaving air.

Finally, wax-coated freezer wrap prevents oxygen and water vapor from passing through to the fish. This material is difficult to make airtight and waterproof, so use it as a final wrap on top of cling wrap. Write the date, fish type, size, and other information on the outside of the package.

Freezing in water—Commercially frozen fish is often glazed with a coating of ice to protect the flavor and table quality. The temperature of home freezers can't be set low enough to accomplish this, but you can seal your fish in water.

Pack the fish tightly in plastic containers (such as Tupperware) and fill the containers almost to the brim with water. Use enough water to cover the fish, but don't leave large empty spaces for water, because water (1) draws nutrients from the fish and causes the fish to freeze more slowly; and (2) crushes the fish when the water freezes. Pack the container with as much fish as possible, minimizing empty spaces. Then seal remaining spaces with water. If fish portions protrude from the ice after freezing, add a little more water.

Freezing Tips

One of the best ways to freeze fish is to tightly wrap it in cling wrap or aluminum foil. Follow with a secondary wrapping of freezer wrap. Write the contents and date of packaging on the outside.

Place fish into a polyester freezer bag and submerge the bag in water to squeeze out the air, or add a small amount of water to the bag to help.

FREEZING TIPS

• Divide cleaned fish into serving-sized portions to eliminate leftover thawed fish.

• The faster fish freezes, the better. Place packages in the coldest part of your freezer and don't overload it. Keep the temperature at 0°F, if possible.

• Thawing fish at room temperature allows thawed parts to deteriorate while the rest thaws. Instead, thaw frozen fish in the refrigerator, allowing 24 hours for a 1-pound package. Or place frozen fish in cold water until it's thawed, keeping it in its vapor-proof wrapping.

• Refreezing thawed fish causes a big loss in table quality. Freezing breaks cell walls, which is why frozen fish is less firm than fresh fish. The flesh turns to mush when refrozen.

• Fish with low fat content may hold its flavor well when frozen for as long as 6 months. Be sure, however, to remove fatty areas and to package the fish properly.

Glossary

Action: Measure of rod performance that describes the elapsed time between flexion and return to straight configuration; ranges from slow to fast.

Adaptation: Biological adjustment that increases fitness.

Adapted: Capable of thriving in a specific habitat.

Algae: Simple plant organisms.

Alkalinity: Measure of the amount of acid-neutralizing bases.

Anal Fin: Fin located on the ventral side of most fish, between the urogenital pore and the caudal fin.

Aggregation: Group of one species of fish within a limited area (see also School).

Backwater: Shallow area connected to a river.

Bag Limit: Restriction on the number of fish that an angler may harvest in a day.

Baitfish: Small fish eaten by predators.

Bar: Long underwater ridge in a body of water.

Bell Sinker: Pear-shaped sinker with brass eye on top.

Brackish: Water of intermediate salinity between sea water and fresh water.

Break: Distinct variation in otherwise constant stretches of cover, structure, or bottom type.

Breakline: Area of abrupt change in depth, bottom type, or water quality.

Buzzbait: Lure composed of a leadhead, rigid hook, and wire that supports one or more blades, designed for surface fishing.

Buzzing: Retrieving spinnerbaits or buzzbaits along the surface so they splash water.

Cabbage: Any of several species of submerged weeds of the genus *Potamogeton*.

Canal: Manmade waterway for navigation.

Carrying Capacity: Maximum density of organisms that a body of water can sustain.

Catchability: Measure of the willingness of fish to bite lures or bait.

Caudal Fin: Fish's tail.

Channel: The bed of a stream or river; the deeper part through which the water flows.

Cline: Vertical or horizontal section of a body of water where water characteristics change abruptly.

Community: Group of interacting organisms within an area.

Coontail: Submerged aquatic plant of the hornwort family, typically found in hard water, characterized by stiff, forked leaves.

Countershaded: Color pattern consisting of dark back and light belly.

Cover: Natural or manmade objects on the bottom of lakes, rivers, or impoundments, especially those that influence fish behavior.

Crankbait: Lipped diving lure.

Creel limit: The number of fish of a species or species group that an angler may legally retain or harvest in a day.

Crustacean: Hard-shelled, typically aquatic invertebrate.

Cultural Eutrophication: Increase in fertility of a body of water due to human alteration of the environment.

Current: Water moving in one direction.

Dam: Manmade barrier to water flow.

Dark-Bottom Bay: Shallow, protected bay with a layer of dark organic material on the bottom.

Debris: Natural or manmade objects in the water; rock fragments or rubbish.

Dissolved Oxygen: Oxygen molecules dispersed in water. Measured in parts per million.

Diurnal: Occurring within a 24-hour period.

Dorsal Fin: Fin located on the center of fish's back.

Downfishing: Level of fishing pressure that reduces fishing quality by decreasing the abundance of large fish.

Drainage: The area drained by a river and all of its tributaries.

Drop-Off: An area of substantial and steep increase in depth.

Eddy: Area of slack water next to current, or reversed current, in a stream or river.

Egg Sinker: Tapered, oblong sinker with a hole from end to end.

Epilimnion: Warm surface layer of a stratified lake or reservoir.

Estuary: Area where a river meets saltwater and has characteristics of both freshwater and marine environments.

Euryhaline: Organism that tolerates a broad range of salinity.

Eutrophic: Highly fertile waters characterized by warm, shallow basins.

Extirpated: Eliminated from former habitat.

Fecundity: Productivity; number of eggs produced by a female in a season.

Feeder Creek: Tributary to a river or reservoir.

Feeding Strategy: Set of behaviors used for capture and metabolism of prey.

Fertility: Degree of productivity of plants and animals.

Filamentous Algae: Type of algae characterized by long chains of attached cells that give it a stringy feel and appearance.

Fingerling: Juvenile fish, usually from 1 to 3 inches long.

Fish Culture: Production of fish in hatcheries.

Fished Down: Fish population adversely affected by fishing pressure, in numbers of fish and percentage of large fish.

Fishery: Group of fish that supports fishing.

Fishery Biologist: Person who studies the interaction of fishermen and fisheries.

Fishing Pressure: Amount of angling on a body of water in a period of time, usually measured in hours per acre per year; its effects on fish populations.

Fitness: Ability of an animal to survive and reproduce.

Flat: Area of lake, reservoir or river characterized by little change in depth.

Flipping: Presentation technique for dropping lures into dense cover at close range.

Flipping Stick: Heavy action fishing rod, 7 to 8 feet long, designed for bass fishing.

Float: Buoyant device for suspending bait.

Fluorescent: Emits radiation when exposed to sunlight.

Forage: Something eaten; the act of eating.

Freeze-Out Lake: Shallow northern lake subject to fish kills in late winter due to oxygen depletion.

Freeze-Up: Short period when ice first covers the surface of a body of water.

Front: Weather system that causes changes in temperature, cloud cover, precipitation, wind, and barometric pressure.

Fry: Recently hatched fish; cooking method using heated oil.

Gamefish: Fish species pursued by anglers.

Genetic Conservation: Management to preserve the gene pool of native fish or local stocks.

Genetics: The study of mechanisms of heredity.

Gradient: Degree of slope in a stream or riverbed.

Habitat: Type of environment in which an organism usually lives.

Harvest: Remove fish with intent to eat. (See also Selective Harvest.)

Hole: Deep section of a stream or river.

Home Range (Area): Defined area occupied by an animal for most activities over an extended period of time.

Hybrid: Offspring of two species or subspecies.

Hypolimnion: Deep, cool zone below the thermocline in a stratified lake or impoundment.

Ice-Out: Short period during which ice on a body of water completely melts.

Ichthyologist: Scientist who studies the biology or taxonomy of fish.

Impoundment: Body of water formed by damming running water.

Invertebrate: Animal without a backbone.

Jig: Lure composed of leadhead with rigid hook, often with hair, plastic, rubber, or other dressings.

Jigworm: Plastic worm rigged on an open-hook jighead.

Johnboat: Flat-bottom aluminum boat.

Jump Bait: Cigar-shaped topwater plug designed to move erratically when retrieved.

Lake: Confined area where water accumulates naturally. (Many impoundments are also named lakes.)

Larva: Immature form of an organism.

Lateral Line: Sensory system of fish that detects low frequency vibrations in water.

Ledge: Sharp contour break in a river or reservoir.

Length Limit: Regulation that prohibits harvest of fish below, above, or within specified lengths.

Littoral: Pertaining to the shoreline of a body of water.

Livebait: Any living animal used to entice fish to bite.

Livewell: Compartment in boat designed to keep fish alive.

Location: Where fish position themselves in response to the environment.

Management: Manipulation of a biological system to produce a fishery goal.

Mesotrophic: Waters of intermediate fertility between eutrophic (fertile) and oligotrophic (infertile).

Metalimnion: Another term for thermocline.

Migration: Movement of large numbers of animals of one species from one region or area to another, often seasonally.

Minnow Bait: Long, thin, minnow-shaped wood or plastic lure designed to be fished on or near the surface.

Monofilament: Fishing line made from a single strand of synthetic fiber.

Mottled: Blotchy coloration.

Nares: Nostrils of fish or other aquatic vertebrates.

Native: Naturally present in an area, as opposed to fish introduced by stocking.

Natural Selection: Process of differential survival and reproduction among individuals that affects the genetic makeup of subsequent generations.

Niche: The role of an organism or species in an ecological community.

Nymph: Larval form of an insect.

Olfaction: Sense of smell.

Oligotrophic: Infertile waters; geologically young, characterized by deep, cool, clear oxygenated waters and rocky basins.

Omnivore: Organism that eats a wide variety of items.

Opportunistic: Feeding strategy in which items are eaten according to availability.

Otolith: Ear bone of a fish.

Overharvest: A level of fish harvest from a body of water that substantially reduces abundance of catchable fish, particularly large fish.

Overwintering Area: Area where fish hold during winter, particularly in cold climates.

Oxbow: U-shaped bend off the main river.

Panfish: Group of about 30 small warm-water sportfish, not including bullheads or catfish.

Pattern: A defined set of angling location and presentation factors that consistently produce fish.

Pectoral Fin: Paired fin usually located on fish's side behind the head.

Pelagic: Living in open, offshore waters.

Pelvic Fin: Paired fin usually located on lower body of fish.

pH: A measure of hydrogen in concentration; therefore of the acidity or alkalinity of a solution. Expressed in values from 0 (most acidic) to 14 (most alkaline); pH7 is neutral.

Phosphorescent: Ability to glow in the dark after exposure to a light source.

Photoperiod: Interval during a day when sunlight is present.

Photosynthesis: Process in which green plants convert carbon dioxide and water into sugar and oxygen in the presence of sunlight.

Phytoplankton: Tiny plants suspended in water.

Point: Projection of land into a body of water.

Polarized: Lenses capable of breaking up sunlight into directional components for clearer vision.

Pool: Deep section of a river or stream.

Population: Group of animals of the same species within a geographical area that freely interbreed; level of abundance.

Postspawn: Period immediately after spawning; In-Fisherman Calendar Period between Spawn and Presummer.

Presentation: Combination of bait or lure, rig, tackle, and technique used to catch fish.

Prespawn: Period prior to spawning; In-Fisherman Calendar Period between Winter and Spawn.

Prey: Fish often eaten by other fish species.

Radio Tag (Transmitter): Device emitting high-frequency radio signals which, when attached to an animal, enables researches to track its location.

Range: Area over which a species or subspecies is distributed.

Rattlebait: Hollow-bodied, sinking, lipless crankbaits that rattle loudly due to shot and slugs in the body cavity.

Ray: Bony segment supporting a fin.

Reservoir: Large manmade body of water.

Recruitment: Process of fish hatching, growing, and surviving to catchable size.

Reeds: Any of several species of tall, emergent aquatic weeds that grow in shallow zones of lakes and reservoirs.

Reef: Rocky hump in a body of water.

Riffle: Shallow, fast flowing section of a stream or river.

Rig: Arrangement of components for fishing, including hooks, leader, sinker, swivel, beads.

Riprap: Large rocks placed along a bank.

Run: A straight section of a stream or river, of moderate depth and little depth change.

School: Group of fish of one species that move in unison.

Seiche: Oscillation of water level in a large lake or reservoir caused by strong directional winds.

Selective Harvest: Decision to release or harvest fish, based on species, size, and relative abundance; selecting fish to keep on the basis of improving the population of that species.

Set Rig: Rig that's cast or drifted into position on the bottom to await a strike.

Shot: Small, round sinkers pinched onto fishing line.

Silt: Fine sediment on the bottom of a body of water.

Sinkers: Variously shaped pieces of lead or other heavy material used to sink bait or lures.

Slip float: Float with a hole from top to bottom for sliding freely on the line.

Slip Sinker: Sinker with a hole for sliding freely on line.

Slot Limit: Regulation that prohibits harvesting fish within a specified length range.

Snag: Brush or tree in a stream or river.

Sonar: Electronic fishing aid that emits sound waves underwater and interprets them to depict underwater objects.

Spawn: Reproduction of fish; In-Fisherman Calendar Period between Prespawn and Postspawn.

Species: Group of potentially inter-breeding organisms.

Spine: Stiff, sharp segment of fin.

Sportfish: Fish species pursued by anglers.

Stock: To place fish in a body of water to increase population or introduce new species; a population of animals.

Stress: State of physiological imbal-ance caused by disturbing environ-mental factors.

Strike Window (Zone): Conceptual area in front of a fish within which it will strike food items or lures.

Structure: Changes in the shape of the bottom of lakes, rivers, or impoundments, especially those that influence fish behavior.

Substrate: Type of bottom in a body of water.

Suspended Fish: Fish in open water hovering considerably above bottom.

Swim (Gas) Bladder: Organ of most bony fish that holds a volume of gas to make them neutrally buoyant at variable depths.

Tailwater: Area immediately down-stream from a dam.

Thermocline: Layer of water with abrupt change in temperature, occur-ring between warm surface layer (epilimnion) and cold bottom layer (hypolimnion).

Tracking: Following radio-tagged or sonic-tagged animals.

Trailer: Plastic skirt, grub, pork rind, live bait, or other attractor attached to a lure to entice fish.

Trailer Hook: An extra hook attached to the rear hook of a lure to catch fish that strike behind the lure.

Tributary: Stream or river flowing into a larger river.

Trigger: Characteristics of a lure or bait presentation that elicit a biting response in fish.

Trolling: Fishing method in which lures or baits are pulled by a boat.

Trophic: Relating to the fertility of a body of water.

Turbid: Murky water discolored by suspended sediment.

Ultraviolet Light: Radiation with wavelengths shorter than 4,000 angstroms; beyond violet in the color spectrum.

Watershed: The region draining runoff into a body of water.

Weed: Aquatic plant.

Weedline (Weededge): Abrupt edge of a weedbed caused by a change in depth, bottom type, or other factor.

Wing Dam: Manmade earth or rock ridge to deflect current.

Winterkill: Fish mortality due to oxygen depletion under ice in late winter.

Year Class: Fish of one species hatched in a single year.

Zooplankton: Tiny animals suspended in water.

Index

(Note: bodies of water are listed under Lakes, Ponds, Reservoirs, or Rivers.)

Shireman, J.V., 140
solar energy, 105
solunar periods, 23, 100, 106, 123-131
   "Best Fishing Times," 123
   celestial positioning, 128-129
   effects on catches, 123-131
   sun-moon interaction, 129
Spoonplug, 56-57
Sport Fish Restoration Act, 182
Sports Afield, 3, 205
stocking, 4-5, 13-14, 17, 120-121,
   159-160, 164-165, 180-181
Strand, Bob, 212
stringer shots, 213
structure, 55-81
   bends, 43-44
   bends, outside, 44
   definition, 55
   fishing, 118-119
   flats, 64-5
   in natural lakes, 56, 58-65
   in ponds, 81
   in reservoirs, 44-54, 73-81, 117-119
   in rivers, 65-72, 119
   modern structure theory, 58
   Perry's theory of, 56-58
   weeds and structure, 60-75
sunfish, 5, 52, 98
"Superbass," 167-168

T-U-V

telemetry (see tracking)
thermocline, 34-35, 105, 107, 121-123
Thurmond, Betty, 196
tides (see rivers, tidewater)
trout, 3, 4, 42, 65, 170, 187
trout, lake, 38, 41
tournaments, 183-198
   contributions, 183-186
   controversies, 187-199
   history, 184-185
   types, 185-186, 197
tracking studies, 133-155
   big bass, 137-139, 140-149
   daily movements of bass 134-136,
     137-139, 140-149
   seasonal migrations, 137-141,
     49-151
underharvest, 202-205
U.S. Fish and Wildlife Service, 1

W

walleyes, 23, 38, 41, 42, 49, 58, 65
Wallop-Breaux Amendment, 182
Ward, Virgil, 185
water
   clarity and color, 106, 113-115,
     121-123
   muddy, fishing in, 108, 113-120
   water color and lure color,
     114-116
   levels, 78-81, 106
   quality
     carbon dioxide, 20
     dissolved oxygen, 20, 85, 108,
       114,121-123, 151-153, 187-190
     pH, 20, 85, 114, 121-123
     salinity, 20, 69-73, 121-123
     temperatures (see Calendar
       Periods)
       bass tolerances, 19-20
       thermoclines, 33-35, 105, 107,
         121-123
       wind and water temperature,
         112-113
Weathers, Ken, 189-190
weeds
   bass use, 84-94, 99-103
   control, 141, 176-179
   definition, 86
   exotic plants, 79, 84, 140, 176-180
   fishing, 86-94
   native plants, 84-87, 178
   seasonal changes (see Calendar
     Periods)
   slop bays, 91-94
   types of, 86-87
   weedlines and weed edges, 87-90
weighing fish, 210-213
Western Outdoor News (WON)
   tournaments, 186
Weybrant, J.R., 174
whitefish, 38
Wilde, G.R., 198-199
wind, 108-114
   Coriolis force, 108-109,
   currents caused by wind, 106-113,
     121-123
   subsurface reversing currents,
     107-110
   Langmuir circulation, 112-113

X-Y-Z

CATCH IT ON VIDEO!

In-Fisherman has an extensive library of the finest bass catching videos in the world. Each video brings you detailed information from the bass experts at In-Fisherman that is guaranteed to help you catch more bass. Plus, there's plenty of big bass action. Here are just a few of the titles you can see at in-fisherman.com or at your local tackle retailer:

LARGEMOUTH BASS: LURE LOGIC

Pick the right lure for the right situation, spring, summer or fall. Learn how variables like cover, clarity, temperature, and the feeding attitude of bass will tell you how to pick the hot lure. *64 min.*

BASS IN THE GRASS

NEW!

Pull the big horses out of the weeds with help from In-Fisherman. Buzzbait Bassin', Rip Crankin', Slow Rollin', Deep Water Toppin', Sloppin', and Cold Water Bassin'. This video is a must for any bass angler who hunts in the weeds. *71 min.*

ADVANCED BASSIN' TODAY

Fine-tuning presentation tactics based on largemouth bass location. Choose the right bait and use it properly! Telly Award Winner. *75 min.*

FINESSE BASS

Sometimes bass need a little finesse to coax them to bite. Deep water, clear water, the In-Fisherman staffers reveal the little things that produce big bites. A must view for every advanced basser. *68 min.*

NEW RELEASE!

JIG TIME BASSIN'

This year jigs will account for more bass caught than any other lure. Learn the five factors to jigging success. Plus jigging bass in shallow water, in dirty water, in the weeds, and dockside. Water breaking big bass action! *60 min.*

TOP SELLER!

ADVANCED SMALLMOUTH BASS

Go toe to toe with bronze fury! Exclusive new tactics for taking big smallmouths in lakes and reservoirs. Line-breaking action! *62 min.*

Start catching more bass today with In-Fisherman videos!
www.in-fisherman.com

241

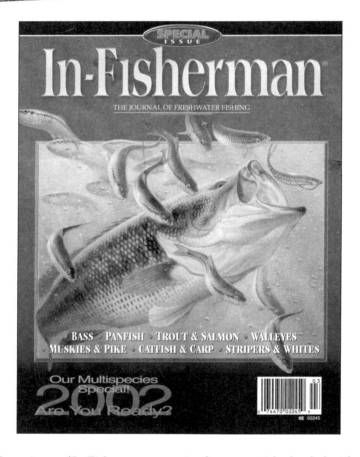

VISIT THE TOP FISHING DESTINATION IN THE WORLD

IN-FISHERMAN MERCHANDISE

Great deals on Award-Winning books, videos and more.

BEST FISHING TIMES

Plan to be on the water when the bite is hot.

TIPS FROM THE EXPERTS

In-Fisherman Pros provide tips and advice to help you catch more fish.

BIG FISH GALLERY

Show off your catch and see what our readers are catching.

in-fisherman.com

FISH ID

Not sure what you just caught? Look it up here!

ASK THE DOCS

Our experts answer your electronics and motor questions.

RECIPES

Fish are nutritious and delicious— especially when prepared from an In-Fisherman recipe.

IN-FISHERMAN TV & RADIO

See what's on tap this week for IF TV and locate the IF Radio station in your area.

In-Fisherman

TEACHING THE WORLD HOW TO FISH!
ON THE INTERNET

7819 Highland Scenic Rd, Baxter, MN 56425

Notes